2|18|10
$29.99
B+T
*5
14day

2|10
W

PETER THE GREAT

Also by Derek Wilson

Rothschild: A Story of Wealth and Power

*Sweet Robin: A Biography of Robert Dudley,
Earl of Leicester, 1533–1588*

Hans Holbein: Portrait of an Unknown Man

*The King and the Gentleman: Charles Stuart
and Oliver Cromwell, 1599–1649*

*In the Lion's Court: Power, Ambition, and
Sudden Death in the Reign of Henry VIII*

*All the King's Women: Love, Sex, and
Politics in the Life of Charles II*

Charlemagne: The Great Adventure

Out of the Storm: The Life and Legacy of Martin Luther

PETER THE GREAT

Derek Wilson

St. Martin's Press ✿ New York

www.stmartins.com

Library of Congress Cataloging-in-Publication Data

Wilson, Derek A.
    Peter the Great / Derek Wilson. — 1st U.S. ed.
        p. cm.
    Originally published: London : Hutchinson. 2009.
    Includes bibliographical references and index.
    ISBN 978-0-312-55099-8
    1. Peter I, Emperor of Russia, 1672–1725. 2. Emperors—Russia—
Biography. 3. Russia—History—Peter I, 1689–1725. I. Title.
    DK131.W75 2009
    947'.05092—dc22
    [B]
                                                           2009031286

Originally published in Great Britain by Hutchinson,
a division of The Random House Group Limited

First U.S. Edition: January 2010

10 9 8 7 6 5 4 3 2 1

Contents

Illustrations

In his hand Peter found only a blank sheet of paper and he wrote on it: 'Europe and the West'. Since then we belonged to Europe and to the West.

Peter Chaadaev

Introduction

Anyone who can remember the televised images of the destruction of the Berlin Wall in 1989 is unlikely to forget them. The dramatic pictures of people tearing at masonry with machines, picks and bare hands, of family members tearfully reunited, of faces radiant with excitement and hope stand vividly in our memories. We felt – rightly – that we were watching history. The Soviet empire was not only crumbling; its people were coming back into the European fold. Integration promised an end to the Cold War. More – it held out the hope that a shared culture embracing East and West could permanently remove the fear of armed hostility. Behind it lay two decades of political and diplomatic activity – arms limitation treaties, rebellions in Soviet satellite states and the progress of European union. It was this last phenomenon that played decisively with Mikhail Gorbachev, the atypical Soviet General Secretary and, subsequently, President, who held office from 1985 to 1991, and who initiated the massive policy changes on the far side of the Iron Curtain. He was impressed by the growing economic strength of the emerging European Union and its apparent success in curbing the nationalism that had been the curse of the twentieth century. Closer contact with western Europe would, he believed, put an end to the crippling arms race, thus freeing revenue for vital modernisation, and provide better access to commercial markets. It would enable Russia to incorporate elements of the Western value system without kowtowing to the USA. His attitude did not fall far short of a 'vision' for civilising Russia by strengthening ties with the family of nations to the west from which it had been estranged since 1917. Most visitors who have seen Russia under the old regime and the new cannot but believe that Gorbachev was right. They are struck by the rapidity and comprehensiveness of the transformation that has come over society since the early 1990s. Creeping capitalism has established itself, for good and ill. City streets are clogged with motor cars. Shop windows glisten with desirable luxuries. Tourism flourishes – both inward and outward. Bars are thronged with middle-class citizens with disposable income. There is a new pride in the country's pre-Soviet heritage. To see all this is to gain some idea of what happened in Russia three hundred years ago.

Peter the Great was no less atypical as a tsar than Mikhail Gorbachev was as a member of the Politburo. He, too, had a vision to Europeanise his country, to end the isolation that he believed was depriving it of its rightful place in the world. Just as the Communist leadership ring-fenced their country against the corrupting influence of capitalism, so Peter's predecessors had protected good Orthodox Russians from the seductions of Christian heresy. Gorbachev had to struggle against his own party caucus to change the direction of Soviet policy. Peter, too, had to contend with the ingrained forces of traditionalism. The difference was that Peter enjoyed the autocratic power that went with being tsar. He was able to turn his dreams into reality, and the scope of his achievement is breathtaking: he created a navy from scratch and provided it with a Baltic base from which to access the world's oceans; he built a whole new city in the prevailing European style; he introduced Western dress fashions and made his nobles shave off their beards; he reformed the calendar; he freed women from their traditional domestic shackles; and he successfully weathered the storms that these and other changes inevitably whipped up among the conservative elements of church and state. The downside of his accomplishments is that they came at incalculable cost in human lives. Hundreds of thousands of men and women perished on battlefields and building sites so that Peter Mikhailov could fulfil his ambitions. He was larger than life, one of the most colourful and remarkable men ever to exercise rule, and his story is, in itself, fascinating. But that story is often told in terms of his Europeanisation of Russia. What is equally fascinating is his impact on Europe. Interaction with the lands to the west was a two-way process. Whatever 'Europe' was at the beginning of Peter's reign, it was something different by the end of it, and Russia was destined to play an increasingly important role in the centuries ahead.

The series of books of which this one forms a part is about Europe: what it is, how it has developed, whether, indeed, it exists at all in any meaningful sense. In *Charlemagne: The Great Adventure*, I considered the emergence of the idea of Europe as an entity coterminous with Latin Christendom, though having its heart not in Rome but north of the Alps. That idea survived for six hundred years and received some kind of political identity in the Holy Roman Empire. But the image of unity was always mythical, not only because of the frequent wars between most of its constituent parts, but because separate cultures, languages and even religious customs developed. In *Out of the Storm: The Life and Legacy of Martin Luther*, I described how one man gave the dolorous stroke to that myth of religious and cultural cohesion by permitting individuals and combinations to question ancient orthodoxies and thus dissolve the already weakened ideological glue that held Western society together. This set the scene for a century of new wars, which were basically political but coloured by a religious discord that gave them a heightened intensity and ferocity. From these conflicts emerged the 'modern' states of western Europe, as religion, culture, dynastic allegiances and commercial rivalries defined boundaries.

The next seismic shift in the fortunes of Europe was its opening up to the vast lands to the east, the lands ruled by the heir to the old crown of Muscovy, who now called himself 'Emperor of All the Russias'. Tentative connections had been developing since the Dutch and English trading ventures of the sixteenth century, which led, in the fullness of time, to diplomatic exchanges, but the reports that came back from Russia were, by and large, far from encouraging. Travellers found the inhabitants of this 'rude and barbarous kingdom' coarse, unsophisticated and addicted to strong drink. As for the political system, it was one of unrelieved tyranny:

> In such a savage soil where laws do bear no sway,
> But all is at the king his will to save or else to slay,
> And that sans cause, God wot, if so his mind be such.[1]

But visitors were also impressed by the spectacular wealth and display of the tsarist court, the elaborate ceremonial that seemed to outshine the splendours to be seen in European palaces. Russia *was* a very different country; that was why it both attracted and repelled visitors from London, Paris, Amsterdam, Copenhagen and Vienna. Serfdom, long since technically abandoned throughout Europe, remained the basis of Russian society, and the concept of sovereign law to which even kings were subject was quite alien to the Tsar's people. The Orthodox church with its elaborate rituals exercised enormous influence and dismissed as heretical both Catholics and Protestants. It erected an ideological barrier against the corrupting influence of the West every bit as effective as the 'iron curtain' with which a later regime sought to protect the Soviet state from bourgeois capitalism. Foreign residents in Moscow were herded into designated ghettos so as not to influence unsuspecting citizens, and the fiercely traditionalist leaders of church and state were as suspicious and contemptuous of Western ways as European travellers were of the 'backward' Muscovites. Despite such adverse reactions, more and more

Westerners responded to invitations from successive tsars to settle for longer or shorter spells. They came to trade, to practise medical and other skills and to advise the government on the latest technical advances, particularly in the arts of warfare. Thus began the love-hate relationship between Russia and the West that has survived to the present day.

But we should not overestimate the differences. The authors who wrote their travellers' tales for a fascinated (and paying) readership almost inevitably exaggerated for effect. Even when they did not, they brought to their narratives a sense of cultural superiority. To them it was self-evident that civilisation was more advanced in France, England or Holland than in Russia, where tyrants lived in magnificence, reigning over a cowed people, and aided by a domineering church hierarchy. Yet it was Louis XIV who regarded himself as God's lieutenant and claimed that 'the humble submission of subjects to those who are set over them' was a maxim 'clearly established by Christianity', and all seventeenth-century European kings were autocrats. It was in Spain that the Inquisition maintained a terrifying regime of autos-da-fé, and in every country state churches persecuted those who were not of their persuasion. It was Frederick I of Prussia who bankrupted himself creating the baroque splendours of the Berliner Schloss and the Charlottenberg Palace, and Louis' Versailles prompted most contemporary rulers to self-glorifying emulation. So Peter I shared with his royal contemporaries most of their political assumptions and the methods they adopted to bolster their image.

But history is not the narrative of the activities of top people. It concerns the ruled as well as the rulers. If royal power had to be buttressed by ostentatious display and appeal to belief in the sacred nature of kingship, it was because ruling elites feared change that might be forced on them from below. The inevitable corollary of absolutism was that discontent with the political status quo, having no legitimate, effective means of expression, could only manifest itself in violence – whether palace coup or military revolt or revolution. Russia experienced several such crises in the seventeenth and early eighteenth centuries. It could scarcely be otherwise in an empire that embraced Muscovites, Ukrainians, Ests, Lithuanians, Don Cossacks, Volga Bulgars and the jigsaw of eastern Slavs extending all the way to the Pacific coastline. The rulers of this vast – and still growing – empire had quite enough to do maintaining some kind of centralised control over their subjects while guarding their backs from court intrigue to concern themselves with events beyond the Dvina.

One man changed all this. The amazingly tall, gawky seventeen-year-old who became de facto master of Russia in 1689 tore up the rule book. He deliberately cultivated the foreign community, appointing several of its members to influential military and political positions. He became the first tsar to travel extensively through other countries. He turned landlocked Russia into a maritime power able to engage militarily and commercially with western nations. He destroyed the Swedish empire and made himself master of the Baltic, ruling from the improbably sited new capital of St Petersburg. His personal impact abroad was colossal. No one knew what to make of this weird phenomenon, who dressed simply, eschewed ceremony, ignored the etiquette of sophisticated courts, reduced his lodgings to a state of ruin through rowdy and boorish carousing and insisted, like the most ardent tourist, on seeing for himself every aspect of European life. Bishop Burnet in his *History of His Own Time* described Peter I of Russia as 'designed by nature rather to be a ship-carpenter than a great prince'. Yet by the end of his reign, this freak of nature, this rumbustious, iconoclastic, crude tyrant had extended Russia's boundaries worryingly westwards, muscled his way on to the top table of the 'political nations' and married some of his relatives into their royal houses. Europe had changed and he had changed it. I hope to show in the following pages that, in opening up Russia to Europe, he also opened up Europe to Russia and began that massive political and cultural realignment that was fundamental to the subsequent history of Europe and the world. We all have to live with the legacy of Peter the Great.

The writing of this book has involved considerable travel, research in libraries and archives and help with translation. It would have been impossible without the generous help provided by the administrators and sponsors of the Elizabeth Longford Grants, which I gratefully acknowledge.

1

Survival

He stood at the top of the Red Staircase between the Cathedral of the Assumption and the Palace of Facets – a dark-haired, wide-eyed ten-year-old, already tall for his age. He huddled close to his mother, who had one arm around him and the other round his half-brother, Ivan. The tension in Tsarevna Natalya's body told him that something was very wrong. She had gathered the two boys hurriedly from their rooms in the palace and rushed them out to face a bewildering scene. Below them, in the square, stood a crowd of soldiers brandishing muskets and shouting. 'Here are Tsar Peter and Tsarevich Ivan,' Natalya cried, and that seemed to calm the angry mob.

Then, three or four soldiers advanced up the steps, intimidating with their calf-length vivid caftans, helmets and vicious pikes. They approached the shrinking Ivan. 'Are you really the Tsarevich?' one of the bearded *strel'tsy* demanded. 'Yes, yes,' the petrified child stammered. Peter stared at the men and felt his mother's grip tighten on his upper arm. He wondered what would happen next.

Two of his mother's friends advanced down the steps and addressed the soldiers. Young Peter wanted to steal back to the quiet and safety of the palace, behind closed doors. But he was rooted to the spot. He could not understand what was passing between the mutineers and the government leaders; did not know what the men intended to do with those terrible sharp halberds. He soon discovered. With a sudden shout, the mob surged forward. They grabbed the two men on the staircase. The screaming victims were impaled on those hideous spikes. Then their bodies were thrown to the ground, and hacked and slashed to pieces. With a cheer, the soldiers rushed

I

up the steps. Did Peter cry and bury his face in his mother's robes, as some people reported, or did he stand, glaring at the murderers with calm defiance, as others would have us believe? One thing is certain. As the rebellious *strel'tsy* surged past into the palace in an orgy of looting and destruction, the scene imprinted itself on Peter's mind and never left him. He would grow up to hate Moscow and all it represented.

'We are Europe.' That claim was made in 1814 by Alexander I, Emperor of All the Russias. He spoke on behalf of the crowned heads of Europe. Bearing in mind the major role the Tsar had played in overthrowing Napoleon's attempt to destroy the old order, none of his fellow monarchs demurred. A century earlier, such a claim would have seemed utterly incomprehensible. The apparently endless territory beyond the Dnieper and the Dvina had been, to most Westerners, a mysterious place peopled by semi-barbarians who espoused alien religions – either Islam or a heretical form of Christianity. The few travellers who did venture into the interior – most of them Polish Jesuit missionaries sent to enlighten the benighted Orthodox Slavs – brought back stories of a brutal land populated by hard people, most of whom were nomads or semi-nomads and knew nothing of broad-streeted cities with elegant palaces and neatly laid-out parks. Cartographers in Amsterdam, Paris and London, struggling to fill the large empty spaces on their maps, thought in terms of 'Russia in Asia' and 'Russia in Europe'. The man who almost single-handedly made his people aware of the world that lay to the west and made the West aware of his people, land and culture was a roaring giant of childlike enthusiasms and psychotic complexity, of whom one English observer recorded, 'I could not but marvel at the depth of the providence of God, that had raised up such a furious man to so absolute an authority over so great a part of the world.'[1] That furious man was the remarkable individual known, with good reason, as Peter the Great. He shifted the whole direction of history, and the fact that, twenty years after the superpower struggles of the Cold War, statesmen of the so-called 'free world' still pay anxious court to the men who rule in Moscow is testimony to the altered relationship inaugurated by the fourth Tsar of the Romanov dynasty.

When, in 1696, Peter became de jure sole master of the world's largest land empire, few people within his territory and fewer outside it understood just how extensive it was. It was bounded by the White Sea in the north and the Caspian in the south, but from east to west it extended more than ten thousand kilometres, from the frontier with Poland to the northern Pacific coast. The exploration and colonisation of Siberia is a story that, for adventurousness, courage, savagery, missionary endeavour and commercial exploitation matches and even exceeds the opening up of the Dark

Continent and the European settlement of North America. It was fired by
the religious impulse to convert pagan tribes and by the quest for furs, which
took the place in the Russian economy that spices and precious metals had
held for the expansionist Iberian nations of the sixteenth century. But it was
the consolidation of Russia's position west of the Urals that preoccupied
rulers in Moscow throughout the two hundred years following Ivan III's
successful emancipation from the Mongols in 1480.

The principality of Muscovy was one of several landlocked Russian
farming/mercantile states periodically harassed by nomadic tribesmen from
the steppes. It never knew a period of sustained peace. Even after 1480, its
rulers constantly struggled with neighbouring chieftains in order to secure
their frontiers or improve their trading positions. Muscovy extended its rule
over other Russian principalities only to find itself hemmed in by Sweden,
Poland and Turkey, who were determined to keep the alien nation out of
their markets. Periodic wars imposed financial burdens on Muscovites and
contributed to political instability. Between 1598 and 1613, Muscovy experienced the 'Time of Troubles', an era of turmoil and bloodshed remarkably
similar to England's Wars of the Roses. Rival noble houses competed for the
crown. Legitimate claimants vied with pretenders. Military leaders changed
sides with an eye to their own advantage rather than the good of the people.
Rulers even hired Polish mercenaries. The conflicts only ended when the
exhausted magnates called an assembly of nobles, gentry, clergy and leading townsmen to elect a new tsar. Their choice fell on Michael Romanov,
distantly connected with the already legendary Ivan the Terrible (1547–84).
The Russians had found a dynasty that would rule them for almost exactly
300 years.

The comparatively stable period that followed did not dispel the basic
problems faced by the state. Muscovy was a country driven in on itself.
Powerful neighbours blocked any intercourse with western European nations
and denied it direct contact with the commercial highways of the Baltic and
the Mediterranean. In the political claustrophobia of Moscow, aristocratic
and dynastic intrigues festered. They came close to destroying in infancy the
child born to Tsar Alexis and his second wife, Natalya Naryshkina, in 1672.

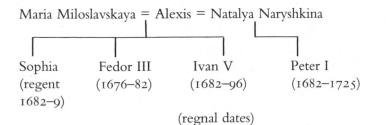

Maria Miloslavskaya = Alexis = Natalya Naryshkina

Sophia	Fedor III	Ivan V	Peter I
(regent	(1676–82)	(1682–96)	(1682–1725)
1682–9)			

(regnal dates)

3

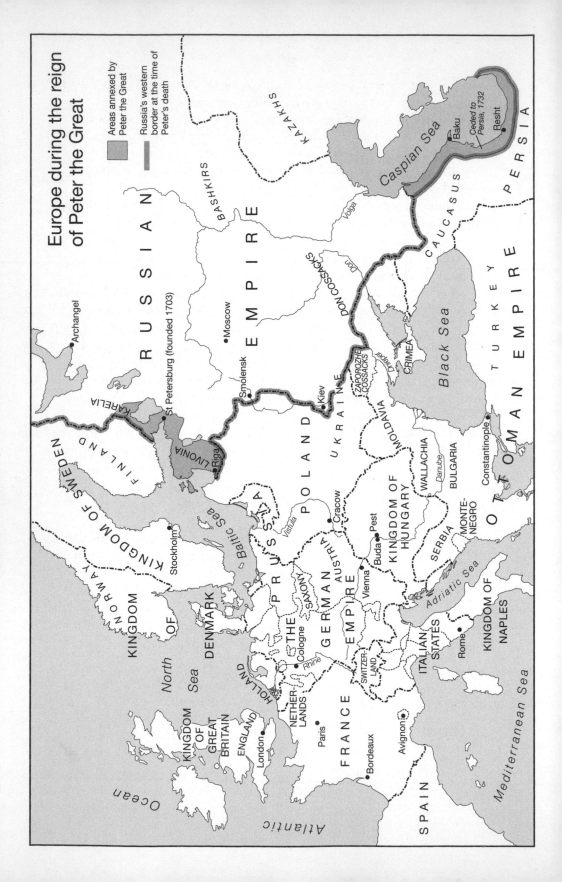

Europe during the reign
of Peter the Great

Areas annexed by
Peter the Great

Russia's western
border at the time of
Peter's death

Atlantic Ocean

North Sea

KINGDOM OF GREAT BRITAIN

ENGLAND

London

Paris

FRANCE

Bordeaux

SPAIN

Mediterranean Sea

KINGDOM OF NAPLES

Rome

ITALIAN STATES

Avignon

SWITZER-LAND

NETHER-LANDS

HOLLAND

Rhine

Cologne

THE GERMAN EMPIRE

SAXONY

AUSTRIA

Vienna

Buda

Pest

KINGDOM OF HUNGARY

Cracow

PRUSSIA

POLAND

Vistula

Danube

WALLACHIA

MOLDAVIA

SERBIA

MONTE-NEGRO

BULGARIA

Adriatic Sea

KINGDOM OF DENMARK

Stockholm

Baltic Sea

KINGDOM OF SWEDEN

NORWAY

KINGDOM OF

FINLAND

KARELIA

St Petersburg (founded 1703)

LIVONIA

Riga

Smolensk

Kiev

UKRAINE

ZAPOROZHE COSSACKS

Dnieper

CRIMEA

Black Sea

Constantinople

TURKEY

OTTOMAN EMPIRE

Archangel

Moscow

RUSSIAN EMPIRE

BASHKIRS

Volga

Don

DON COSSACKS

CAUCASUS

Caspian Sea

Baku

Ceded to Persia, 1732

Resht

PERSIA

KAZAKHS

The Tsar was in theory an autocrat and in reality dependent on the support of the boyars. These were the top noble families, normally around thirty in number. Their ranks were augmented, usually annually, when the Tsar conferred the title on favoured individuals. Their loyalty was a matter of personal and religious adherence to the divinely anointed Tsar; there were no legal or constitutional ties. It was a loose arrangement that inevitably lent itself to the forming of factions and obliged the ruler to be negotiating constantly for support. Naturally he turned first to his own family and the families with which he was connected by marriage. In his need for men he felt he could trust, he might also raise up favourites and place them in positions of power. It was a system, if such it can be called, that encouraged jealousy, corruption and court intrigue. Weak tsars were manipulated by those around them. Strong tsars had to be ruthless.

Alexis Mikhailovich enjoyed a long reign (1645–76) thanks to his ability to balance the leading boyar families. However, in his later years, desiring to give the crown greater independence, he raised up a low-born favourite, Artamon Matveev, and it was this man who more than any other created the circumstances that coloured the early years of Peter's life. Matveev was the son of a clerk who rose up the ranks in the diplomatic service. Artamon chose a military career, and by the 1660s he had his own regiment of musketeers, whose duties included guarding the Tsar. Alexis was impressed with the young man and entrusted to him various administrative and diplomatic tasks, which he performed with both efficiency and flair. Thereafter his rise was rapid, and by 1670, Matveev was the Tsar's right-hand man. This coincided with important developments in the royal family. Alexis' first wife, Maria Miloslavskaya, had recently died. She had presented him with thirteen children, but only three had survived infancy: a girl, Sophia, and two boys, Fedor and Ivan. Both sons had weak constitutions, and in the hope of providing Russia with a healthy heir, Alexis decided to marry again. A shortlist of suitable high-born maidens was drawn up and, inevitably, the leading boyar families fell to scheming and manoeuvring over the rival candidates for the royal bed.

Matveev favoured the seventeen-year-old Natalya Naryshkina, who came from a family of moderately wealthy landowners to whom he was distantly related. Natalya's father, Kirill Naryshkin, was a member of Matveev's regiment of musketeers. The favourite could thus count on the support of the Naryshkins as he made his plans to safeguard his position in the event of Alexis' death. Everyone knew that the two Russian princes were unlikely to be long-lived. Fedor was described as 'very unhealthy and melancholic', while Ivan was 'humpbacked and nearly blind'. Matveev intended to put in place a strong-minded tsaritsa who would underpin his own position and,

God willing, provide Russia with another heir who would come into his own as soon as his stepbrothers were no more. The situation was quite plain to Matveev's enemies, and they immediately swung into action. Poison-pen letters accused Natalya of having an affair with a Polish nobleman, and rumours were spread that Matveev was using drugs to influence the Tsar. Their schemes came to nothing. In February 1671, Alexis and Natalya were married. Fifteen months later, the new Tsaritsa gave birth to a healthy son.

The favourite certainly stood to gain from the success of his candidate, and, after Alexis had chosen Natalya, further rewards were not slow in coming Matveev's way. In 1674, he received the ultimate accolade, the rank of boyar. All the political activists in Moscow were now looking to the future, when Alexis would be replaced by one of his weak and malleable sons. Matveev had the immediate advantage, and he used it to remove the relatives of the late Tsarina, the Miloslavskis, from Moscow and appoint them to positions in distant regions. Other boyars were also dismissed from high office in favour of men of lower rank who owed their positions to the favourite. Natalya's relatives were, of course, among those brought to the Kremlin and given important jobs. Her father was also raised to boyar status. But Matveev's enemies kept a close eye on him and used every stratagem to hamper his attempt to build up a 'party'. He was obliged to proceed with caution and fate was not on his side. Tsar Alexis fell suddenly ill in January 1676 and died within a few days.

This resulted in thirteen years of turmoil that ultimately degenerated into a reign of terror. Natalya and her young son were seldom out of danger. The majority of the boyars resented her because of her humble origins and her connection with Matveev, but the more conservative among them had other, personal grievances. They thought her an ambitious, 'liberated' woman, contaminated by foreign influences. She had spent some of her impressionable teenage years in Smolensk, where her father held a military post, and had come into close contact with the hated Catholic Poles. She lacked the submissive, unthinking respect for ancient institutions that was expected of Russian women. Her open-mindedness communicated itself to Peter during his early years, when mother and son were thrown especially close together by shared adversity.

One of the first acts of the new Tsar, Fedor, was to recall and reinstate members of his mother's family, the Miloslavskis. The tables were turned on Matveev, who was dispatched into exile at Pustozersk, in the treeless wastes of the Malozeml'ska Tundra, three thousand kilometres from Moscow. Prominent members of Natalya's family were also ordered away from the capital and placed under virtual house arrest. Natalya herself kept a low profile in the Kremlin palace with her three children (Natalya was born in 1673 and Fedora, who died at the age of four, in 1674). However, she could not fail to be aware that Peter was the subject of increasing interest and speculation. He was obviously more robust than his half-brothers, and it soon became clear that he would grow to be very tall. Young Peter was a bright, intelligent lad who responded well to the instruction of his excellent tutor, Rodion Streshnev. Calculating members of the political class realised that the son of Alexis' second marriage might yet succeed. But not if the current Tsar and his relatives had anything to do with it. In July 1677, Fedor got married and everyone at court watched the new Tsaritsa carefully. They had to watch for a long time. Not until July 1681 was Fedor's wife brought to bed of a child. And then the rejoicing was cruelly cut short. The Tsaritsa died during the birth and her baby son followed within hours. Seven months later the desperate and ailing Tsar tried again, taking a fifteen-year-old bride, against the advice of his physicians.

Every move in the roller-coaster adventures of the royal family affected the fortunes of Peter and his mother. In the spring of 1682, restrictions against Matveev and the Naryshkins eased. The ex-favourite returned to his estate near Moscow, and Natalya's relatives were readmitted to the court. Their reinstatement was an attempt by the Tsar to assert his independence by displaying favour for men his father had trusted. But his strength for the task was rapidly failing. On 27 April, the semi-invalid Tsar Fedor died. Faced with the choice between the fifteen-year-old half-blind, mentally impaired Ivan and the nine-year-old healthy Peter, the majority in the boyar council, the duma, voted to proclaim Peter tsar. It seemed that the Naryshkins' long ordeal was over. But the worst was yet to come.

Over the next few months two events occurred, and it is not altogether clear exactly how they related to each other. Behind the scenes the Miloslavskis moved to safeguard their position. Peter's election meant that Ivan's family now risked being sidelined – or worse. They might well have feared a backlash once Matveev and the Naryshkins were back in power. What they needed was to have Peter set aside in favour of Ivan. There was no law of primogeniture in Russia and there could be no doubt that Peter had the potential to make the better ruler. Any contest, therefore, was entirely governed by family rivalries and not by considerations of what might be best for Russia. The person who emerged as leader of the Miloslavski challenge was Tsar Alexis' third surviving daughter, Sophia (born 1657). She had the support of one of the leading boyars, Vasily Golitsyn (who may also have been her lover).

The other event was the revolt of the musketeers, the *strel'tsy*. The *strel'tsy* were the nearest thing Russia had to a corps of crack troops. They were armed with primitive (by Western standards) firearms. Originally recruited by Ivan the Terrible from among the ranks of the urban trading communities, they combined military duties with civilian pursuits. This tended to create a tension between rival loyalties. They were very proud of their elite status in the military but often reluctant to be away on campaign for long periods of time because this interfered with their business interests. The *strel'tsy* of Moscow formed the Kremlin guard, and this was where their political influence rested. Their closeness to the court enabled them to bring pressure to bear on their betters. The nation's leaders relied on the loyalty of the *strel'tsy* but were wary of their potential power. The revolt of 1682 began as a protest over pay and conditions, and the soldiers' discontent was focused on certain unpopular officers. One of the first acts of the new Naryshkin-packed government was to pacify the malcontents by demoting and publicly flogging some of the protesters' bêtes noires. But appeasing mobs is always a self-defeating stratagem, and once the *strel'tsys'* blood lust was up, they looked for other victims. Their complaints were directed against the new regime and they declared their loyalty to Ivan.

Sophia and her collaborators decided to ride the tiger of *strel'tsy* wrath for their own ends. The princess was described by one foreign diplomat as an accomplished and ruthless schemer: 'Her mind is as sharp, subtle and political as her figure is broad, short and gross and, without ever having read Machiavelli or learned about him, she has a natural grasp of all his maxims.' As tension in Moscow rose, with bands of disaffected soldiers swaggering through the streets, someone began spreading rumours that were deliberately intended to inflame the situation: the Naryshkins were strutting about the palace as though they owned it; one even had had the temerity to sit on the royal throne; Tsar Ivan had been attacked. On 15 May, an angry musketeer mob appeared before the palace demanding to know that Ivan was safe. Natalya brought Ivan and Peter out to the top of the steps. That did not satisfy the rebels. Their leaders now wanted a conference with boyar leaders to discuss a long list of grievances. Principally they required Ivan to be made tsar and the Matveev–Naryshkin caucus to be exterminated. However it was managed, the *strel'tsy* had become a violent armed force doing the bidding of Sophia and Golitsyn. The situation was approaching flashpoint. Then Matveev appeared accompanied by Michael Dolgoruki, one of Golitsyn's enemies. With a roar, angry soldiers dragged them away from the royal party and threw them down the stairs into the courtyard where they were hacked to pieces by the *strel'tsy* mob.

The bloodletting continued for three days. Bands of soldiers rampaged through the capital and its environs, hunting down men they believed to be their enemies and carrying out summary executions. Peter lost several relatives in the rebellion. He shared his mother's fear and anguish, and might even have been present when she pleaded tearfully for her father and brothers to be spared by the musketeers' leaders. Meanwhile, Sophia and her allies were seeking a way of bringing the situation under control. The 'loyal' demands of the rebels for Ivan's election had given them what they most wanted, and it was not in their interests to allow mob rule to continue. Golitsyn negotiated a compromise with the duma and the *strel'tsy* whereby Ivan and Peter would be jointly crowned as senior and junior tsars respectively, with Sophia acting as regent. The Naryshkin tree was pruned but not uprooted. The victorious party did not want to provoke an ongoing feud between families. They needed concord among the boyars in order to re-kennel the hounds they had unleashed. The *strel'tsy*, inevitably, were continuing to flex their muscles, making ever more extreme demands. In late summer Sophia removed the royal court from Moscow to tour various country estates, leaving the capital virtually under the control of the musketeers and their commander, Ivan Khovansky. The story was that their majesties had to be removed because they were in danger of being attacked by traitors. A letter (probably forged) accusing Khovansky of plotting against the Tsars was then circulated among the political elite. Having assured herself of boyar support, Sophia now summoned Khovansky to be present at a court ceremonial occasion. As soon as he and his son arrived, they received the summary justice they had meted out to others in recent weeks. Bereft of their leader, the rebels rapidly caved in and were only too ready to accept a royal pardon in return for swearing a new oath of loyalty. When the court returned to the Kremlin in November, a major constitutional crisis had been averted and firm government established under the leadership of Tsarevna Sophia, who held the reins of power for the next seven years. But the trauma of the bloody summer of 1682 had left an indelible mark, not least on Peter.

The end of the violence and Sophia's triumph did not signal the end of rivalry in Moscow. A Swedish diplomat summed up the situation graphically in a report home:

> Between the two tsars there is great jealousy. The younger has the greatest following, especially among the nobility, although the older has given the nobility great gifts and favour and lets everything be governed by his sister ... Most people are of the opinion that the younger tsar would separate from the elder and easily get the government alone. A few weeks ago various writings were found in the tsar's [i.e. Peter's] apartments in which among other things it was stated that the princess would keep the government to herself and the older tsar would go to a monastery, in which also the lord Miloslavski and others who support

the older tsar were threatened, and for this reason a great investigation was done to find out whence these came.[2]

Sophia began to adopt an increasingly authoritarian pose. In royal decrees she coupled her name with those of the Tsars. For the time being, she could rule in the name of her brother, but the likelihood of his living a long life was remote, and without him she would have to face down Peter's supporters. Success then would depend on her ability to build and maintain a secure power base.

The most enduring effect on Peter of all the unpleasantness was his alienation from Moscow. Ivan IV had called his capital the 'third Rome' and prophesied that no city would ever surpass it, but Peter spent as little time there as possible, preferring his country residence in Preobrazhenskoe, a village in the northern suburbs. Moscow held bitter memories for him, and he had no taste for the heavy formality of traditional church and state ceremonial. His physical separation from the trappings of Muscovite convention helped him to look critically at a way of life he might not otherwise have questioned so closely. He developed a gift for what we might today call 'thinking outside the box'. Whenever possible, the teenage Tsar escaped from court ritual and the claustrophobic small-windowed rooms of the Kremlin to enjoy a simple open-air life at Preobrazhenskoe. He had a wooden house built for him, and this became the centre of a court very different from that presided over by Sophia. Peter also avoided being moulded by formal education. He was not 'bookish' and his handwriting remains the despair of historical researchers, but he was intensely inquisitive. He was always intrigued to know how things worked and how they were made. He sought out carpenters and metalworkers and from them learned how to handle tools.

It was inevitable that, in his quest for knowledge, Peter would be drawn to Kokui. This was the place near Preobrazhenskoe that Tsar Alexis had designated as the settlement for foreigners – the diplomats, merchants and military advisers he had encouraged to come to Russia to share their expertise and help develop the economy (see p. 31 below). It was a cosmopolitan community where Germans, Hollanders, Swedes, Englishmen, Scots and Frenchmen, Catholics and Protestants rubbed shoulders, maintaining their national rivalries yet drawn together by their 'foreignness'. Peter was fascinated by this ghetto and its inhabitants, with their strange (and rather more comfortable) clothes, the modern machines and gadgets in their houses and the stories they had to tell of a wider world beyond Russia's enclosed culture. The growing boy visited Kokui often, made friends there and accepted several of them as his guides and mentors.

What made the foreigners even more attractive in Peter's eyes was the prevailing attitude of the Russian establishment towards them, as expressed by the Orthodox patriarch Joachim:

> May our sovereigns never allow any Orthodox Christians in their realm to entertain any close friendly relations with heretics and dissenters – with the Latins [Roman Catholics], Lutherans, Calvinists, and godless Tatars (whom our Lord abominates and the church of God damns for their God-abhorred guiles); but let them be avoided as enemies of God and defamers of the church. May they command by their tsarist decree that men of foreign creeds who come here to this pious realm shall under no circumstances preach their religion, disparage our faith in any conversations, or introduce their alien customs derived from their heresies for the temptation of Christians; they should be strictly forbidden to do all this on pain of severe punishment ... For these dissenters do not agree in faith with us, Christians, who are in possession of true Orthodoxy; they are completely at variance with us in interpreting the tradition of the [holy] fathers; they are alien to our mother, the Orthodox church. Of what help could such accursed heretics be to the Orthodox host? They only bring on the wrath of God. The Orthodox pray to God according to the rules and customs of the church, while they, the heretics, sleep, and perform their abominable deeds, despising Christian prayer. The Christians honour the most pure Mother of God, the Virgin Mary, and invoke in every way her aid and that of all the saints; but the heretics – the military commanders – being ungodly, revile it and blaspheme; in no way do they respect the most holy Mother of God and all the saints; they do not honour the holy icons, they scoff at all Christian piety. Christians observe the fasts; heretics – never.[3]

For young Peter, association with these 'heretics' had the delicious flavour of forbidden fruit.

Peter could not be a cipher. In Moscow his position was ambiguous and he could do nothing to change it. At Preobrazhenskoe he created his own pond in order to be its big fish. By pursuing there his own passions, he was, perhaps without realising it initially, laying the foundations for Russia's army and navy. The young Tsar spent much of his time in what seemed to most observers to be military games but which formed the basis of something much more important. Not for him playing with toy soldiers; Peter formed his own little regiments – the Preobrazhensky and the Semenovsky – composed of local young men and the sons of courtiers. They had uniforms, ranks and training methods, all based on the latest innovations in Western military techniques. The two regiments had their own barracks and a small fort, named Presburg. From about 1687, Peter enjoyed the benefit of advice from General Patrick Gordon, a Scottish soldier of fortune who had served his father for many years and who became a close personal friend. Peter had a profound respect for professionals and always formed his own opinion of a man's worth. In the nearby royal estate of Izmailovo, at the age of sixteen, he made an exciting discovery. It was an old sailing dinghy. Though much in need of repair, it caught the boy's imagination. He had it refitted and was soon taking sailing lessons from a Dutch expert. He was joined in his new sport by some of his soldier friends from Presburg, and as they tacked to and fro on Lake Pleshcheevo, the grand vision was formed: Russia should have an ocean-going navy. Muscovy had never been a maritime power, for the very good reason that it had no outlet to the world's oceans other than the White Sea, which was frozen for several months of the year.

From his new friends in the foreign diplomatic and mercantile community, Peter heard something of how the trading network to the West operated; Russia's furs, hemp and tallow finding their way, via Archangel, in Dutch, English and Swedish ships to distant markets. Why should Russia not have a more active role in this profitable commerce? In the summer of 1693, he set off for Archangel to see for himself the great trading vessels. He stayed till late in the season, gobbling up every scrap of information on the construction and handling of ships, despite the entreaties of his mother, who viewed with suspicion anything to do with the alien environment of the sea, terrified that Peter might meet a watery death. He returned home brimming with ideas that he immediately began putting into practice. Within three years he had laid the basis of a fleet made up of armed merchantmen and galleys commissioned from the Archangel dockyards or bought from the Dutch.

The young Tsar's preoccupation with such activities suited Sophia and Golitsyn well. Their political situation was essentially insecure. Peter was popular with the nation's elite and becoming steadily more so. Their own power base was the Miloslavski network, the more reactionary boyars and church leaders and the *strel'tsy*. To widen their support they needed the disabled Tsar Ivan to marry and sire an heir, and also to originate some popular policies. They failed on both counts. In 1684, Sophia managed to arrange her brother's nuptials. The unfortunate bride was Praskovia Saltykova, who had, almost literally, to be dragged kicking and screaming to the altar. There followed for the Regent five years of impatient waiting. At last the Tsarina became pregnant, but Sophia's relief was short-lived. The baby was a girl. Luck just was not with Sophia (Ivan and Praskovia had no fewer than five children between 1689 and 1694 – all girls). There was no male who could be presented to the people as a potential alternative to Peter. This could be put down to misfortune, but the fiasco of Russian foreign policy was of the government's own making. In 1687 and 1689, Golitsyn personally led military campaigns against the Turks in the Crimea. They were intended, in part, to divert attention from the failings of the regime by producing rousing national victories. They failed spectacularly. Both were disastrously costly in terms of lives and money and brought Russia no increase in land or treasure. Sophia laid on a hero's welcome for her returning colleague, but it fooled nobody.

Now Sophia had another problem. In January 1689 Peter had got married, and within months it was known that his wife, Eudoxia Lopukhina, was pregnant. If she were to be delivered of a healthy prince, Sophia's ambition to hang on to power would be doomed. The following summer she had to swallow the humiliation of the second Crimean campaign. Peter now began to assert himself. He had rarely stood up to the Regent. He had his own interests, and he might well have reflected that the best strategy was to allow Sophia enough rope to hang herself. But now he challenged government policy and declined to automatically endorse the Regent's enactments. It is from this year that we have a pen picture of the young Tsar from a French visitor who had his detailed information from Peter's close companions. It is not an altogether endearing portrait.

Tsar Peter is very tall and quite well proportioned, with a handsome face. His eyes are big but so wild that he is pitiful to look at. His head shakes continually. He is twenty years of age. He amuses himself by making his favourites play tug-o-war with each other and often they knock each other out in their efforts to pay court. In the winter he has large holes cut in the ice and makes the fattest lords pass over them in sleds. The weakness of the new ice often causes them to fall in and drown. He also likes having the great bell rung but his dominant passion is to see houses burn, which is a very common occurrence in Moscow.[4]

We must suspect a certain amount of deliberate sensationalising in this report by a traveller wishing to impress, but some elements of the account are supported by other testimony. Peter was restless and found it difficult to sit through long church services and court rituals. He always had to be up and doing and was possessed by an energy that was at times manic. As a compulsive enthusiast, he stopped at nothing in his pursuit of the latest idea, and he drove his companions and courtiers to do his bidding, whether that involved fighting mock battles with the real risk of serious injury or carrying out experiments to test the strength of ice. He had witnessed appalling scenes of violence at an early age and had known what it was to experience personal danger. This had left him desensitised to the pain and suffering of others. He did not shrink from bloodletting, and the kind of buffoonery he classed as practical jokes sometimes had fatal consequences. Peter grew into manhood with an emotional void at the centre of his life. He avoided several of the religious ceremonies that the sovereign was expected to attend and which, it was believed, connected him with the God in whose name he claimed to reign. His actions were increasingly governed by his desires, plans and ambitions. He had withdrawn from Moscow because there his self-expression was restricted. In Preobrazhenskoe, by contrast, no one could or did thwart him. If ever he felt that he was not receiving appropriate respect, that his whims were not being sufficiently indulged, he responded with hot rage or cold determination to make the offender pay. Men like Peter Mikhailovich usually achieve great things – at great cost.

It comes as something of a surprise that a man so proactive did not launch the political coup that, at long last, unseated Sophia. He might well have decided that she would undo herself. However, the eventual crisis seems to have been a case of spontaneous combustion. Clashes between tsar and regent were becoming more frequent, and in July 1689, Peter refused to sanction rewards the regime wanted to give to the 'victors' of the second Azov campaign. In Moscow, rumours (probably started by the reigning clique) now spread that Peter, under the pernicious influence of foreigners, had no respect for Russia's ancient religious and cultural institutions. More inflammatory was the suggestion that he was preparing to strike at the *strel'tsy*, on whom Sophia still relied. The musketeers themselves were caught in a dilemma, not clear who had the first call on their loyalty. On the evening of 7 August, one of Peter's leading supporters was arrested. At the same time a large body of *strel'tsy* was mustered, ostensibly to accompany the Regent to Donskoi monastery for religious observances. These events provided the spark. Messengers rushed to Preobrazhenskoe to waken the Tsar and warn him of impending peril. Peter leaped from bed and, without stopping to get dressed, took horse and galloped to a vantage point in nearby woods. Hither his servants followed him with suitable clothes, and having changed out of his nightshirt, the Tsar rode at full speed to the Trinity monastery, some twenty kilometres north-west of Moscow.

Peter's mother and wife, along with other family members and leading boyar supporters, hastened to join him. The young Tsar issued orders for the musketeers to rally to him at the monastery. Sophia countermanded these instructions. For three weeks the stand-off continued. More and more influential figures came to the Tsar's camp, including Joachim, Patriarch of Moscow, Russia's leading churchman. But the outcome was not a foregone conclusion. Although Peter was popular, the Naryshkins were not. Several of the boyars found the royal family overbearing and feared that handing power to them would simply be to exchange the frying pan for the fire. Thus, some of the nation's most influential men waited on events, particularly the outcome of negotiations between the parties. Sophia sent messengers to the monastery to discuss a possible compromise. Peter did not respond, and eventually Sophia herself left Moscow for talks with her rival. Peter simply refused to see her and she was obliged to return, humiliated. Now, in this first political crisis of his life, the seventeen-year-old Tsar revealed one of his strongest characteristics – stubbornness. He was essentially straightforward in his thinking and no scheming politique. When he had made up his mind on any course of action he pursued it with the energy and focus of a blinkered racehorse. He paid little attention to counsel. If his project failed, he merely set a different course, without anguishing over events or laboriously analysing the reasons for failure. Intriguingly, Peter's attitude towards politicians contrasts markedly with the respect he showed military, naval and technical experts. He was always ready to learn from those who had useful things to teach, and would spend hours in humble tutelage with men who could reveal to him the mysteries of a ship's rigging or novel battlefield manoeuvres.

As the days passed, Peter became bolder. Some *strel'tsy* units had come over to him, and he now ordered the surrender of commanders who failed to do so. He also demanded the surrender of Fedor Shaklovity, one of Sophia's favourites and the prime anti-Naryshkin rumourmonger. Now the tables were turned against Shaklovity: he was accused of plotting to assassinate the Tsar. The Regent tried strenuously to protect her ally, but on 7 September, she was forced to sacrifice him. Shaklovity was sent in chains to Trinity monastery. Four days later, after excruciating torture, he confessed to his 'crimes' and was executed. This was the end for Sophia. Golitsyn had already thrown himself on Peter's mercy and been happy to accept a sentence of banishment. Peter now consigned his half-sister to a convent and purged the government of all her supporters. The seven-year struggle was over.

2

The Third Rome

Nations largely define themselves by what they are not. They may be and usually are racially diverse. Numerous dialects and even languages may be spoken within their borders. They may tolerate different religions or denominations (though variations of belief tend to create more problems than any other kind of division). Centralisation of political power may be incomplete. Yet citizens will have a sense of belonging to something and they will identify that something by contrast with other nations. In the two centuries before Peter and Ivan came to exercise joint rule, Russian identity had been forged as its people defined themselves as a distinct nation with a destiny that marked them out as different from their neighbours. That process was still going on – and a remarkable process it was. We will not understand the changes that occurred in Russia under Peter the Great, nor the altered relations with Europe, if we do not see them in the context of deeper and longer-term developments that were already in train.

In the fifteenth century, Muscovy was a small, landlocked Slav nation surrounded by peoples who were certainly different and frequently hostile. Like their neighbours, Muscovites had fallen under the control of the Mongols (or Tatars), but this did not impose any cultural unity. The western Mongol tributary states (which would eventually become Lithuania and Poland) were evangelised from Rome and experienced all the creative and destructive features of the Reformation and the Renaissance. Most of the Tatars to the south and east of Muscovy were Muslims. Muscovy, by contrast, and the surrounding region was brought within the fold of Orthodox Christianity by missionaries from Constantinople. In 1453, Constantinople was overrun by the Ottoman Turks and the great cathedral of Hagia Sophia became a mosque. The churches that had owed allegiance to the Byzantine patriarch were left to their own devices, and this inevitably involved disintegration of unity. Some national churches looked to Rome and approved a degree of assimilation. Muscovy, however, not only remained true to the old tradition, but went further. Its religious and secular leaders identified their regime as the heir of Byzantium and the sole defender of Orthodox truth. Moscow, they asserted, was the Third Rome. The first, in Italy, had forfeited its leadership of the Christian world by falling into heresy. The second had been sacked by the infidel. It fell to Moscow to recover the standard from where it had fallen on the field of battle and hold it boldly aloft. This gave the ruler of Muscovy spiritual justification for expansionist policies. Wars of aggression, whether against Muslim or Catholic enemies, took on the nature of crusades. It was the reign of Ivan III, Grand Duke of Muscovy (1462–1505), that launched his people on a remarkable path of conquest that would see a tiny Slav nation become master of the world's largest land-mass empire. Ivan married as his second wife Zoe Palaeologos, daughter of the last Byzantine emperor, assumed the title of tsar, threw off the Tatar yoke, employed as his personal emblem the double-headed imperial eagle, which hitherto had represented the emperors ruling from Constantinople and Vienna, called his territory the land of the Rus (the part-legendary agglomeration of Slav peoples once ruled from Kiev), and extended it 1,800 kilometres to the east. By the time of his death, Russia's borders were established on the White Sea, the Dnieper and the Urals. This new political entity was a mix of territorial imperialism and cultural isolationism.

The next initiatives in projecting Russia on to the world stage were taken by Ivan IV (1533–84). The title by which he is best known – the Terrible – is a poor translation from the Russian and should more accurately be rendered 'the Awesome'. Our judgement must depend on what benchmark we lay down by which to measure him. Some rank him with the more notorious sadists of history such as Nero, Robespierre and Stalin, but we should not judge him apart from the age in which he lived. The grandson of Ivan III, he dominated Russia for half a century, murdered his own son while in one of his frequent rages, summarily sentenced to death thousands of his own subjects, involved his country in long and unproductive wars and instilled fear in all who came in contact with him. He was the complete autocrat and a bloody tyrant. That means he does not stand out as markedly different in kind from several contemporary monarchs. He was as warlike as Suleiman the Magnificent. Like Henry VIII, he married six times (his seventh wife was not recognised by the church) and disposed of most of his wives when they had outlived their attraction or usefulness. His capacity to justify cruelty with the excuse of devout necessity matched Philip II's ruthless imposition

of Catholic orthodoxy. The appalling purge he authorised in the years
1565–72 does have a parallel in Catherine de' Medici's St Bartholomew's
Day Massacre. It might also be argued that Ivan faced and dealt with the
same kind of problems as his European counterparts. If the Russian crown
was to be secure, he had to bring the boyars to heel. Tudor and Valois kings
also had to curb the ambitions of their potentially overmighty subjects. For
Russian trade to develop fully and cease being dependent on foreign traders,
the country needed an outlet to the world's shipping lanes. This was why
Ivan devoted years of military endeavour to gaining permanent access to
the Baltic, in the same way that European governments backed merchant
adventurers looking for routes to the wealth of the Orient around Africa and
South America and through the frozen seas to the north-west and north-east.
Ivan the Terrible was a man of his age, an age remarkable for the emergence
of autocratic monarchies. Autocracy always carries the seeds of morally unacceptable excess. Thomas More urged Henry VIII's councillors to advise the
King not what he could do but what he should do. When every allowance
has been made, the story of Ivan IV is that of an intelligent and genuinely
devout ruler degenerating into a power-crazed psychopath. He did indeed
share the traits of many of his contemporaries, but what he managed to
achieve was the combination of *all* their vices.

Such a man inevitably changed profoundly the nature of Russia. Ivan
was the first Russian ruler to have himself crowned with the title of 'tsar',
an indication that he intended to be an absolute monarch. He also vowed
to govern in the interests of the people and to use his power for the public
good. In the early years of his reign, he demonstrated his intentions with
a series of reforms in several areas of national life – law, local and central
government, the army, and church–state relations. The responsibility of
administering an expanding country under constant external pressure from
hostile neighbours and internal disruption by boyar rivalries, and without a
clear constitutional framework, should not be underestimated. The peoples
over whom he came to rule had their own very diverse political institutions
and ideas about what did and did not accord with the principles of justice.
It is no surprise, therefore, that Ivan preferred to sever the Gordian knot of
conflicting advice and self-interested counsel with the sword of royal diktat.

The Russia that emerged from Ivan the Terrible's tyranny was one of
growing interest to the outside world. This was because of its manifest commercial and political importance and also because to most Westerners it was
a land of fable and mystery. Visitors to Moscow brought back eye-widening
accounts of the splendour of the Tsar's court. The English explorer Richard
Chancellor, who travelled on campaign with the Russian army, described
Ivan's pavilion in breathless prose. It was 'covered with cloth of gold or

silver and so set with stones that it is wonderful to see'. He insisted that for exuberant display, it exceeded the war tents of Henry VIII and Francis I.[1] A seventeenth-century English ambassador who appeared before the Tsar to present his credentials was overwhelmed by the experience: 'I observed betwixt 20 and 30 great princes and councillors of state sitting upon the left hand of the emperor, who were all in long robes of cloth of gold, embroidered with pearls and precious stones and high caps either of sable or black fox about three quarters of a yard high upon their heads.' When he was invited to advance and kiss the Tsar's hand, four sumptuously attired attendants stepped forward holding rods beneath which he was obliged to prostrate himself. Thus, only by grovelling was he with difficulty able to reach the outstretched hand of the great autocrat.[2] Other visitors were also impressed by the religious ceremonial of the Kremlin, the gorgeous costumes and banners, the icons glowing with gold and the heady atmosphere of the candlelit interiors, thick with the smell of incense. The stories that reached Western capitals painted the Tsar's realm as extreme in every way – magnificent, vast and barbarous. Russia was a backward land, untouched by the scientific and technological revolutions that had transformed Europe (it took almost a century for the printing press to reach Russia). Its people and ruler were wild and morally inferior. Jeremy Bowes, Elizabethan ambassador to Moscow, was appalled when Ivan ordered a man to jump from a high window and break his neck to demonstrate his obedience and loyalty. Such stories circulated round the chancelleries and fashionable salons of Europe and were given as much credence as the tales mariners brought back from the New World of cannibals, winged creatures, and men with heads in the middle of their chests. Everything about this land seemed to be extreme – the exuberant beards, the gratuitous cruelty, the combination of regimented ceremonial and anarchic buffoonery at the royal court, the power of the church, the capacity for alcohol consumption, the subservience of the large serf population, the intense nationalism that resisted outside influence. The worst excesses of the tsarist regime were reported and deliberately exaggerated by German and Polish writers, who had their own reasons for wanting to discourage visitors to Russia. It was not only Ivan's rule that was portrayed as an insane and bloody regime perpetrating every conceivable atrocity, such as roasting children over open fires and perfecting instruments of torture that would have been the envy of the Inquisition.

But visitors were not to be put off. This was the age of the merchant adventurer. The lure of profit and the impulse of national rivalry impelled bold spirits to seek new markets and new routes to the trading empires of the Orient. Religious conflicts were seriously disrupting traditional commercial life, and just as in the nineteenth century manufacturing nations needed to develop colonies to absorb their output, so, for example, English cloth exporters were desperate to find fresh outlets in order to avoid the recession of their industry. Catholic Iberia and Muslim Turkey and Barbary dominated the sea lanes to the Levant and the Indies, so Protestant England and Holland turned some of their attention to the north-east. It was difficult to gain access to Baltic trade, which was dominated by the powerful Hanseatic League of German towns and frequently disturbed by the rivalry of Sweden, Denmark and Poland. So, in 1553, a pioneering voyage financed by the Company of Merchant Venturers for the Discovery of Regions, Dominions, Islands and Places Unknown set out from London and sailed northwards, coasting Norway, into the formidable Arctic. Only one ship, captained by Richard Chancellor, survived, finally reaching the mouth of the Dvina river, near where the port of Archangel would soon be founded. It was a timely arrival. Ivan IV had recently brought the region under his sway and was delighted to hear of the arrival of English merchants. He had Chancellor and his men brought to Moscow, bestowed trading privileges upon them, sent them home with a cargo of furs and other goods originating in Russia and lands beyond, and gave them letters for Queen Elizabeth, requesting the establishment of diplomatic relations. Ivan was principally interested in acquiring allies who would support him in his wars with Poland and Sweden (at one point he even offered Queen Elizabeth his hand in marriage) and in availing himself of superior armament technology.

Foreign merchants, it must be said, were not initially much interested in their Russian counterparts as trading partners. The Company of Merchant Venturers became the Muscovy Company (later the Russia Company), but its agents and backers were still captivated by the East as a source of exotic merchandise – spices, silks and gems – and determined to establish routes, either by sea or land, to the markets where these commodities were to be bought. Ivan's territory stood as either a barrier or a bridge to their ambitions. Within a few years, English traders had penetrated thousands of kilometres beyond Moscow, to Astrakhan, on the Caspian, and Bukhara, not far distant from the mighty mountains frontiering Persia and Turkestan. These journeys literally put Russia on the map. Information supplied by these travellers was incorporated in the *Theatrum Orbis Terrarum*, the magnificent world atlas issued by Abraham Ortelius, in Amsterdam, in 1570. Russia's principal export of interest to the West was hemp for the rapidly developing naval and mercantile marines, and in the seventeenth century Russia became the largest supplier of this commodity. But dramatic developments during Ivan IV's reign opened up a supply of a unique range of luxury goods – furs. The Tsar granted to the Stroganov family the right to exploit lands beyond Muscovy's eastern boundary and thus began the historic advance into Siberia. The inhabitants of this forbidding land of forests, lakes and extreme climate were relatively primitive and divided into small communities, but they excelled at fishing, felling and trapping. The Stroganovs and their commercial rivals were soon supplying to foreign merchants ermine, sable and beaver skins destined to trim the robes of Europe's royalty and nobility.

The establishment of regular commercial and diplomatic relations between Russia and the leading nations of Europe was accomplished only slowly and with difficulty. Sweden and Poland-Lithuania, which blocked Russia's access to the Baltic, did their best to hinder its access to the outside world. They were incidentally aided by reactionary forces within the country. Leaders of the Orthodox church feared 'contamination' by contact with the West. The nations of Europe were either Catholic or Protestant. Either way they were under heretical regimes. The religious hierarchy could always count on a substantial body of pious and/or nationalistic sentiment within the upper echelons of Russian society. This explains why it fell to the tsars to respond to overtures from England, Holland and Germany or to take their own initiatives in maintaining international contacts. But the greater barrier was always geography. The trade route to the White Sea pioneered by Chancellor was hazardous, and the port of Archangel, established in 1584, was only ice-free in the Arctic summer. It says much, therefore, for the tenacity and determination of successive tsars and western merchants that communication was kept up. Residential quarters were created in both Archangel and Moscow for the foreigners. Diplomatic missions were sent to and received from Denmark, Holland, Poland, Sweden, England and various German states, though only on an intermittent basis.

Nevertheless, such facilities did encourage a flow of visitors to Russia. They did not only come to trade. There were those who saw opportunities for their talents and expertise (particularly in matters military) in the service of a monarch who was in the market for any service that would increase his prestige, power or wealth. Things did not always work out well for new arrivals in Moscow. Dr Elisei Bomel, aka Eliseus Bomelius, was one of the more colourful characters who established himself at the tsarist court but who eventually came to a sticky end. Bomel originated in Holland but travelled to England, where he studied medicine at Cambridge. He subsequently enjoyed a lucrative career as physician and astrologer to some of the leaders of Elizabethan society. However, his overexuberant prognostications brought him to the attention of the government and he was forbidden to practise his craft. Bomel had by now become accustomed to the high life and the adulation of his clients. In 1570, unwilling to face a reduction in his circumstances, he resolved to emigrate to Russia. Ivan and his court had never seen anything like Elisei Bomel, and he became the latest fashion with a reputation for magic and healing. Fame soon went to his head. He represented himself as an intimate of Elizabeth, who, he told Ivan, was a young woman eager for marriage with the great Russian monarch. This was not the sum total of his dabbling in political matters. Inevitably he overreached himself, and the Tsar, who had previously showered his wonder-worker with costly gifts, now suspected him of intriguing with his Polish and Swedish enemies. Bomel soon saw the other side of Ivan the Terrible. He was subjected to the most excruciating torture in order to make him reveal details of a supposed plot against the paranoid Tsar, dying in or about 1574, in great agony. His fate provides a kind of parable on the life of foreign visitors to Moscow in the century or so before the accession of Peter the Great. In the uncertain world of the royal court, they might be feted or hated. They were valued for their commercial and diplomatic contributions but were confined to specified residential areas and were always aware of the suspicion directed at them by some sections of the Russian top brass.

It was the church leaders who provided justification for xenophobia. They pointed to the fissiparation of the Western church following the revolt of Martin Luther as evidence of the inevitable result of Rome's descent into heresy. But in the middle of the seventeenth century, Russia experienced its own version of the Reformation. Like the upheaval that sundered Latin Christendom, it had its roots in spiritual intensity and scholarly innovation. And like the European reform movements, it involved church–state relationships. The Orthodox Patriarch, Nikon, instituted a much-needed revision of several old theological and liturgical texts that had become corrupted over the centuries. This infuriated powerful reactionary elements in the hierarchy, who banded together in defence of what they called the Old Belief. Year by year the schism widened and became more violent. Nikon wielded the secular machine against his enemies. Monasteries were sacked. Dissident priests were burned at the stake. Eventually success went to the patriarch's head. When he claimed superiority of church over state, and, therefore, of the patriarch over the monarch, Tsar Alexis promptly demonstrated where the real power lay. He deposed Nikon and exiled him to a distant monastery. This did not signify the end of the reform. On the contrary, Alexis endorsed the changes and a church council proclaimed the new orthodoxy. Persecution of the Old Believers continued. Countless numbers suffered the full rigour of the law, but there were others who chose the path of self-martyrdom. It has been estimated that more than twenty thousand monks perished in communal immolations by fire over a twenty-year period. That sobering statistic places the religious turmoil of sixteenth–seventeenth century Europe in a different perspective, and indicates the spiritual intensity (some might call it fanaticism) that alone could inspire widespread resistance to the Tsar's claimed authority.

Once again, we must return to the reign of Ivan IV to discover how the foundations of tsarist absolutism were laid and to understand the purged society that emerged from his refining fire. A letter from the Tsar to Elizabeth I in 1570 reveals the gulf between their two regimes: 'We had thought that you were sovereign in your state and ruled yourself, and that you saw to your sovereign honour and to the interests of the country. But it turns out that in your land people rule besides you, and not only people, but trading peasants ...'[3] There is a sense in which this tells us more about the developing governmental system in England than about the distinctive autocracy of Russia. The share in the political process that Lords and Commons had come to expect in the Queen's realm and the rights and privileges protected by law were unique. They were already fuelling debate about sovereignty – whether it was bestowed from above or rose from the people. There was no such discussion in Russia. There was no independent judiciary, and while custom played its part in determining the relationships of groups and individuals to the government, the concept of 'rights' did not exist in any sense that a citizen of London, Amsterdam or Paris would have understood it. There was no established mercantile class whose accumulation of wealth was independent of the land and of tsarist patronage and who might, therefore, act corporately to ensure a share in the political process. Ivan asserted that he who carried the responsibility of government had it laid upon his shoulders by God. His will and the Creator's were as one. There could be no appeal against royal decree. The Tsar could do whatever he wanted, and if that implied tyranny, the people must accept it as they accepted any other manifestation of the inscrutable will of God. Some version of the divine right of kings (though by no means uncontested) existed in all Christian states, founded on the Bible and supported by the church. It seemed inconceivable to most political thinkers that society could be held together without it. The kind of autocracy espoused by Tsar Ivan was simply the most extreme version of this principle.

It did not go wholly unchallenged. In any state there are three elements that may compete for power with an established regime: the religious leadership, the nobility and the army. As we have seen, the Orthodox hierarchy claimed at least partnership with the Tsar. It was a potential rival, in terms of both the wealth at its command and the spiritual authority it wielded. The church, and particularly the monasteries, had benefited over the centuries from the gifts of its rich and devout sons. By 1550 it owned a third of Russian land and over half a million serfs. Many monasteries were little fortified towns, equipped to resist foreign invasion but also able to withstand military pressure from the Tsar. During the great schism, the Solovetskii monastery, a stronghold of the Old Believers, was able to hold out against a sporadic siege that lasted eight years. Religion dominated the thinking of the people. The illiterate masses went in awe of their robed and bearded priests, the glowing, gilded church interiors, the emotive chants, the glittering icons viewed through a haze of incense smoke. For the educated minority, there was little to challenge traditional assumptions. No new ideas were spread by the small printing industry; virtually every book and pamphlet that came off the presses was a devotional or liturgical text. With no corpus of innovative philosophy and no body of independent-minded scholars to espouse it, intellectuals were effectively insulated from any political theories that might challenge the status quo. This left the church, the guardian of all formal education, in a position to train the minds of the Tsar's subjects. Thus, church and state working together were formidable, and on the rare occasions that they had clashed, the Tsar had been able to assert his will.

What of the boyars? Did they act as a potential constitutional check on autocratic power? As we have seen, they could be subject to feuds and the formation of factions centred round royal favourites or family members. Their constitutional position was ill-defined. They came from leading families whose status was determined by heredity, wealth and royal service. Some – and the number could vary very widely – were members of the boyar council or duma. Theoretically, they advised the Tsar and were associated with him in the issuing of edicts. Below them in rank were well-defined groups of royal attendants, court functionaries and government officials. Customarily the Tsar made annual appointments to the rank of boyar. All major court, civil and military appointments were made from the ranks of the Muscovy elite. The monarch was thus the only source of patronage, and this in itself kept potential 'overmighty subjects' loyal to and dependent on him. Louis XIV assembled the great magnates of France around him at Versailles and involved them in a highly elaborate ritual of 'Sun King' worship, but this was but a pale shadow of the court regime that had evolved naturally in Moscow. Boyar and official families were intensely jealous of their status. Disputes over precedence were frequent. Every duty and privilege, from rank in the army to the seating plan at state banquets, was a matter of 'honour'. On a daily basis the opulent ceremonial of the royal court was both an expression and a reinforcement of the Tsar's control over the political elite.

But the basis of the Tsar's power over the boyars was his ability to exercise naked force and the fear that such ability engendered. The horrors of the *oprichnina* still lingered in the collective memory. Exactly a century before Peter was born, Ivan IV had ended the bloodiest period in pre-Stalinist Russian history. For eight years he had carried out a series of ruthless purges that had decimated the ranks of the boyars and, in effect, defined tsarist autocracy. Angry with the pretensions of the duma and the church leaders, the Tsar had divided his territory into two sections. One continued to be governed under the existing political regime of tsar and duma. The other, the larger, comprising a network of profitable lands, important towns and even individual buildings, was the *oprichnina*, a personal state administered by officials of Ivan's own choosing and mainly from non-boyar families. Supervisory powers were invested in the sinister black-robed *oprichniki*, a combination of secret police and secular inquisition. They confiscated lands, carried out summary executions and terrorised whole regions. The purge culminated in the siege of Novgorod, during which a vast but unknown number of the population were put to death (estimates vary from 15,000 to 60,000). In 1571, an army of Crimean Tatars, taking advantage of the internal dislocation, marched into Moscow, looting, destroying, murdering and carrying off many citizens into slavery. Ivan was obliged to put an end to the *oprichnina* experiment. Whatever its failings, the purge left the Tsar in a position that was almost unassailable. He had removed troublesome boyars and replaced them with men he could trust. He had accumulated a personal estate that provided him with an enhanced power base. By rewarding *oprichniki* with lands and serfs, he had created a 'new nobility' and bought its loyalty. Most importantly, his ruthlessness had made a lasting psychological impact. In sixteenth-century Spain, France and England, the monarchy had asserted control over the church and the nobility. Ivan IV and his successors had essentially achieved the same political authority.

Yet that authority would not have been accepted had the landowning class not been able to exercise a similar power over those beneath them in the social scale. The vast majority of Russia's families were serfs, people tied to the land and prevented by law from moving from their estates or selling their labour to other employers. This institution also dated from the reign of Ivan IV. His Russia was not, and could not be, a complete money economy. The normal expenses of government could just about be met from taxation, but foreign wars overburdened the financial system. One answer was to repay state service with land and serfs. Serfdom well served the needs of an expansionist state. Not only did it provide, as we have seen, a supply of soldiers for the Tsar's wars; it also meant that when there were new lands to be colonised, the chosen pioneers could be supplied with the necessary labour force. By and large, therefore, the structure of Russian society in the seventeenth century was one that served reasonably well the tsars and their more powerful subjects.

But what of the army? We have seen that the *strel'tsy* were a disruptive influence in the years following the death of Fedor and affected the political situation. Does this imply that the Russian army possessed the ability to wrest power from the Tsar or impose some limitation on autocracy? In a nation committed to a series of offensive and defensive wars, the position of the military was obviously of central importance. The survival of the tsarist regime was dependent upon it. If it did not constitute a major threat, it was because no opponent of the Tsar was ever able to take control of the military machine and turn it against the government. In fact 'machine' is not a very appropriate word for the haphazard collection of armed units with which Peter's predecessors went to war. The bulk of them were levies of serfs dragged from their estates and led by their boyar masters. They were, for the most part, ill-equipped and poorly commanded. Their main advantages, as far as the Tsar was concerned, were their numbers and their expendability. He could enlist thousands upon thousands for a campaign, and if they did not overwhelm the enemy they simply became so much unmourned cannon fodder. This unsophisticated way of waging war was so obviously wasteful that successive tsars addressed themselves to military reform. Ivan IV was interested in the latest technology. He imported cannon to give his army artillery teeth and invested in arquebuses, the first hand-held guns for battlefield use. It was this innovation that enhanced the reputation of the *strel'tsy*, who were trained in the use of the new equipment. The *strel'tsy* and their weapons had to be kept in working order during peacetime, and this had the disadvantage of being expensive, which was why they were allowed to engage in trade and became something like a citizen militia, performing guard and ceremonial duties when not involved in training exercises or war. This self-confident armed brotherhood was a new element in Russian society and, as we have seen, could become a tool in the hands of unscrupulous politicians.

The seventeenth century was a time of rapid development in the art of warfare. For more than four decades, large armies were employed across Europe, from Ireland to Poland, from the Baltic to the Mediterranean, fighting in the English Civil War, the Thirty Years War and the First Northern War. This era of conflict produced such great tactical generals and original military strategists as Gustavus Adolphus of Sweden, Oliver Cromwell, and Johann von Tilly of Austria. If they were to stay in the military race, tsars had no option but to keep up with foreign developments. They did not have to go out of their way to find experts to advise them of the latest innovations or to train their troops. This was the great age of the professional soldier. Footloose, battle-hardened mercenaries looking for employment were available in plenty. Like modern football managers, they travelled from country to country building their reputations, changing their loyalties and selling their services to the highest bidder. Some found their way to Moscow. The result was a steady modernisation of the Russian army. New light and heavy cavalry and infantry regiments were formed under the command of foreign officers. As so often happens, war was the stimulus for industrial and technological development. In the middle years of the century, the first munitions factories were set up to produce cannon, muskets, swords and other military equipment, under the guidance of experts brought from Holland and Germany. Prospectors were sent out to seek deposits of iron and copper, and in the fullness of time, a Russian metallurgical industry evolved.

Russia, as was suggested at the beginning of this chapter, was an agglomeration of peoples that identified itself largely by what it was not. Two factors in this process remain to be considered as we attempt to gain some impression of the land that Peter Romanov came to rule. They are the twin threads of internal disintegration and external pressure. Hereditary autocracy only works as long as the line of succession remains unbroken, or at least undisputed. When the last of Ivan IV's sons died, childless, in 1598, the Riurikid dynasty came to an end and the realm was plunged into fourteen years of constitutional crisis. While rival claimants battled it out within Russia, powerful neighbours swooped on the failing empire. The Swedes seized Novgorod, and Sigismund III, the ruler of Poland-Lithuania, Europe's largest territorial state, tried to add Russia to his empire. He had the support of some indigenous factions, and for three years his troops occupied Moscow. The reunification of the nation's disparate elements in order to see off the Polish threat may be regarded, if not as Russia's 'finest hour', then certainly as one of its better ones. Against all the political and military odds, a majority led by the ecclesiastical top brass rejected rule by a heretic monarch. They asserted the nation's Orthodox identity and the people rallied behind the traditional faith. In 1613, most of the rival camps united behind a newly elected tsar, Michael Romanov.

Recovery after the 'Time of Troubles' was slow, but now luck was on Russia's side. Her powerful neighbours were distracted by more pressing problems. From 1618 to 1648, Sweden and Poland were caught up in the Thirty Years War. The perpetual 'battle for the Baltic' went very much Sweden's way until 1658, but thereafter the nation's very success acted against it because its neighbours were jealous and resentful. Denmark, Holland (fully independent from Spain after 1648), Prussia and Russia were equally determined not to allow Sweden a commercial stranglehold or the ability to prevent the passage of warships through the Sound (between Scania and Zealand), and were ready to make common cause against their overmighty neighbour. Meanwhile, in the south, the long decline of the Ottoman Empire began in the mid-century. The attempt by Sultan Mehmed IV, in 1683, to accomplish the capture of Vienna, a prize denied to his predecessor, Suleiman the Magnificent, was the last opportunity to revive former glories. It ended in failure, thanks to the heroic defiance by the Viennese and the intervention of a multinational relief force. Muslim pretensions were checked once and for all, and the Turkish Empire was seen to be disastrously overstretched.

It is against this international background that the emergence of Russia as a European power must be seen, an emergence that began well before Peter came to the throne. The appalling devastation of the Thirty Years War, the cynical accepting and betraying of treaty commitments and the internal disruption to which fighting and crippling taxation gave rise had profound psychological effects. Royal chancelleries throughout Europe were shocked by the establishment of republican rule in Holland, its temporary establishment in England and the revolutions know as the Frondes in France (1648–53). The abyss of chaos seemed to open up before the feet of men accustomed to regard kingly authority as part of the divinely ordained schema for human society. Recovery would involve the firm reassertion of autocracy, not just for the 'top nations', but for those able to take advantage of the weakening of neighbouring regimes to elbow their way to the front of the crowd. It was Frederick William, the 'Great Elector', who described the philosophy that enabled him to weld his inheritance of scattered north German states into the mighty Brandenburg-Prussia: 'Alliances, certainly, are good but one's own forces, on which one can more surely rely, are better still. A ruler receives no respect [from his peers] if he has no resources and folk of his own.'[4] Frederick William was not the only European prince to understand the maxim 'if you desire peace (internally or externally), prepare for war'. The successful royal governments of the later seventeenth century were those backed by well-equipped and trained standing armies. The *ancien régime* was forged in the fire of the Thirty Years War.

In 1648, the year the Peace of Westphalia put an end to that war, three significant events occurred in the realm of Tsar Alexis. There were demonstrations against taxation on the streets of Moscow. The Cossacks of the Ukraine offered homage to the Tsar. Pioneer explorers/traders reached the Bering Strait.

Alexis was a cultured and prudent ruler who understood well that it was necessary to look westwards for those ideas and technologies that would modernise his country. We have already considered his military reforms, but he also introduced Western-style drama at his court and authorised the publication of newssheets carrying information about the latest events in Europe. But reform and maintaining an army come at a price, and Alexis' government found itself cash-strapped. Old methods of raising revenue had to be fully exploited and new ones found. The most controversial ways of adding to the exchequer were the increased salt tax and the introduction of tobacco, which carried a heavy state premium. Hitherto, the church had forbidden the sale of the noxious weed but any moral objections were now swept aside to meet the government's need for ready cash. In addition, there were complaints of institutional corruption by the Miloslavskis (undoubtedly justified). Alexis' subjects thus had genuine grievances, which could be cloaked in religious indignation. In the resulting Moscow riots, some of the Tsar's officials were lynched, and disaffection manifested itself in other towns. The Tsar calmed the situation by summoning representatives of all parties concerned, sacking some officials and promulgating a new, comprehensive legal code. It had been an uncomfortable interlude and it demonstrated that Russian autocracy was by no means absolute yet.

The eastward expansion of the Tsar's empire was a long-term endeavour whose full impact would not be felt for several years, but it too was tied up with the government's need for money. The steady penetration of Siberia and the incorporation of its scattered communities in the empire made Russia the world's largest colonial power in the seventeenth century. In a surprisingly short space of time, her adventurers penetrated six and a half thousand kilometres of inhospitable forest and permafrost to reach the Bering Strait and the borders of the Chinese empire, which made Alexis master of the most extensive territory on the planet. Neither he nor his ministers were interested in extending 'civilisation' to the hunter-gatherers of northern Asia. The well-armed frontiersmen they dispatched with their authority were charged with exacting tribute from newly subjected peoples. This took the form of ever-valuable furs, which could then be traded for the specie the government so urgently needed. It was the same motivation that launched a settlement programme. The government offered land and cash grants to serf families prepared to move to designated areas of virgin territory and bring it under cultivation. Once established, such settlers would, of course, be able to contribute to the national tax take.

Alexis was concerned not to add to his financial problems by plunging into unnecessary war. For this reason his initial response to the appeal of the Ukrainian Cossacks in 1648 was decidedly cool. 'Cossack' is an imprecise term used to cover diverse communities dwelling within or without Russia's southern borders. Originally these peoples were independent Tatar bands who owed no fixed allegiance to any ruler of the lands in which they set-tled or through which they passed. They were brilliant horsemen and fierce warriors, and their 'economy' had its basis in plunder and mercenary service. Both Russian and Polish governments found uses for these rootless people, and not just as supplementary army units. Cossacks were the right sort of settlers for newly conquered or disputed frontier lands because they could be depended on to defend fiercely their homes and farms. With the passage of time, many of these communities inevitably changed their way of life, becoming full partners in the agricultural and mercantile life of the regions where they lived. But they held firmly to their own traditions and spirit of independence. Such were the Ukrainian Cossacks. They were under Polish sovereignty but found obedience to their overlords increasingly irksome. The influx of Polish settlers and the land-registration laws of their masters made the Cossacks second-class citizens in their own country. But religion was at the root of their main grievance. They were Orthodox Christians who found themselves coming under mounting pressure from the government of the Catholic Polish state. By 1648 their position had, they felt, become intolerable. They launched a rebellion and turned for protection to Tsar Alexis. He rejected their plea, and subsequent repeated pleas, and watched from a distance as the Cossacks launched themselves with some success against their overlords. Anything that destabilised Poland-Lithuania was good news for Russia, especially if it did not involve Russia in military or financial commitment. However, the tide of war eventually turned and the plight of the Cossacks became more desperate. It was obvious in Moscow that Russia's co-religionists would be forced to bend beneath the suzerainty of a powerful neighbour – if not Poland, then Turkey – with potentially unacceptable risks for the stability of the southern border. In 1654, Alexis accepted the proffered loyalty of the Ukrainian Cossacks. Thus began the Thirteen Years War.

It lasted so long because it became increasingly complicated from campaign to campaign. As well as the original combatants, Sweden, the Ottoman Empire and the Crimean Tatars were drawn into the conflict, and Alexis had to cope with divisions that opened up in the ranks of his Cossack allies. There were moments when Russia was brought almost to its knees. In 1662 another spate of demonstrations was sparked off, this time by a debasement of the coinage that the government had set in hand in order to pay for the war. Alexis was forced to order the withdrawal of the copper kopeks, but this only meant that money had to be raised through fresh taxation, which was scarcely less onerous. The war went from bad to worse. Poland made a separate peace with Sweden and a Russian army was massacred in the Ukraine by combined Tatar, Cossack and Polish forces. The only crumb of comfort Alexis could draw from the situation was that his enemies were as exhausted as he was. Inevitably, compromise was the order of the day, and peace talks were at last held in 1666–7. Thanks to some clever negotiating, Russia made significant gains. The western boundary was pushed to the Dnieper, which effectively brought half of the Ukraine, as well as the cities of Smolensk and Kiev, under Russian rule.

★

If the young Tsar who came to power in 1689 was an enigma, so was the land over which he ruled. It was westward-looking and eastward-leaning. As we have seen, it rejected 'contamination' by heretic neighbours but was growing increasingly dependent on foreign expertise in matters commercial and military. It was territorially vast and becoming politically more significant as its immediate neighbours declined. Yet its borders were vulnerable. No one challenged the authority of the divinely appointed Tsar and no political philosophy existed that urged the rights of subjects, but boyar factions, the flexing of military muscle or the revolt of racial minorities could destabilise the government. In later years Peter acknowledged that he had been influenced by Ivan IV and by Alexis, his father – and therein lies another apparent contradiction. Ivan was unscrupulous and power-crazed (perhaps literally). Alexis was a prudent and peace-loving tsar, who thought of himself as the father of his people, rather than their master. What Peter valued about these contrasting ancestors was their intelligence, their ability to think outside the box. They were rulers who looked to the wider world and were not blinkered by tradition. Russia was changing, growing, becoming aware of new opportunities. Whether they or their people liked this or not, it was a fact, and they were clear-headed enough to recognise it. Alexis was only seven years into his reign when he established the foreign quarter at Kokui. The residents of this ghetto were able to ply their trades, worship in their own ways and follow their own customs. Like all ghettos, it existed as a means of restricting the access of the native population to their 'inferiors', and like all ghettos, it only served to arouse the curiosity of the native population about its inmates. Long before Alexis' death, some wealthy Muscovites had begun to dress in Western-style clothes and remove that most Russian of all appendages, the flowing beard. But a country that still had its own calendar, alphabet, intense and exclusive religious life and sense of divine destiny was not yet in a position to ride the wave of history.

3

The Travels of Peter Mikhailov

It suited Peter very well to share the throne with his pious, handicapped half-brother. Ivan could mope around the Kremlin in his heavy robes, fulfilling the ceremonial functions of the Tsar's office and performing the tedious round of religious duties, which left Peter free to begin putting his own ideas into practice. At the age of seventeen, his head teemed with plans and his dreams possessed him. This was evident from his appearance. Not only was he a head taller than most of his companions, he was constantly restless. Unable to sit still for long, he would stride about with jerky, energetic steps, his eyes darting to and fro and his lips twitching. He could not bear to be idle. If he was not in the German quarter, quizzing foreigners about events in the wider world, or sailing his boat or drilling his play regiments, he was amusing himself in boisterous, drunken revels.

If you marry teenage exuberance, arrogance, bravado and scorn for tradition with unlimited wealth and a passion for strong drink, you might very well end up with something like Peter's All-Mad, All-Drunken, All-Jesting Assembly. This mock court came into being around 1690, and testifies perhaps more clearly than any of the Tsar's policies and enactments to his disrespect for the conventions of the Kremlin. The revels associated with this unrestrained band of Peter's friends have some similarities with the festivals of misrule common in Western courts and the drinking clubs frequented by young European aristocrats, but they were entered into with more abandon combined with a baroque attention to the ornate embellishment of the absurd. The Assembly's meetings were enacted parodies of royal and ecclesiastical ceremonies, and usually descended into orgies. Their antics verged on the blasphemous and are reminiscent of those of England's Hellfire Club, half a century later. One of their minor revels involved a naked Bacchus wearing a bishop's mitre blessing the unrestrained proceedings in the name of Venus with a cross fashioned from two clay pipes. There were two elaborate establishments, that of the Prince-Caesar and the Prince-Pope, each with its own officials and prescribed rites. They usually held solemn court in the German quarter, and from the beginning, foreign residents played an important part in the festivities alongside boyars and men of humble birth who enjoyed Peter's patronage. However, later the Tsar had appropriate 'church' and 'palace' premises built at Preobrazhenskoe.

For Peter, there was much more to these irreverent revels than high-spirited escapism from the arduous task of running the country. The distinction between mock court and real court was blurred. Indeed, the two overlapped. Just as the play regiments developed eventually into units of the Russian army, so the pseudo-governmental assemblies merged with the executive departments. Several of Peter's roistering friends held important posts in government. This was because fact and fiction were intertwined in the life of the Tsar himself. Here we touch an important and extraordinary aspect of Peter's personality. Throughout history there have been many kings and queens who have longed for the simple life of ordinary people; have wanted to escape from the restrictions imposed upon them by their station. We might cite the 'disguisings' of which Henry VIII was so fond, or Marie Antoinette's playing at being a shepherdess. The masque and the pageant were popular entertainments in Europe's courts, and royalty often took part in them. Peter, however, went further than his contemporaries, taking the 'dual role' idea as far as it could go. There was a practical reason for this: only by mixing with artisans on equal terms could he learn the variety of skills, from shipbuilding to dentistry, that so fascinated him. But that does not fully explain the split personality of Tsar Peter and Peter Mikhailov. He loathed the pomp and ceremony that inevitably went with his role as head of state. In his mind there was a distinction between the trappings of monarchy and the business of ruling. This was demonstrated most pointedly in later years when he built magnificent palaces to rival Versailles while preferring to live in a log cabin. He distanced himself from 'empty' church–state rituals by avoiding them whenever possible and by ridiculing them in the mock rites of the All-Drunken Assembly. But what was more important was that in the latter he did not play the role of Prince-Caesar. He was a mere acolyte in the train of the pretend tsar, which title was bestowed on one of his friends. When writing to his 'superiors', he would sign himself 'Archdeacon Peter'. This paralleled the subordination he affected in military and diplomatic affairs. In the army and navy he assumed minor officer rank, and on his famous Grand Embassy of 1697–9 he pretended to be an official in the train of the ambassador. Again, there were practical reasons for this. He wanted his armed forces to be led by experienced professionals who knew more than he did about warfare. When visiting foreign countries he wanted to be free to travel at will, without the time- and energy-wasting business of official receptions, formal banquets and welcoming ceremonies. But, again, that does not tell the whole story. Peter's love of play-acting revealed a detached, almost sardonic attitude to the role destiny had allocated him. He would join in the game of monarchy, but only if he could rewrite the rules.

By creating a parody court, Peter could also find positions for his foreign friends. This was very important to him. He discovered in the cosmopolitan atmosphere of Kokui a vital release from the claustrophobic, introverted world of Russian traditionalism. In her biography of the Tsar, Professor Lindsey Hughes advances a persuasive argument about the foundation of the All-Drunken Assembly, suggesting that it may have come about as a direct response to the revival of Muscovite rituals and protocols that followed the overthrow of Sophia. Having rid themselves of the anomaly of female rule, church leaders reasserted traditional ways with a vengeance. In March 1690, the death of the old patriarch left a vacancy for the top ecclesiastical job. The conservative majority set aside Peter's nominee in favour of Adrian, a martinet and stickler for tradition. The young Tsar correctly saw conflict ahead between himself and the new leader of Russian Orthodoxy. This became very clear when, at the ceremony of Adrian's installation in August, Peter had to listen to a long sermon castigating the heresies of Catholicism and Protestantism and rejecting all contact with those who sought to seduce pious Russians from the truth. It was an ill-concealed attack on Peter's social preferences by an adviser who saw it as part of his responsibility to keep the head of state on the straight and narrow. Peter's reaction was that if he could not have enlightened foreigners in his court and government, he would create a court where he *could* have them, and in the course of time, he would introduce them into important positions in the state.

For the time being, Russia's government remained in the hands of the boyar faction, which had emerged triumphant from the downfall of Sophia. This was the caucus that had as its nucleus the family of the Tsaritsa Natalya – the Naryshkins. Power in Moscow was still finely balanced, and to those who watched political events, the future was still far from clear. Dynastic rivalries were as strong as ever. Sophia and Golitsyn watched from their respective places of exile and were kept informed by their agents of events at the centre. The *strel'tsy* were still a force to be reckoned with, and as we have seen, the Orthodox leadership gave divine sanction to the conservative majority of the people. Had events turned out differently, as in these years they might very easily have done, Peter I would have gone down in history as a mere eccentric, an aberration who took a political byway that ended in a cul-de-sac. In 1692 he fell seriously ill, and for ten days his life was despaired of. Several members of the Naryshkin party packed their bags ready for instant departure. Two years earlier, Peter's unloved wife Eudoxia had given birth to a son, Alexis (another boy, born in 1692, survived only for a few months), and briefly the possibility existed of another palace power conflict. But Peter's constitution proved strong enough to fight off the fever. Nevertheless, the scare brought home to friends and enemies alike just how precarious the regime was. Small wonder that Natalya was alarmed beyond the limits of natural maternal anxiety every time her son went playing about in boats or visited distant Archangel. Eventually, death ended that concern. The remarkable woman who had sheltered Peter throughout his troubled childhood died in January 1694.

Peter's grief was deep and genuine. 'It is hard for me to tell you how bereft and sad I feel: my hand is incapable of describing it fully or my heart of expressing it,' he wrote to a friend. But his emotion was also private and personal. Though he visited Natalya's tomb the day after her funeral, he did not attend the ceremony itself and he left his half-brother to represent him at the requiem masses. Such rites brought him no comfort, and in all probability, he had by now ceased to believe in them. 'A little rested from my misfortune,' he told his correspondent, 'and leaving behind what cannot be restored, I write of what is alive.'[1] There was work to be done, there were sights to see, and initiatives to take. Not even mourning could deflect him from the vital and exciting tasks ahead.

Almost immediately, Peter began planning something that, possibly, he would not have contemplated while his mother was alive – going to war. His target was Azov, which Golitsyn had so signally failed to capture in the previous decade. The very fact of that failure was doubtless one reason why Peter decided to make the fortress-port at the mouth of the Don the scene of his military debut. To achieve what the previous regime had been unable to would be an important coup in Russia's internal politics. However, there were wider issues involved. Peter wanted to dislodge the Turks from the riverain access routes to the Russian heartland and to minimise influence over the Cossacks. Foreign policy considerations also came into play. When the Ottomans had been repulsed from Vienna in 1683, Europe had grasped the opportunity to press home the war against the reeling Muslim foe. In 1684, urged on by the Pope, the Holy League of Linz was formed, which pledged Austria, Poland and Venice to expel the Turks from the Danube basin and lands bordering the Black Sea. Such activity brought the threat of war to the area that lay in Russia's sphere of influence. If the country was to profit from any territorial realignment in the region, it would have to be involved in the fighting.

Peter's first experience of real war gave him a salutary shock. In the summer campaign of 1695 he served as a bombardier in the Preobrazhensky regiment, which spent several weeks investing Azov. It was a formidable undertaking, because the army's supply lines were extended and it was unable to prevent the fortress being supplied by sea. The defenders were easily able to sit out the siege, and the Tsar and his men returned home with nothing to show for their exertions and all the government money that had been spent on the campaign. Sage heads nodded in Moscow. So much for the pretensions of their impulsive young ruler!

For his part, Peter was not worried by the political fallout, or if he was, he did not show it. He had more important things to do – preparing for the next season's campaign. He analysed the reasons for failure, then threw himself into the monumental effort of equipping himself with a force that would be able to dislodge the Turks. Expressed in simple terms, Russia needed a navy. Very well, Peter would create one – within months! He moved to Voronezh, on the middle Don, and established his headquarters there. He recruited from Venice, home of the Mediterranean's leading mariners, men who were experienced in building and operating galleys. But he supervised all the construction in person and was prepared to roll up his sleeves and set his workers an industrious example. In this winter of 1695–6, Peter discovered his vocation as an inspirer and organiser of men. It was his enthusiasm, his energy, his attention to detail and his anger when things did not go according to plan that accomplished the seemingly impossible. He had thousands of labourers and artisans drafted in and set them a punishing schedule. He organised the delivery of timber and other necessary materials. He imposed new taxes on the church and landlords to pay for his navy. By the early summer, when the Sea of Azov thawed, he had ready a fleet of a thousand transport barges to convey his army downriver, plus thirty galleys and sailing vessels not only to attack the fortress but to patrol the sea approaches to prevent Turkish supply ships getting through. The new tactics and the enormous industry that made them a reality paid off spectacularly. 'Impregnable' Azov capitulated within three months.

This triumph was celebrated in the capital with public celebrations the like of which Muscovites had never seen. Hitherto, church leaders had been accustomed to leading thanksgiving parades in their sumptuous robes and carrying icons. They still featured in Peter's procession, but what grabbed the attention of the crowds was the sight of their tsar in his European dress, the columns of Turkish prisoners; the triumphal arches bearing Julius Caesar's legend '*Veni, Vidi, Vici*' extolling the accomplishments not of God, but of his representative; the images comparing Peter to classical heroes – and the presence of a carriage carrying the Prince-Pope, who waved and smiled at the gawping spectators. Peter made full propaganda use of his victory to demonstrate that a new era had dawned. At the beginning of this year, 1696, Tsar Ivan had died. Peter was now sole ruler of Russia, and he left his people in no doubt that they must prepare themselves for change.

The Tsar was too impatient and too convinced of his own rightness to proceed with any degree of caution. He had waited many long years for the chance to impose his will on the nation. He had spent those years defining and refining his political views. Now was the time to advance boldly. The only choice he offered to his advisers and officials was to hoist their sails to the wind of change or be dashed by it on to the rocks. This was certain to provoke conservative elements to plots and rebellions. Peter knew this perfectly well. Bearing in mind the terrifying episodes that had studded his early years, he could not be ignorant of the potential danger in which he was placing himself. Even if he purged his memory of such events, he could not ignore the letters that reached him from various sources. Most were anonymous, but there were some brave men who were ready to oppose the Tsar to his face. One such was Father Avraamy, a Moscow monk, who presented Peter with a list of complaints and urged him to return to the pious ways of his ancestors. The Tsar, he accused, was under the evil influence of foreigners. He was holding the church up to ridicule. He wasted his time with games and profane amusements. Without his restraining hand his government was slipping into a pit of corruption. Peter contented himself with wafting the presumptuous monk away, as one might an annoying fly. Avraamy was dispatched to another monastery at Kolomna, some hundred kilometres to the south-east of Moscow.

The Tsykler conspiracy had to be treated more seriously. Soon after his return from Azov, Peter selected fifty young men of good birth to be sent to Europe to learn languages and skills, and it soon became known in higher circles that the Tsar himself proposed to make a personal tour of foreign courts. Both of these developments alarmed traditionalists, and the prospect of the Tsar's absence from the country suggested that an opportunity might exist for some kind of a coup. The so-called Tsykler conspiracy seems to have amounted to nothing more than unguarded talk among malcontents. Ivan Tsykler was a duma official who had made vague references to 'something happening' to the Tsar while he was away and speculated about who might succeed him. This, however, was sufficient to set off a witch hunt. Tsykler was tortured to reveal the names of others who were in contact with Sophia, Golitsyn and disaffected *strel'tsy*. Rapidly the net of suspicion spread wider until it had encoiled scores of unfortunates. In March the offenders were tried and those pronounced guilty suffered penalties ranging from exile and confiscation of lands to death. The Tsar had a particularly gruesome lesson to teach any men connected with the culprits or who might feel some sympathy for them. He had the body of Ivan Miloslavski disinterred and conveyed to the execution site, where it was placed beneath the scaffold so that the blood of the traitors dribbled on to it. It was a moment of revenge for which he had waited fifteen years. The appalling bloodshed he had witnessed in the revolt of 1682 had been a triumph for Sophia's Miloslavski relatives, and Peter's mother had always claimed that Ivan was the brains behind the *strel'tsy* atrocities. Ivan had died peacefully in his bed, but that did not put him beyond the reach of Peter's vengeance. For several days his rotting cadaver was left on public display alongside the bodies of the latest crop of traitors – a pungent warning that the Tsar knew where to look for his enemies.

Peter was impatient to see for himself various European countries and the technologies they had mastered. He had long been developing his plans for what would come to be known as his 'Grand Embassy'. But there were sound political reasons for him to choose this particular year to make his appearance on the European stage. All governments were aware that 1697 would be a significant year. In Poland, John III Sobieski, the warrior king, had just died, leaving a nation internally divided and facing increasing external pressures. No fewer than eighteen members of European houses were competing for election as John's successor, and the outcome of the election would largely determine whether Poland continued as a powerful central European state or whether it dwindled into one easily manoeuvred by its neighbours. At the same time, it became obvious that France and her enemies had fought themselves almost to a standstill and that peace negotiations would soon be underway. Peter did not want to be receiving out-of-date news of decisions that would impact considerably on Russia. It was important for him and his delegation to be where the action was. There were, therefore, compelling reasons for his westward trek, but that did not make it any the less unusual.

For a reigning monarch to leave behind affairs of state and spend more than a year travelling abroad was in itself unprecedented. For the head of a traditionally 'closed' nation to do so was bold to the point of foolhardiness. But Peter was not politically naïve, as his ruthless dealing with the Tsykler conspiracy shows. He had no intention of leaving Russia without ensuring that it would be in the hands of men who were both effective and loyal. Now it became clear what the teenage Tsar had been up to for the last decade, when he had seemed to be merely amusing himself with war games and drunken revels. He had been building up a personal court, staffed by men whose only qualifications were talent and loyalty to himself. Men who did not rely on boyar factions or family alliances. Men who were not necessarily even Russians.

The late seventeenth century was a good time to recruit foreign advisers. Recent wars, particularly the Thirty Years War and the Civil War in England, had produced a class of military officers, many of whom were either unable to settle to civilian life or were *personae non gratae* in their own countries. One such was Patrick Gordon, a Scottish adventurer who from the age of sixteen had sought his fortune in the pay of foreign rulers. By 1661, he had served in the armies of Sweden, Poland and the Holy Roman Empire. Then, at the age of twenty-six, he offered his sword to Tsar Alexis. He was still footloose, but he married the daughter of a prominent member of the German community in Moscow and took part in various campaigns. The young Peter was attracted by this swashbuckling Scot and drew him into his inner circle. This was an important political coup, for Peter gained the support not only of an experienced officer, now raised to the rank of general, with extensive international contacts, but also one who had fallen out with the Sophia–Golitsyn faction. As a Catholic and a supporter of the Stuart cause, Gordon wanted to work for the restoration of James II. However, he had become stuck in Russia as a result of the intransigence of Golitsyn. Sophia's regime had become so reliant on the Scot's military expertise that they simply could not allow him to leave. Golitsyn feared that, if he gave Gordon, his most senior officer, permission to go home, others would follow. This led to a long-running argument until, as Gordon reported, eventually the minister 'did fall out in a great passion against me' and he feared exile 'to the remotest places of their empire'.[2] Gordon had proved invaluable to Peter in training the Preobrazhensky and Semenovsky regiments in the latest military techniques. His support during the 1689 crisis had been absolutely crucial. Peter ordered Gordon to come to his assistance, and it was the Scot's decision to back the young Tsar that brought other officers to his standard. By 1695, he had raised the Tsar's personal guards to a high level of competence, and he led them in Peter's first and second Azov campaigns. When Peter set off on the Grand Embassy in March 1697, the veteran Gordon was prominent among those entrusted with maintaining order at home.

Gordon was a Scottish Catholic. Another member of Peter's motley 'gang' was the Swiss Calvinist François Lefort. Since, in Russia, both men shared the stigma of being regarded as heretics they were able to work together in a way that would have been more difficult elsewhere. As for Peter, he set little store by religious differences. Lefort, some twenty years younger than Gordon, had been schooled in the great Swiss infantry tradition and brought different skills and experience to the modernisation of Peter's army. Those who criticised Peter's favourites dismissed Lefort as a debauched wastrel, and he certainly seems to have been a leading light in the lecherous and irreverent revels of the All-Drunken Assembly. It was Lefort who set Peter up with his first mistress, the German Anna Mons, the daughter of a wine merchant. For whatever reasons, the Tsar reposed complete trust in his Swiss friend and mentor. Lefort took command of Peter's Azov campaigns and held the ranks of both general and admiral. The extent of the sovereign's confidence was revealed when he put Lefort in charge of the Grand Embassy.

Despite the prominence of Gordon and Lefort, most members of Peter's inner circle were his fellow countrymen, sons of well-established noble or gentry families. However, as if to underscore the fact that neither birth not court contacts were passports to royal favour, Peter chose his closest lifelong friend from among the Moscow plebs. Alexander (Peter's pet name for him was 'Aleksasha') Menshikov was almost the same age as the Tsar and was widely believed to have been the son of a pastry cook. In fact, it is difficult to discern the truth about Menshikov's lowly origins because he never advertised them and jealous commentators delighted to exaggerate them. His was a rags-to-riches story par excellence, and the immense power and wealth he came to enjoy he owed entirely to Peter's affection. According to one story, the two met when Menshikov, a member of the Preobrazhensky regiment, was on guard duty. When the Tsar approached his post clad, as usual, in the garb of anonymity, which fooled no one, the young soldier challenged the tall 'stranger'. Though arrested for his effrontery, Menshikov was pardoned and commended by Peter for his diligence. However their friendship came about, it proved to be extremely close. Peter and Alexander were kindred spirits. Their letters expressed the kind of endearments often associated with lovers – 'my heart', 'my dearest friend', 'my beloved comrade' – and they were suspected of having a homosexual relationship. This may well have been the case. Peter was not the sort of man to deny himself any kind of experience and had little regard for conventional morality. Menshikov was selected as a member of the Tsar's personal entourage during the Grand Embassy, and it seems that it was this shared 'holiday' that cemented their friendship. Like all intense relationships, this one had its downs as well as its ups. Peter bestowed phenomenal gifts and important positions on his 'brother', but there were also occasional 'tiffs' when Menshikov felt the edge of Peter's tongue or even the force of his fist. In purely political terms, the Tsar knew that he could rely on men like Menshikov. They were his creatures, tied to him by personal bonds and totally dependent upon his continued goodwill. Menshikov responded to Peter's trust and generosity with undivided loyalty and conscientious hard work. He was dashing and brave in battle, diligent in carrying out numerous administrative duties, and always ready with considered counsel. He often acted as the Tsar's personal envoy, particularly in situations involving difficult or unpleasant confrontations. The supreme example of Peter's confidence was his entrusting of the upbringing of the young tsarevich into Menshikov's hands.

The makeup of Peter's inner circle was so idiosyncratic and rainbow-hued as to make it difficult to see any pattern in his appointments. Alongside the new men were others of boyar rank. Peter prided himself on being able to spot potential among the hereditary nobility, a class that he largely held in contempt. He told a group of his intimates that 'from time to time an individual member of their or some other clan distinguished himself, but that was all; all the rest were complete idiots, of which their own brothers were examples'.[3] Yet it is not easy to discern obvious skills and talents in the close attendants the Tsar *did* choose. Among the confidants to whom he addressed the remark just quoted were Fedor Golovin and Fedor Apraksin. The only trait obvious to cynical observers that the two men had in common was a considerable capacity for strong drink. Golovin had no diplomatic experience before he was given joint command of the Grand Embassy. Apraksin was made an admiral before he had ever been to sea. Yet both fully justified the confidence the Tsar had reposed in them. Apraksin was tireless in building a royal navy and the administrative structures for maintaining it. Golovin oversaw a variety of initiatives, from control of the royal armoury, to building a new theatre and establishing a corps of foreign doctors. What Peter valued, encouraged and rewarded in those he sought out to share his work of building a new Russia was open-mindedness, eagerness for reform, readiness to join with him in what he saw as an exciting crusade. The approved attitude was that expressed by one of Peter's devotees, who urged him to 'be merciful to the people of your state, continue to labour unceasingly that they may be delivered from their old Asiatic customs and taught to behave like the Christian peoples of Europe'.[4]

The Grand Embassy of 1697–8 was Peter's first major exercise in pursuing that principle. In March the cavalcade set out – two hundred and fifty diplomats and attendants, complete with an honour guard drawn from the Preobrazhensky regiment. Among the junior officers of the latter was Captain Peter Mikhailov. According to the diplomatic correspondence that laid the preparatory ground for this expedition, its purpose was 'the confirmation of ancient friendship and love and the weakening of the Turkish sultan, the Crimean khan and all their Muslim hordes, the enemies of the cross of our Lord'.[5] The subtext of this diplomatic-speak was Peter's desire for a place in the sun alongside the monarchs of the Christian West at a time of increasing instability. The slow decline of the Ottoman Empire and the gradual disintegration of Poland made it vital for the Russian monarch to understand the intentions of the leading European states and to impress them with his country's military and naval strength. Peter's conquest of Azov had earned him the respect of his allies and he had just renewed the treaty with Austria and Venice. Further west, however, kings and statesmen knew little more about Russia and its ruler than the sensational reports brought back by travellers.

These countries were caught up in their own conflicts. The year that witnessed the overthrow of Sophia and the effective beginning of Peter's reign was also the year that Mary II and her Dutch husband, William, became joint rulers of England, having ousted the last Stuart king, James II. This event was the coping stone on the League of Augsburg, a coalition of states brought into being to check the ambitions of Louis XIV, the expansionist autocrat who ruled from the symbolic magnificence of Versailles and had dominated Europe for a quarter of a century. His armies had outfought and his diplomats outthought his rivals. He had extended France's boundaries to the north and the east. His subjects and many foreigners had come to share his own belief in his invincibility. But eventually his very success forced his neighbours to unite against him. It was not just the French king's awesome power, backed by his army of 140,000 well-trained and equipped troops, that concerned other rulers; Louis had unleashed a ferocious reign of terror at home that drove hundreds of thousands of his subjects to seek refuge abroad and stripped him of moral authority, not only in the Protestant states of Europe. In 1685 he had revoked the Edict of Nantes (1598), which had extended religious toleration to France's considerable Huguenot population. Soon, horrifying stories of the *dragonnades* (persecution by bands of soldiers) were reaching foreign capitals. Churches were burned, communities massacred, women raped and children orphaned. Protestants were ordered to convert or face the consequences. No other single act did more to damage Louis' international reputation than the revocation of the Edict of Nantes. Even his ally, James II, opposed the French king's policy as 'not being politic, much less Christian'. Other states opened their borders to the pitiable bands of refugees queuing to find asylum. Russia was among their number. In 1687, a decree was published whose title left no doubt about the government's official policy: *A Declaration of the Tsars of Muscovy against the French King in Favour of the Poor Protestants' Distress in this Present Persecution.*

Bearing in mind the opposition of the Orthodox church to all contact with heretics, this policy is, at first sight, surprising. There were, I believe, two reasons for it. One was the poor diplomatic relations between the two countries. In order to distract the Empire from events in the West, Louis had formed an alliance with the Turks. Embassies sent from Moscow to the French court seeking aid against the Muslims were rebuffed, and in 1689, two Jesuit missionaries en route from France to China were expelled from

Russia. As we have seen, Peter formed close personal links with German, Dutch and British residents in Moscow, and mercantile contacts came via the northern routes that bypassed French territory. The other reason for Peter's antipathy to the regime of Louis XIV was his genuine revulsion at the French autocrat's treatment of religious minorities. The Tsar was by temperament opposed to coercion in matters of faith. In the foreign quarter and during his trips abroad he often debated religious issues with church leaders, and his sympathetic attitude towards Protestant churches encouraged some Lutheran theologians to believe that Peter was at heart 'one of us'. In later years he instigated reforms of the Orthodox church designed to eradicate 'obscurantism' and over-ornate ceremonial and to encourage lay people to study their faith. Although just as much an absolutist as Louis, Peter's style could scarcely have been more different. He was an Enlightenment monarch *avant la lettre*. While he would employ the most draconian measures to ensure loyalty to his person, he saw no need to enforce unity of belief.

By 1689, the alliance of anti-French states embraced Spain, the Empire, Sweden, Saxony, England, Holland, Bavaria and Savoy. The War of the League of Augsburg raged throughout the years that Peter was establishing his authority. To observers in Russia it demonstrated two facts: that French military power had passed its zenith and that a ruler of stature had emerged in the person of William III. The English king and Dutch stadtholder pursued the war against Louis with tenacity. Despite a string of defeats and inconclusive battles, as well as difficulties with his parliaments, William held the alliance together and kept its armies in the field. The French were eventually worn down and Louis was obliged to enter into secret negotiations with William, which led to a peace conference being convened at Ryswick (Rijswyk), near The Hague, in the summer of 1697. This gathering of plenipotentiaries caused Peter to change his travel plans.

He had journeyed westwards along the established trade route that led to the port of Riga in Swedish-occupied Livonia. Here he was eager to learn all he could about the military and political situation along the southern Baltic littoral. Charles XI of Sweden had maintained his dominance of the region by a series of wars and treaties early in his reign, by courting the friendship of Louis XIV and, in latter years, by judicious neutrality during the War of the League of Augsburg. Charles XI was another member of the seventeenth century's 'autocracy club'. By a series of enactments he had reduced the power of the nobility and established himself as an absolute monarch with the backing of a large, well-trained conscript army and an efficient bureaucracy. One of his major domestic reforms was the institution of a table of ranks, which made promotion and royal favour dependent not on birth, connections or wealth, but on service to the crown. Charles employed men on merit, regardless of social station. The similarities between these policies and those adopted by Peter are striking, but they owe more to what we might call the 'temper of the time' than to actual emulation. In this age of absolutism, intelligent and perceptive rulers adopted similar policies. Charles was certainly intelligent and perceptive, a hard-working king who did not waste time or money on the prestige projects that obsessed some of his royal contemporaries.

Peter could not help but regard Sweden as potentially hostile, a nation that barriered his access to the West, and his reception in Riga did nothing to change his perception. Having arrived incognito ahead of the main embassy, he naturally gravitated to the harbour. Here he tried to make drawings of the ships and fortifications. Just as naturally, the local authorities objected and ordered Mr Mikhailov to desist. Peter complained bitterly that he had not been treated with the honour due to his station. Apparently, he could not see the illogicality of his position. He insisted on playing the anonymity game his way, which meant not being recognised when he did not want to be, but being accorded all the dignities of royalty when he did. Peter left Riga in a huff on 8 April before the arrival of Lefort and Golovin. It was left to them to smooth over the situation and re-establish cordial relations with a trade treaty. This was no storm in a teacup. Peter's reaction to being, as he believed, snubbed by his fellow monarch was to have far-reaching, bloody consequences. What the Tsar did not know before his hasty departure was that on 5 April, Charles XI had died suddenly of cancer in Stockholm, at the age of forty-one. He was succeeded by his fourteen-year-old son, who was cast in a very different mould from his father. As Charles XII, he would play a dramatic part in the life and fortunes of Tsar Peter.

The reception in Brandenburg-Prussia Peter found altogether more agreeable. He had much in common with the ruler of this state, just emerging into full nationhood. Frederick III (soon to become King Frederick I of Prussia) inherited from his father, Frederick William, the Great Elector, the mission of turning a disunited, ravaged land into a powerful centralised monarchy with a military reputation that could claim the respect of its European neighbours. Brandenburg had suffered terribly in the Thirty Years War. Much of its territory had been annexed by Sweden, and though it had given loyal support to the Empire, it had gained very little from the Peace of Westphalia, which concluded that war. Caught between the ambitions of Sweden and Poland, Brandenburg-Prussia could easily have been crushed, but Frederick William turned danger into opportunity. Internally, he established autocratic control and used it to build a large standing army. Externally, he successfully played the balance-of-power game by lending support to either France or the Empire in order to increase his own prestige. When courted by both sides, it was his policy always to choose the one that was currently weaker. This placed him in a position to profit in the subsequent peace negotiations. Frederick III was not cut from the same cloth as his father. He was more interested in the glittering trappings of royalty, and overspent hugely on the building of palaces and the maintenance of a cultured and luxurious court. However, the momentum built up by the Great Elector did not slow down disastrously. Frederick was related through his mother to the House of Orange: William III was his cousin. Family ties as well as practical politics inclined him to support Holland in the War of the League of Augsburg. It was in the interests of both countries to prevent Sweden, by judicious neutrality, from strengthening its position in the Baltic. He was also appalled at the fate of his French co-religionists and threw his borders open to the fleeing Huguenots.

His host, presumably knowing the Tsar's passion for pyrotechnics, welcomed Peter with a firework display, concluding with a set-piece tableau extolling the Russian monarch. Again, while Lefort and the diplomats were holding serious talks with their counterparts, Peter was exploring the docks and military headquarters. He spent most of May and June in Brandenburg-Prussia and was there when two pieces of important news arrived. Frederick Augustus, Elector of Saxony, had won the Polish election by setting aside his Lutheran faith and converting to Catholicism. Peter was anxious to meet the new ruler of Poland, but that, and also a courtesy visit to Vienna, had to wait. Information arrived that the peace negotiator had been summoned to Ryswick. This made it imperative for Peter to set off for the Netherlands without delay.

However, he was not allowed to pass through Hanover without engaging the attention of the Electress Sophia, who was curious to meet this strange Oriental phenomenon. She was not the only one to be attracted by the newcomer. A crowd gathered outside the appointed rendezvous, and the first problem his hostess faced was getting Peter into the building. She later recalled, 'We negotiated for a long time, and finally my son had to disperse the crowd with the help of the guards. While the ambassadors with their retinue were approaching, the tsar sneaked by a hidden staircase into his room, which was next to the dining room.' That embarrassment safely negotiated, the party went in to dine. Peter seems to have been on his best behaviour. He certainly made an impact on the Electress – and her daughter.

> The tsar is a very tall, fine man, with a handsome face and good posture. His mind is very lively and his retorts are quick and incisive. But with all these great gifts of Nature, he could well have better manners. We went to table without delay. Mr Koppenstein, who acted as master

of ceremonies, offered His Majesty a napkin, which puzzled him, for in Brandenburg they would offer him a fingerbowl after a meal. My daughter and I placed His Majesty between us, with an interpreter on either side of him. He was very gay and quite unconstrained, and we struck up a great friendship with him. My daughter and His Majesty exchanged snuffboxes. The tsar's snuffbox is ornamented with His Majesty's initials; my daughter values it very much. We remained at table for a long time, but it did not seem long to us for the tsar never stopped talking and was very gay. My daughter made her Italians sing for him. He liked their singing, though he admitted that he was not a great lover of music. I asked him whether he liked hunting, and he answered, no, but that his father had loved it very much, as for himself, his own real passions, since youth, were sailing and fireworks. He told us that he built ships himself; he showed us his hands and made us feel how hard they were because of work. After supper, His Majesty ordered his violinists to be brought in, and we danced after the Muscovite manner, which is much more graceful than the Polish one. Our dance continued until four in the morning ... [The tsar] is quite an extraordinary person, one can neither describe nor picture him without having seen him; he has a good heart, full of just and noble sentiments. He did not drink to excess in our presence, but the men of his retinue got drunk after we had left.[6]

Peter continued on his way to Holland. The great maritime republic had always been his primary objective. He knew several Dutchmen, from ambassadors to mariners and shipwrights, and had taken pains to learn their language. He longed to see for himself the harbours from which great ships set out for the world's farthest oceans and returned bearing all manner of exotic merchandise. He wanted to examine the yards where the gun-bristling men-of-war were built and listen to sailors' tales of furious naval battles. It was with one of his acquaintances, Herrit Kist, that he lodged on his first arrival in the country on 6 August. Kist was no commercial prince or Dutch oligarch, but a humble smith who lived at Zaandam, near Amsterdam, and worked in the shipyard. True to his custom of preferring simple dwellings to grand palaces and maintaining the anonymity that would free him to pursue his own interests, Peter slept in a cramped bedroom in the artisan's house and took his simple meals with the family. By day he went to work with his host, eagerly observing the way metal cleats and bolts, gun mountings and chains were fashioned, and trying his own hand at the forge. But the pantomime could not be sustained. In polite society people might indulge the Tsar in his quaint masquerade, but Kist's neighbours were inquisitive men and women who made no effort to hide their curiosity. It was not every day they had an exotic stranger in their midst, particularly a giant of a man who was rumoured to be a king. They came to stare at the phenomenon, to peer in at windows, to clamber on to rooftops, to accost him. Some, according to newspaper reports, were hostile and threw stones at this 'freak' who had appeared in their midst. Peter was forced to acknowledge that playing the commoner had its hazards. As soon as the official contingent arrived in Amsterdam on 16 August, he rejoined them.

From here, the Russians kept closely in touch with the negotiations at Ryswick. The main terms had already been agreed in secret deals between Louis and William. They involved territorial compromise in which France gave up some, but not all, of its recent acquisitions and re-established trade with the Dutch Republic. Louis' main – and humiliating – concession was recognising William as King of England (his wife, Queen Mary II, had died in 1694) and, by extension, his kingdom as Protestant. The two states now united under the rule of the King-stadtholder constituted a powerful maritime entity and one that virtually controlled the narrow seas linking the trade areas of the Atlantic, the Mediterranean and the Baltic. On 10 September, the treaty was signed by France, the United Provinces (the Dutch Republic), England and Spain, and the Empire accepted its terms a few weeks later. There now followed a couple of years of peace, but unresolved issues ensured that it would be an uneasy peace. The Emperor was moving towards an understanding with the Ottoman sultan, which would undermine Peter's principal objective in the Grand Embassy. There were new rulers in Poland and Sweden and, therefore, new diplomatic relations to be established with those lands. And the last of the Spanish Habsburgs, Charles II, was a doddering, childless imbecile, approaching the end of his days. Peter's concerns were with events in the east and north, but the eyes of most European statesmen were fixed on Madrid and the fate of the vast Spanish empire. Would its European and overseas territories fall into the hands of France or the Empire, both of whose rulers could claim inheritance through family connections? There could be little doubt that stormy days lay ahead.

However, for the moment, Peter was enjoying his grand tour. He spent four and a half months in the Netherlands, during which time he worked in the shipyard of the Dutch East India Company as a carpenter. He was employed on the construction of a new frigate, and it was with great pride and satisfaction that he saw it launched on 9 November as the *Peter and Paul*. His stay in Amsterdam was enlivened by a series of events laid on by his hosts. Always participating as a member of the Golovin and Lefort entourage, Peter attended, among things, banquets, a play (a novel experience for him), firework displays, a mock naval battle and a visit to an orphanage. Everything about this energetic young republic impressed the Tsar. In turn, he and his companions made an impression on Dutch high society, though not in all respects the one they might have wished to make. The clash of cultures was considerable. Russian table manners were less refined than those of their hosts, and the Muscovites' prodigious capacity for strong drink never failed to amaze the ladies and gentlemen of the Dutch *haut monde*. Inevitably the guests from the East cut a poor figure on the ballroom floor and their attitude to women generally was considered boorish. Probably the biggest hurdle of etiquette the visitors had to overcome related to class distinctions. For all Peter's playing at being a humble artisan, sailor or soldier, he could not rid himself of the rigid mental barrier that segregated the servers and the served. He and his companions saw no reason to treat Dutch councillors and officials with the respect to which their rank entitled them. Notions of equality dear to the merchant princes of Amsterdam were quite alien to the Russians.

Peter had a list of the men he most wanted to meet. High on that list was Antonie van Leeuenhoek, the great microscopist. The Tsar made a special visit to Delft to spend time with this pioneer scientist. Here he was able to examine the most sophisticated instruments currently available for the study of infinitesimal entities. Leeuenhoek ground his own lenses, some giving as much as three-hundredfold magnification. Peter discussed Leeuenhoek's theories about the minute organisms he called 'animalcules' and which, he claimed, always existed in water and air. The Dutchman overturned old beliefs about the generation of tiny creatures such as weevils and fleas. They were not, he asserted, bred from matter or spontaneously created, but went through similar reproduction processes to those of larger members of the animal kingdom. The same, he suggested, must be true of his 'animalcules'. Peter's fascination with this groundbreaking research is one more indication of his own freedom of thought. He was determined to liberate himself from old ideas and stifling prejudices.

At the beginning of September, Peter met another man about whom he had heard much and whose accomplishments he admired. William III received the Russian ambassadors at Utrecht and the formal reception was followed by a private meeting between the two monarchs. This was not a unique flouting of protocol, but it was unusual for heads of state to confer together without aides or advisers at their elbows. What passed between the twenty-five-year-old Tsar and the seasoned monarch almost twice his age has long been the subject of speculation. What is clear is that it launched a genuine friendship, which, though not destined to be of long duration, was important at the time. According to copies of Peter's speech of greeting that circulated later (and that may or may not be genuine), the visiting monarch expressed his admiration in most fulsome terms. Peter avowed that he could not adequately express 'the veneration I have for your sacred person'. He explained that the primary objective of his long journey had been 'to see the most brave and most generous hero of the age'. In military matters, Peter insisted, he had taken the Dutch leader as his model. Nothing would please him more, if the war against France were to be resumed, than to fight under William's banner against the man who was trampling the liberties of Europe. Whatever the future might hold, he offered his fellow monarch's subjects favoured-nation treatment in all their commercial dealings with Russia.[7]

This is important as the first self-declaration of Peter the European. To emphasise the point, the Tsar ordered his delegation to abandon their national dress in favour of Western fashions (what he called 'German style'), a decision as fraught with significance as nineteenth-century Japanese diplomats forsaking the kimono for the top hat and frock coat or their later Chinese Communist counterparts taking up the business suit. It certainly made an impact. Newspapers eagerly reported the advent of this new celebrity and speculated about the effect he might have on the wider political scene. The timing of Peter's debut was perfect. Diplomats from all nations were gathered at Ryswick, and they were, to a man, intrigued by the Russian embassy. Just as ordinary citizens were fascinated by the foreign giant who worked alongside them at the lathe or forge and society hostesses wondered how to cope with the uncouth manners of their strange guests, plenipotentiaries pondered the implications of the involvement of this vast Eastern nation in the affairs of Europe. What they saw in terms of the immediate situation was an ally in the conflict with France. Russia was backing the new Saxon ruler of Poland, who had been elected in preference to candidates favoured by Louis. That would block one avenue to French ambition. Western chancelleries were impressed by news of fresh Russian victories over the Turks, and the prospect of this nation joining the anti-French alliance, perhaps even with military assistance, was one that would dramatically change the balance of power. At this stage, Western diplomats had little understanding of Russia's primary foreign policy concerns. There was scant enthusiasm for becoming involved in the ongoing struggle against the Ottoman Empire, and interest in Baltic affairs was largely restricted to matters of trade.

The English were particularly concerned with commercial possibilities. In 1649, the privileges established by the pioneering Muscovy Company (later known as the Russia Company) had been suddenly terminated as a protest against the execution of Charles I. Its directors had long been anxious to regain the company's position, and they recognised the vast potential Peter's realm offered for trade in one particular commodity. The principal export of the New World colonies was tobacco, which the producers exchanged for the much-needed manufactures of the home country. The problem was that there was a glut of tobacco; there were simply not enough customers for the fashionable weed. Russia presented an alluringly vast new market. Smoking was a habit outlawed by the Orthodox church, which represented it as yet another proof of Western decadence. But the Tsar's desire for closer contacts with William III's realms suggested that it might be possible to break the embargo. The Muscovy Company's principals were not the only people to see this exciting commercial opening. They were outmanoeuvred by one of the most unscrupulous sharp operators of the age, Peregrine Osborne, Marquess of Carmarthen.

Carmarthen was the son of Thomas Osborne, Duke of Leeds, who, as Earl of Danby, had been the most successful – and the most corrupt – of Charles II's ministers. It was he who had headed the cabal that offered the crown to William of Orange. Unsurprisingly, therefore, he was in high favour with the new King, who elevated him to the dukedom of Leeds. The Duke held, and profited from, numerous offices, and, thanks largely to William's support, survived various scandals involving bribery and corruption. His son elected to follow a naval career, and in the astonishing space of three and a half years from his first command, he had risen to the rank of rear admiral. His service was quite undistinguished, and after a bungled engagement in 1695, he was quietly removed from the active list. Carmarthen may have been useless as a commander on board, but he did know something about the theory of ships and shipbuilding. In 1697, he designed for the King a state-of-the-art, sleek and well-armed vessel christened the *Royal Transport*. As a gesture of friendship he knew Peter would appreciate, William gave this fine ship, which was still being fitted out, to his guest. This gave Carmarthen an excellent opportunity to draw himself to the Tsar's attention, and he did not shirk it. From England he wrote, in suitably obsequious terms, to offer his services. He was sure, he observed, that the Tsar, from his own superior knowledge, would want to make improvements to the vessel. Naturally, Peter was excited at the prospect and eager to inspect his gift.

The Grand Embassy was officially over, and there were no plans for it to move on to England. Peter, however, decided on a personal visit, in order to take possession of the *Royal Transport*. He also wanted to learn the secrets of English shipbuilding. He later recollected (writing in the third person as was his custom) that this was the sole reason for his voyage across the North Sea. He was, apparently, annoyed by the technical limitations of his Dutch hosts:

> ... he asked Jan Pool, the master shipwright of [the East India] ship-yard, to teach him the proportions of ships, which he showed him in four days. In Holland, however, this art is not perfected in accordance with the principles of geometry but is guided by a few rules only, and

for the rest it is based on practical experience of long standing; the above-mentioned master shipwright also told him this and said that he was incapable of showing him everything on a draft, then he felt disgusted that he had undertaken such a long journey without attaining the desired aim. Several days later His Majesty happened to be at a gathering at the country house of the merchant Jan Tessingh, where he sat very unhappy for the reason mentioned. When, in the midst of the conversation, he was asked why he was so gloomy, he explained the reason. Among those present there was an Englishman who, upon hearing this, said that in England naval architecture had been perfected as much as any other and that it was possible to learn it in a short time. His Majesty was overjoyed at these words, and without delay he went to England, where he mastered this science within four months, and, returning from there, he brought with him two master shipwrights – John Deane and Joseph Ney.[8]

Leaving all his other fellow countrymen in Amsterdam, Peter embarked, on 7 January 1698, with Menshikov and fifteen companions on what would turn out to be a rollicking jaunt his English hosts would long remember.

Peter's four-month stay in London fell into two periods. When he arrived in the capital, he hired a house off the Strand for himself and his party that was so small, visitors found it crowded and evil-smelling. To them, Peter's preference for confined, intimate spaces was further proof of his uncivilised upbringing. For him, the little dwelling was a retreat from the unwelcome attention he could not help attracting wherever he went. Londoners were just as inquisitive as the people of Zaandam, and the Tsar often had to flee their gaze, sometimes quite literally. Nor was it just hoi polloi who tried to invade his privacy. When the King provided his guest with servants, some of the gentlemen of the royal court disguised themselves as menials in order to gain admittance to his lodging. On one occasion, a prominent nobleman called on the Tsar without an appointment, whereupon Peter 'suddenly rose from table and went upstairs, locked himself in his chamber and said 'twas strange he could not eat without being stared at'.[9]

For the most part, however, he did not allow the attentions of celebrity-seekers to disturb his programme. He was intent on seeing the sights of the capital, and though he could have elected to travel in a closed carriage, he preferred, as always, to go about on foot. He was the eager, experience-hungry tourist par excellence. He was given tours of the Royal Observatory and Woolwich Arsenal. The easy accessibility he was allowed to naval and military installations contrasted starkly with the treatment he had received in Swedish territory. He visited the Tower, where he was particularly interested in the working of the mint. He made a flying visit to Oxford, but was put off by being stared at by students and townspeople. He climbed to the top of the London Monument, from which he could view the layout of the city, now rebuilt after the Great Fire of 1666. What he could not see was the Palace of Whitehall, which had also succumbed to fire immediately before his arrival. On the night of 4–5 January, the ramshackle royal residence had been almost completely gutted, some hundred and fifty buildings being burned down, or blown up in an attempt to hinder the progress of the flames. This catastrophe was, inevitably, the talk of the town, and Peter may have joined the crowds that went to view the mounds of ash and broken, blackened walls which were all that was left of Henry VIII's palace, once the largest in Europe. He certainly viewed it from the water on his trips up and down the Thames. Perhaps he discussed with William what plans were in train regarding its re-building, for the King had vowed to create a more impressive court/government complex on the ruins of the old. Peter saw the elegant classical addition the King had made to Hampton Court and the refurbishment of Kensington Palace, William's preferred London residence. He was particularly interested in the naval hospital currently being built at Greenwich. What we may be sure about is that the Tsar, who had an amazing mental capacity for storing information, noted for future reference all the latest architectural details. He took back to Russia several books of architectural designs, and it would be only five years before he began his own prodigious programme of palace- and city-building.

The strangest item on his itinerary was his visit to Parliament. Because he was anxious to see how England's governmental system worked, arrangements were made for him to witness a joint session of Lords and Commons at which the King presided. There being no Strangers' Gallery and, apparently, no arrangements for visitors, Peter was 'placed in a gutter upon the house-top, to peep in at a window, where he made so ridiculous a figure that neither king nor people could forbear laughing'.[10] The Tsar cannot have understood very much of what he heard, but the spectacle of subjects expressing themselves freely to their sovereign certainly made an impression. It contrasted with the formal subservience of the boyar council. There were aspects of this dialogue that he admired, but he concluded that such liberty would not be appropriate in Russia. 'You have to know your people and know how to govern them,'[11] he insisted. Free thinker though Peter was, he could not break out of the autocratic mould. The distinction between ruler and ruled was a political given, to be preserved not so much because it reflected the divine order of things, but because strong personal government was the only bulwark against that anarchy of which he had witnessed distressing examples.

When he was not taking in the sights, Peter was engaged in a shopping spree. He accumulated a variety of novelties, from blackamore servants (then regarded as essential fashion accessories by society ladies) to clothes and a coffin. The latter purchase illustrates both his openness to unfamiliar customs and his determination to appropriate any that he could make use of. What struck him about the English way of death was that coffins made from deal planks were much easier to construct and less wasteful of natural resources than their Russian counterparts, which were hollowed out from tree trunks. But it was gadgets that intrigued Peter most. As in Holland, so in England, he made a point of talking with leading scholars such as the Astronomer Royal, John Flamsteed, and visiting the workshops of the lens-grinders and scientific instrument makers. London boasted several of Europe's finest craftsmen producing navigational and astronomical aids, and dozens of watches, compasses, telescopes, sextants and other intricate items were soon being crated up for transport back to Russia.

While he was staying in town, the London season was in full swing and Peter's guides were intent on initiating him into its pleasures. Carmarthen lost no time in introducing himself to the Tsar and the Tsar to some of the current entertainments. It was probably the Marquess who arranged for a performance of *The Prophetess, or the History of Diocletian*, an opera with words by the veteran actor/impresario Thomas Betterton and music by the late Henry Purcell. It was an intelligent choice for a visitor with limited command of English. Contemporary opera was more about music and spectacle than words and plot. Audiences attended more to be dazzled by sumptuous costumes and ingenious effects than by dramatic subtlety. One of William's protégés, the French exile and man of letters Charles, Sieur de Saint-Évremond, was dismissive of this theatrical fashion: 'I confess I am not displeased with their magnificence; the machines have something that is surprising, the music in some places is charming; the whole together seems wonderful. But it is very tedious, for where the mind has so little to do, there the senses must of necessity languish.'[12] Doubtless the opera appealed to Peter for the very reasons that the fastidious critic found it boring. His initiation into theatrical performances in Amsterdam had clearly not put him off, and Carmarthen's agents had probably intimated that arranging a special performance would help to ingratiate him with the Tsar. During February, Peter made at least one other visit to the theatre. The attraction was not limited to what was happening on stage. Visits by gentlemen to the actresses' dressing rooms, backstage parties and private assignations were routine events in the lives of the London demi-monde. Among their number was a certain Letitia Cross, a singer and actress in her prime and at the height of her fame. Observing that the Tsar was much taken with her, his 'minders' made the necessary arrangements, and Letitia – briefly – became Peter's mistress.

By such means Carmarthen strengthened his relationship with the Tsar. The two men got on famously, partly because the Marquess and his cronies were more than ready to join in the heavy drinking and rowdy behaviour their guests enjoyed. But Peter was just as much at home with religious leaders as he was with roisterers. He had several interviews with the most notable churchman of the day, Gilbert Burnet, Bishop of Salisbury. This forthright and controversial cleric had suffered exile for his opposition to James II and was a warm supporter of the current regime. He opposed Catholicism but was, by the standards of the day, a champion of religious toleration. His first impressions of the Russian monarch were favourable. The two men agreed in their condemnation of French support for the Turks, and Burnet opined that God had raised up Peter to be the scourge of Islam. For his part, Peter found in the Bishop a sympathetic supporter for his determination to simplify Orthodox worship and, in particular, to dilute the cult of saints and the exaggerated veneration of icons.

At the beginning of February, Peter and his small entourage left their London lodging for a house further downriver. 'The Tsar Emperor of Muscovy, having a mind to see the building of ships, hired my house at Sayes Court and made it his court and palace, lying and remaining in it, new furnished for him by the king.'[13] So John Evelyn recorded on 6 February. Sayes Court was a fine manor house near Deptford where the venerable diarist had spent the greater part of his life. He was particularly fond of his garden. He had spent over forty years developing it and during that time had become a leading horticultural expert. In 1694, he had, with some reluctance, left the house in order to help run the family estate at Wotton, Surrey. Instead of selling the property, he let it to Vice Admiral John Benbow, the master of Deptford dockyard. This tenant, however, was often sent away on naval business, and early in 1698, he was ordered to the West Indies on anti-pirate patrol. It may have been the King or Carmarthen who suggested that Sayes Court would make a suitable short-term residence for the nation's distinguished guests. Peter and his friends had already been living in England for several weeks at royal expense, and in the opinion of some of William's councillors, they were beginning to outstay their welcome. Since the Tsar's predominant interest was in naval matters, it was felt that moving him to Deptford would enable him to complete his itinerary quickly. Benbow was willing to sublet, and Evelyn was probably not unhappy to oblige the King. Benbow had not been an ideal tenant, and the gardens their creator was so proud of were suffering from neglect.

Over the next couple of months, Peter was in his element, messing about in boats – and ships, and boatyards. Most days he walked the short distance to the naval docks, where the King's ships were repaired and new ones laid down. He talked with the master builders, studied their plans and learned the basic principles of their craft. On 2 March, he took possession of the *Royal Transport* and proudly sailed it up and down the river, aided by Carmarthen and a hand-picked crew. Later in the month, a trip was arranged to Portsmouth, England's main naval base. Here the visitors had a great time watching and participating in mock battles and reviewing some of the finest men-of-war afloat. Yet it was not only information about ships that Peter took back to Russia with him in written notes and details committed to memory; he did not hesitate to poach men. Whenever he came into contact with someone he believed could be useful to him, he tried to lure him into his service. As a result, hundreds of captains, lieutenants, engineers, mathematicians and artisans of all kinds were recruited for the Tsar's navy and shipyards and the academy he set up to train a whole generation of ship's officers.

For Peter's companions, the round of visits and formal functions among people whose language and customs they imperfectly understood was a punishing schedule. They needed opportunities to let their hair down, and in the seclusion of Sayes Court they did so with a vengeance. Their wild parties and drinking bouts reduced poor Evelyn's house to a wreck. After the Russians' departure, Admiral Benbow complained to the King, who sent Sir Christopher Wren to survey the damage. He was shocked by the shambles he discovered – broken furniture, slashed paintings, shattered windows, torn curtains and ruined bed linen. If anything, the state of Evelyn's beloved garden was worse.

1. All the grass work is out of order and broke into holes by their leaping and showing tricks upon it.
2. The bowling green is in the same condition.
3. All that ground which used to be cultivated for eatable plants is over-grown with weeds and is not matured or cultivated, by reason the tsar would not suffer any men to work when the season offered.
4. The wall fruit and standard trees are unpruned and unnailed.
5. The hedges nor wilderness are not cut as they ought to be.
6. The gravel walks are all broke into holes and out of order.[14]

The government picked up the bill for the vandalism. Benbow received £158 2s. 6d. for damage to his belongings, and Evelyn was paid a similar sum.

The King seems to have accepted the embarrassment caused by his guest with equanimity. Perhaps he could see, beneath Peter's eccentricities and barbaric behaviour, a man who was not only a useful potential ally, but also likeable. Certainly, the two monarchs got on very well and their relationship went beyond diplomatic courtesy. During the course of the visit they had several meetings, both formal and informal. The King went to considerable lengths to ensure that his guest was well entertained. He assigned his Groom of the Chamber, Admiral Sir David Mitchell, to convey the Tsar's party to and from the Netherlands and to look after them during their stay. He instructed that Peter was to be shown every courtesy and allowed to see whatever he wished. One introduction that was made was to the leading portrait-painter of the age, Sir Godfrey Kneller, who created the first likeness of the Tsar and the one destined to become his defining image. The full-length painting, which William caused to be hung in Kensington Palace, showed the subject in heroic pose, wearing armour and with ships in the background. Peter, who seldom in later life had the patience to sit for portraits, approved of this one, and had several miniature copies made and set with diamonds as gifts for Carmarthen, Mitchell and others who had made his stay in England so enjoyable. But the impact of Kneller's portrait was felt far beyond court circles. Almost immediately an engraving was made and was soon on sale in the print shops. In the seventeenth and eighteenth centuries, this was the only visual medium of mass communication, and many Englishmen were sufficiently intrigued by what they had seen and heard of this exotic celebrity to spend good money on his picture.

It is one of those accidents of history that the Grand Embassy coincided with the unique linking of England and the Dutch Republic under one ruler. Had it been otherwise, Peter might well not have visited England or, if he had, would certainly not have been so accommodatingly received. He set great store by personal relationships. Just as his 'insulting' treatment in Riga coloured his attitude to Sweden, with dramatic consequences, so the warmth of his reception led to the forging of ever closer links with the two leading Protestant states of Europe. One man who had considerable cause for satisfaction over the Tsar's visit was the Marquess of Carmarthen. His careful cultivation of the King's guests (including a call upon his father, the disreputable Duke of Leeds, currently living in disgraced seclusion at Wimbledon) and, no doubt, his enthusiastic sharing in their drunken revels secured for him the Russian tobacco monopoly. Carmarthen and his consortium had to negotiate hard for this valuable concession and eventually clinched the deal by making an advance payment of £12,000, which went a long way towards defraying the Grand Embassy's costs. The nobleman's considerable income from the monopoly contributed to his turbulent and, frankly, treasonable lifestyle. Only weeks after Peter's departure Carmarthen was almost fatally injured in a duel, and in later years he intrigued with Jacobites abroad for a restoration of the Stuart dynasty.

Peter eventually left England on 25 April, intent on continuing his European tour at a leisurely pace. News from home was to cause a change of plan. What impression did he leave behind him in the various countries in which he stayed? Several of those who met him saw no further than his uncouth behaviour. Peter of Russia was, as might have been expected, a barbarian. That said, we need to remember that one aspect of the rigid class divisions of society was an acceptance by the lower orders of the excesses and whims of their masters. There were certainly members of the English aristocracy who behaved with an arrogance and disregard of the rights of others not dissimilar to Peter's. But he was a monarch, and that meant that people expected from him a certain stereotypical dignity, reserve and *royauté oblige*. This they certainly did not get from Peter Mikhailov. He was as much an enigma abroad as he was at home. Probably the prevailing attitude towards him was the patronising comment of one observer: he came 'to see countries more civilised than his own and ... to take patterns for civilising his own rude people'. But the Grand Embassy was much more than a cultural tour, and after it Europe would never be the same.

4

Avenging Angel

The most important outcome of the Grand Embassy was Russia's emergence as a leading member of the European diplomatic club. Several foreign courts now had first-hand experience of the Tsar and his people, and those he did not visit heard colourful stories about him on the international grapevine. Undoubtedly, many observers failed to grasp the significance of the fact that this bizarre ruler had turned his gaze westwards. They still thought of him as an exotic Oriental on a par with the Sultan of Turkey and the warrior princes of Tatary. The events of the next few years would oblige them to revise their estimate. Peter's travels through Europe might have excited curiosity similar to that inspired by the passage of a comet across the night sky, but unlike rare astronomical phenomena, the Tsar did not disappear back into the black void whence he came. He was about to make a strong – and bloody – impact on western Europe.

After a brief second visit to the Dutch Republic, the main points on Peter's itinerary were Vienna, Venice and Warsaw, the first two to renew with his Holy Alliance partners the war against Turkey, and Warsaw to make the acquaintance of the newly elected King Augustus II. The first objective was foiled by events. In 1697, Austria had won a historic victory against the Ottomans at Zenta (modern Senta, Serbia). Caught crossing the Tisa river, the Turkish army had been all but annihilated, with the loss of all its artillery and a substantial treasure chest. Peace talks were now underway (concluded in the Treaty of Karlowitz of 1699), which would result in the expulsion of the Turks from Hungary and the emergence of Austria as the major central European power. This meant that Louis XIV could no longer use his eastern ally to distract his enemies from the main theatre of war and Austria could turn all its attention to strengthening its position against France. The overwhelming concern of Emperor Leopold I was to reunite all the Habsburg lands when the heirless Charles II of Spain should die. The experienced and wily monarch calculated that he no longer needed Russia, and in his negotiations with the Sultan, he ignored Russia's interests. This, of course, was not how Peter viewed the situation. He regarded the capture of Azov as having contributed materially to the halting of the Muslim menace. Even during his absence his armies had been engaged on the lower Don, warding off an Ottoman counteroffensive.

Despite cold-shouldering his guest diplomatically, Leopold extended every hospitality to the Russian delegation, even to the extent of entering enthusiastically into the fiction of the Tsar's anonymity. By now he knew well what to expect of his odd guest. Among the many reports he had received, one from London read:

> While he was here [the Tsar] went around all the time dressed as a shipwright, so who knows what sort of dress he will assume when he is in Your Imperial Majesty's court. He did not see much of the king as he refused to change his lifestyle and had his lunch at 11 a.m. and his supper at 7 p.m., then went straight to bed and got up at four in the morning, which was very trying for the Englishmen who had to attend him.[1]

At a banquet where Lefort was the guest of honour, the ambassador asked permission to allow the attendant behind his chair to taste the excellent wine. The 'servant' was, of course, Peter. The Tsar's love of masquerade found expression at an elaborate fancy-dress ball laid on by his host.

> ... on this occasion, Joseph, king of the Romans, and the countess of Traun, represented the ancient Egyptians. The archduke Charles, and the countess of Wallenstein, were dressed like Flemings in the time of Charles V. The archduchess Mary Elizabeth, and Count Traun, were in the habits of Tatars: the archduchess Josephina, and the count of Workslaw, were habited like Persians, and the archduchess Mariamne, and Prince Maximilian of Hanover, in the character of North Holland peasants. Peter appeared in the dress of a Friesland boor, and all who spoke to him addressed him in that character, at the same time talking to him of the great czar of Muscovy. These are trifling particulars; but whatever revives the remembrance of ancient manners and customs is in some degree worthy of being recorded.[2]

The Emperor vied with Louis XIV for the accolade of being the most cultured ruler in Europe. He spent extravagantly to make his court as ostentatiously lavish as possible. During his long reign he refashioned Vienna and began its transformation into a baroque city worthy to be the capital of the Holy Roman Empire. But it was not only the old town that was in the process of being refurbished when Peter arrived. The latest fashion was for summer palaces in the countryside beyond the city walls. The tone was set by Schönbrunn, conceived by Leopold as a rival to Versailles. It was only partly completed in 1698, but other out-of-town residences built by members of the Austrian nobility were to be seen, and the idea must have impressed itself firmly on Peter's imagination. With no shipyards to visit, he was able to give his mind to the innovations in architecture that were all the rage in civilised society. The Russian delegation stayed almost a month in Vienna, and Peter seems to have been on his best behaviour at the balls and banquets held in honour of the 'absent' Tsar. His entourage had by now learned much about the etiquette of Western courts, and no 'barbaric' incidents marred their visit. There was serious diplomatic work to be done trying to persuade the Austrians not to negotiate a separate deal with the Turks, and when Peter departed, he left one of his officials, Prokopy Voznitsyn, to continue talks. They proved fruitless, and Peter became permanently disillusioned with his erstwhile ally.

But there were new diplomatic friendships to be made, and this was why the Tsar was anxious to meet Augustus II, King of Poland. Russia's successful backing of Frederick Augustus of Saxony for the vacant throne of Poland was one of the most important – and ultimately devastating – events in that country's history. John III Sobieski, who died in 1696, was one of the great military heroes of Poland. A series of victories over the Turks was crowned by his lifting of the Ottoman siege of Vienna in 1683. Yet in all other respects, Sobieski's reign was a disaster. Constant warfare weakened the economy and the crown's control of the nobility. Externally Poland became the tool of more powerful states intent on using it in their own war games. France, Austria and Sweden all at one time or another courted Poland without any concern for the country's own interests. Lithuania descended into anarchy and was to all intents and purposes lost to the Polish crown. Sobieski's designs on Prussia, which threatened his access to the Baltic, were frustrated. But most damaging of all, Poland failed to regain control of the grain-rich Ukraine. The area east of the Dnieper had been ceded to Russia in 1667. The Poles regarded this as a temporary arrangement, but in Moscow it was considered as a restoration of territory that belonged to Muscovy as of ancient right. Then, in 1686, Russian diplomats pulled off the amazing coup of having their claim to the whole Ukraine recognised. Possession of this vast territory of over 600,000 square kilometres was vital to both countries. Peter understood well that his nation's wealth and well-being depended on retaining it. That was why his government watched closely events in the neighbouring state in the 1690s. The great Sobieski had degenerated into a fat, disillusioned old man whose death could not be long delayed. When it happened, in June 1696, the Russian resident, Nikitin, was ready. As we have seen, other countries were no less interested in the Polish succession. It was widely assumed that the crown would go either to the candidate backed by Austria or to France's protégé. It was while the supporters of these two contestants were locked in their intrigues with members of Poland's electoral college that Nikitin made his move. In a stirring speech to the assembly, he sang the praises of Frederick Augustus. Church opposition to the Saxon on religious grounds was disposed of by the candidate's declared readiness to convert to Catholicism. At the same time, the nobles were sweetened by bribery. Frederick Augustus pawned his crown jewels in order to distribute gifts among the electors. He was duly installed but had to fight a brief civil war to confirm his position. It was Russian aid at this crucial time that gave him the edge over rival factions. It also turned Poland into a virtual vassal state.

There was a great deal of economic sense in the union of Poland and Saxony. The German state was one of the most developed industrial nations of Europe, while Poland was rich in raw materials. But the potential of the new entity depended on the skill of its king in overcoming internal divisions and manipulating foreign relations to the benefit of Poland. Unfortunately for Poland, and fortunately for Russia, Augustus II was not equipped to cut the nation free from the Laocoön political coils that were crushing it. At the age of twenty-eight (two years older than Peter), he had already established a creditable military reputation. The Tsar knew of his exploits (and may have met him) as one of the commanders of Holy League armies. He was certainly aware of the dashing King's reputation in other areas. Augustus was a pleasure-loving prince who spent hugely on jewellery, art and elaborate parties and could drink most of his courtiers under the table. But he was most celebrated as a Don Giovanni *avant la lettre*, whose sexual adventures in various European capitals might well have inspired Mozart to write Leporello's famous catalogue aria. The King was credited with siring at least three hundred bastards. It is not difficult to see why Augustus, a young man of unbridled appetites, soaring ambition, personal courage and contempt for convention, who had attracted the nickname 'the Strong', appealed to Peter. This king was, like himself, a member of a new generation, unhampered by tradition and, particularly, free from religious restraints. In Lutheran Saxony he levied discriminatory laws against Catholics and in Poland he removed privileges from Protestants. He aimed to be the complete autocrat, an ambition that, under different circumstances, he might have achieved.

The discussions held by these two self-confident extroverts in August 1698 at Rawa Ruska, near Warsaw, were brief but pregnant with consequences, not only for their own nations but for the whole of Europe. They agreed that their mutual interests lay in establishing firm control of parts of the Baltic coastline. Sweden stood in their way. Peter explained then and reiterated frequently thereafter that he regarded the snub he had received at Riga in 1697 as a *casus belli*. It is hard to believe that a reproof delivered (quite reasonably) by a mere regional governor should have been considered sufficient reason for inflicting twenty years of war on eastern Europe, but a closer look at the situation as it existed in the summer of 1698 might help us to understand what was going on in Peter's mind. During his travels he had been taking soundings about the situation in northern Europe. He wanted a Baltic Sea open to international commerce in which Russia would play a prominent part. Sweden was opposed to any such development, so conflict between the two nations at some time was inevitable. There were also scores to be settled – and not just the recent rebuff Peter believed he had received. During the reign of the great Gustavus Adolphus (1611–32), Sweden had nibbled away at Russian territory, taking Karelia and other land along the common border and the Gulf of Finland. Peter's predecessors had made repeated, vain attempts to regain it. A case could certainly be made for righting an eighty-year-old wrong. But other countries with interests in the region might not look favourably on a northern war. The formation of an anti-Swedish alliance would, therefore, demand careful diplomatic preparation. Claiming that his motivation was one of revenge and not territorial aggression was a useful ploy. (That is not to say that Peter had not been genuinely stung by the 'Riga Incident'. He was extremely sensitive to any slight against his royal person.) He calculated that he might gain his objectives from a brief campaign. In 1698, he was certainly not thinking in terms of a major conflict. He simply let Augustus know that he would look favourably on a Saxon strike at Livonia, where many of the nobles, as he knew, were looking for a chance to shake off Swedish rule. To both men the time seemed to be ripe for a military initiative. The ruler in Stockholm was a sixteen-year-old boy, Charles XII, and the support of Denmark, which had its own quarrel with Sweden, could probably be relied upon. A short war fought successfully by his ally could only be to Russia's advantage. Time alone would tell what might follow. Thus it was only the basis for an alliance that was established before Peter had to hurry on his way. He abandoned his proposed visit to Venice. Bad news from Moscow necessitated his immediate return.

While Peter was away, there were two *strel'tsy* revolts. The first, in

May 1698, was a small-scale affair and was dealt with expeditiously (as they thought) by the government Peter had left in charge. However, a month later, trouble flared again, and although this second mutiny was also suppressed, the Tsar decided that the situation in Moscow was too flammable to leave to underlings. There were two strands to the discontent. The *strel'tsy* regiments had real grievances, and these merged with the anxiety felt by traditionalist elements within the political class that Peter would be coming back with a sackful of alien and heretical customs to be imposed upon the people.

The musketeers' specific complaints were about arrears of pay and unusually long periods of employment. They were accustomed to fairly short campaigns that allowed them to return to their homes and businesses for parts of the year. In 1697, several regiments were dispatched to the lower Don to guard Azov against the Turks. Then, without any respite, they were sent the following winter to the Lithuanian border to help ensure the election of Frederick Augustus. But what lay at the root of their anxiety was their sense of being marginalised by the changing pattern of warfare brought about by Peter's army reforms. They resented having foreign officers foisted upon them. They were jealous of the new guards regiments, who seemed to be trusted with the more important tactical manoeuvres. They believed that they were being used as mere cannon fodder while the Tsar's favourites, the Preobrazhensky and Semenovsky regiments, won all the glory. Peter's navy also played its part in changing the pattern of warfare and added to the bewilderment and hostility of the old military elite.

Meanwhile, in Moscow, other discontents were brewing against both real and imaginary horrors. Patriarch Adrian had taken it upon himself to resist the Tsar on two counts. He opposed the importation of tobacco (and excommunicated the man to whom Peter had granted the monopoly) and he challenged Peter's decision to have Tsaritsa Eudoxia dispatched to a nunnery. There had never been love between the royal couple, and Peter found his wife increasingly irritating, not least because of her stubborn conventionality. Now he had decided to divorce her and had instructed Adrian to see to it. Stories reaching Moscow about the travelling Tsar and some of his friends fanned the imagination of devout Orthodox believers. It was known that Peter had established close relations with Catholic and Protestant leaders, and Boris Sheremetev, one of the Tsar's most accomplished generals and diplomats, had actually had an audience with the Pope! Fear of creeping Catholicism gripped many members of the Muscovite elite. One fanatical group vowed that if Peter tried to change the religion of Russia, they would assassinate him.

In the summer of 1698, some of the *strel'tsy* on the western front left their posts and set out on the road back to Moscow. For the government it was vital that they should not reach the capital and link up with other dissident elements. That would almost certainly turn a mutiny into a political coup. Boyars and officials who had not declared themselves would be drawn into a movement that would depose the Tsar *in absentia*. The military leaders Peter had left in command, Aleksei Shein and Patrick Gordon, acted promptly. Shein forced the members of the boyar council to sign a document granting him emergency powers. This manoeuvred them into declaring their support for the Tsar and made it difficult for them to contemplate changing sides. All available troops were mobilised and the royal family were taken to Trinity monastery for their safety. Leaving a thousand soldiers to guard the city, Gordon marched out at the head of three thousand men to intercept the rebels. It was a close-run thing. The mutineers were heading for Voscresczinskii monastery, where they could establish an almost impregnable base. Gordon cut them off a short distance away at the River Vidnia. He parleyed with their leaders and, finding them obdurate, issued an ultimatum. When the *strel'tsy* refused to lay down their arms, Gordon opened fire with his artillery. It was all over in less than an hour. Sixty or seventy of the mutineers were killed; the rest surrendered.

The aftermath of the aborted coup was to leave a permanent stain on Peter's reputation. After the prisoners had been tried, Gordon sent word to the Tsar that 130 had been executed, 1,845 jailed and 25 held for further interrogation. He considered this a reasonable response, but others in Moscow were pressing for more draconian retribution. It is not difficult to see why. The coup having been aborted, there were those in the capital who were desperate to distance themselves from it. It was important to silence any offenders who might be able to point the finger at them. Gordon was in no position to carry out a purge, but he urged Peter to hasten his return in order to instigate a fuller inquiry. In fact, the speed of Peter's return took the general by surprise. On 25 August, Gordon had retired to his country house some fifty kilometres from Moscow and was preparing for bed when he received the news that his master was back. Word spread rapidly, and Moscow's political leaders hurried with great nervousness to greet the Tsar next morning at the house of his mistress, where Peter had spent his first night home. None of them could have expected the welcome they received. Peter was all affability. He forbade the visitors to prostrate themselves as was the custom, and instead embraced them. Then he suddenly brandished a razor. One wonders how many hands flew nervously to throats. But the only things to be cut were beards. With laughter and smiles, the Tsar personally removed the luxuriant growths adorning the chins of his boyars and officials, starting with General Shein. This famous event had a double significance for those who experienced it. It presaged a deep cultural shift in the life of the nation, but it also warned traditionalists that their days were numbered if they resisted their tsar. Beards today; heads tomorrow.

Peter's mood soon changed. Over the next few days he made searching inquiries into what had been happening in his absence, and he was quick to find fault with what he discovered, lambasting his officials as 'dogs and brute beasts'. In an oft-reported incident he rounded on Shein. Banging his sword down on the table, he bellowed, 'As I strike this table I will skin you to the ears!' He accused the general of selling commissions and also of mishandling the aftermath of the revolt. Shein, the Tsar said, had been too quick to have the culprits executed. He should have subjected them to extreme torture to discover the true extent of disaffection. Peter was not slow to make good the omission. He appointed ten interrogators to work systematically on every one of the imprisoned mutineers and others whom their testimony implicated. This was payback time. Now Peter was able to avenge himself not only on those responsible for the recent revolt, but on the *strel'tsy* and their friends as a body for their opposition ever since that grim day in 1682 when he had been forced to witness the brutal murder of his relatives and their friends. There may have been a sense in which Peter actually welcomed the mutiny, because it gave him the opportunity to root out with great thoroughness every hostile element in the upper reaches of Muscovite society. Very little escaped the examiners. Their work began in September 1698 and was not concluded until February 1700. Even then the Tsar may have been disappointed that no well-constructed plot came to light. From the start he seems to have been convinced that there had been a conspiracy to oust him from power, and that his old adversary, Sophia, was its originator (Bishop Burnet recorded in his *History of His Own Time* that Peter had cut short his European peregrination 'on a suspicion of intrigues managed by his sister'[3]). He himself pursued all lines of inquiry that seemed to be linked to his half-sister, and he interviewed her personally (it was their first meeting in nine years), but although there were certainly connections to Sophia, nothing emerged to suggest that she had co-ordinated the rebellion. The mutineers had harboured nothing more sinister than vague plans to remove Peter and return Russia to its old ways, and many looked to the former Tsarevna as the obvious replacement for the heretical Tsar, but they were not part of an organised plot. Peter could not, therefore, remove the person who was the focus of traditionalist hopes, but he could and did send out to her and all who might harbour disloyal thoughts the message that their sins would be sure to find them out and that retribution would be swift and terrible.

The executions began immediately. They did not stop until almost 1,200 rebels had perished in the Moscow killing fields. Hundreds more were permanently disabled by their torture, and those not condemned to death were sent into exile. No citizen could go about the streets without seeing rotting corpses and heads on poles. The stench of death was everywhere. Peter was not just concerned with carrying out the due punishment prescribed by law. He was determined to extract maximum propaganda advantage from it. He obliged some of the boyars to behead their own condemned friends, and showed them how to do it by wielding the axe himself. As for Sophia in her distant convent, Peter hanged forty-seven mutineers within sight of her window and left the bodies dangling there so that she could reflect on the cost of dabbling in politics. This persecution did not eradicate dissent and there were to be more revolts in the years ahead, but Peter's prompt and thorough action certainly softened up the people and made it easier for him to set in motion a radical programme of reform that went well beyond the removal of facial hair. In fact the Tsar's atrocities seem to have shaken his reputation abroad more seriously than in his own country. Friends and acquaintances he had made on his recent tour followed closely the news coming out of Russia, and many were the letters sent home by members of Peter's enlarged foreign workforce. Bishop Burnet, who had been impressed by the Tsar's theological knowledge, and had been prepared to see in this exotic monarch God's appointed champion against Islam, radically revised his assessment on receipt of the latest news. He described the Tsar as 'a man of a very hot temper, soon inflamed, and very brutal in his passion ... a want of judgement, with an instability of temper, appear in him too often and too evidently'. Burnet came to regard Peter's self-imposed crusade against the infidel Turk as empty boasting. This bad-tempered Muscovite was 'designed by nature rather to be a ship-carpenter than a great prince'. All in all, the bishop found Peter a disagreeable enigma. He thought it a divine mystery 'that such a person ... has such multitudes put, as it were, under his feet, exposed to his restless jealousy and savage temper'. Regarding the suppression of the *strel'tsy*, Burnet adjudged Peter to be guilty of atrocious sadism. 'So far was he from relenting, or showing any sort of tenderness,' Burnet wrote, 'that he seemed delighted with it. How long he is to be the scourge of that nation, or of his neighbours, God only knows.'[4]

What seems to have particularly outraged the good bishop was not the extent of government reprisals, but that 'it was said that [the Tsar] cut off many heads with his own hand'. Burnet would have been the first to agree that treason against divinely appointed authority must be punished and that rebellion was a threat to Christian civilisation. What he could not condone was Christian monarchs giving way to savage bloodlust. Throughout Europe, opinions about Peter Romanov varied widely, from those who applauded his 'civilising' regime to those, like Daniel Defoe, who condemned his 'unjust and arbitrary exercise of despotic government'.[5] We who have the advantage of the long view need to put Peter's revenge against the *strel'tsy* into perspective. He was not the only monarch of the period to be faced with dangerous opposition, nor was he alone in responding violently. While the Tsar was dealing with his rebellious troops, Leopold I was carrying out a ruthless purge in Hungary. Having driven out the Turks, the Austrian 'liberators' more than matched Ottoman atrocities in their determination to bring the Magyar kingdom firmly under Viennese control. Peasants sold their children into slavery to meet the financial demands of the Emperor's officials, and Protestants fled abroad to avoid the imposition of Catholicism at swordpoint. Unsurprisingly, as soon as Austria was preoccupied with the War of the Spanish Succession, Hungary rose in revolt. In France, as we have seen, it was only a few years since Louis XIV had outlawed Protestantism and deliberately unleashed the murderous *dragonnades* on thousands of loyal French men and women whose only crime was their wish to worship differently from their Catholic neighbours. Set beside such contemporary examples, Peter's treatment of men who had actually threatened his regime does not look quite so extreme or disproportionate.

Having given traditionalists this severe warning, the Tsar was now in a strong position to set in hand cultural and administrative changes. All the impressions he had gained during his travels now issued in innovations that he never for a moment doubted were necessary to ease the passage of Russia into the community of European nations. The first necessity was to introduce his country into the same time frame as its western neighbours. The Muscovite calendar was reckoned from the creation of the world, computed by ancient Orthodox scholars as having taken place on 1 September 5509 BC (it had obviously occurred in the autumn so that Adam and Eve could harvest the fruits of the earth!). Peter now decreed that on 1 January 1700, the Russian calendar would be brought into line with the Julian calendar used in most Protestant countries. Moreover, the change was to be ushered in with scenes of compulsory rejoicing:

> To commemorate this happy beginning and the new century ... after solemn prayer in churches and private dwellings, all major streets, homes of important people and homes of distinguished religious and civil servants shall be decorated with trees, pines and fir branches ... friends should greet each other and the New Year and the new century as follows: when Red Square will be lighted and shooting will begin ... everyone who has a musket or any other firearm should salute thrice or shoot several rockets.[6]

*

To pious Orthodox believers, this was a breathtakingly audacious, if not blasphemous, innovation. Times and seasons were set by God, and the church geared itself and its rituals to the divine rhythm. Now, at a stroke and by a merely human edict, not only had the old computation system been swept aside, but the conventional religious celebration of New Year had been declared obsolete. This was widely regarded as the not particularly thin end of a secularising wedge.

It was easier to introduce changes in public ceremonial and the dating of official communications than to force ordinary Russians to adopt new habits in their day-to-day lives, but this was what Peter now set out to do. The long arm of royal decree reached into his subjects' wardrobes. The instructions issued in January 1700 were extremely specific:

> Western dress shall be worn by all the boyars, okol'nichie, members of our councils and of our court ... gentry of Moscow, secretaries ... provincial gentry, deti boiarskie, gosti, government officials, strel'tsy, members of the guilds purveying for our household, citizens of Moscow of all ranks, and residents of provincial cities ... excepting the clergy (priests, deacons, and church attendants) and peasant tillers of the soil. The upper dress shall be of French or Saxon cut, and the lower dress and underwear – [including] waistcoat, trousers, boots, shoes, and hats – shall be of the German type. They shall also ride German saddles. [Likewise] the women-folk of all ranks, including the priests', deacons', and church attendants' wives, the wives of the dragoons, the soldiers, and the strel'tsy, and their children, shall wear Western dresses, hats, jackets, and underwear – undervests and petticoats – and shoes. From now on no one [of the above-mentioned] is to wear Russian dress or Circassian coats, sheepskin coats, or Russian peasant coats, trousers, boots, and shoes. It is also forbidden to ride Russian saddles, and the craftsmen shall not manufacture them or sell them at the marketplaces.[7]

People were given only a few days to effect the necessary changes to their appearance, and were threatened with fines for non-compliance. This time the Tsar had to stifle his impatience. Even those willing to obey were not able to do so at such short notice, and many were not clear about the details of the prescribed new fashion. The deadline had to be extended by several months, and models sent out into the streets to display the required Western-style dress. Even then, conformity to the new regulations did not extend very far from the capital. The problem that has always faced reforming autocrats (and we might instance Henry VIII and Kemal Atatürk) is that the necessity for change that is blindingly obvious to them is not at all clear to the bulk of their subjects. Winning hearts and minds is the work of generations, and tyrants, even if they realise the fact, lack the patience to instigate slow-moving gradualist educational programmes.

Peter did take opportunities to explain his policies to xenophobic critics:

> The monarch, however, soon perceived that several Russian noble-men censured, in secret, the favour he showed to foreigners in general … One day, when he saw himself surrounded by a great number of these noblemen, all Russians, he availed himself of the opportunity, and turned the conversation on the foreigners – 'I well know,' said he, 'that the favour I am obliged to grant them publicly does not please all my subjects: but I have two kinds of subjects; I have intelligent and well-meaning ones, who see very plainly that if I endeavour to retain foreigners in my dominions, it is only for the instruction of my people, and consequently the good of the empire: I have others who have neither sufficient discernment to perceive my good intentions, nor candour to acknowledge, and cheerfully to comply with them; who, in short, from want of reflection, despise all that appears new, feel regret on seeing us emerge from our ancient state of sloth and barbarism, and would hold us down, if it were in their power. Let them reflect a little what we were before I had acquired knowledge in foreign countries, and had invited well-informed men to my dominions: let them con-sider how I should have succeeded in my enterprises, and made head against the powerful enemies I have had to encounter, without their assistance!'[8]

Peter was conscious of having so much to do and so little time in which to do it. A favourite saying of his was that wasted time is like death; one can never recover from it. He slept little, regularly rising before dawn, and put in several hours' work before most of his officials had reached their desks. If he upbraided them for laziness, as he frequently did, it was because he needed less rest than they did. The demon driving him forced his body to keep pace with a mind constantly conceiving new ideas. Thus it was that a spate of institutional reforms poured forth from the office of the industrious and effervescently enthusiastic Tsar in the years following his return. He over-hauled the taxation system. He established a department of state to oversee the ecclesiastical courts, the administration of church lands and even the daily routine of monks and nuns. Just because some Russians were devoted to a life of religion, that did not absolve them from being efficient and account-able to the Tsar. With the aid of leading academics from Britain, Peter set up the Moscow School of Mathematics and Navigation. He established a printworks and gave his literate subjects their first regular newspaper.

All this indicates a new phase in the reign and in the government of Russia. Tsar Peter Romanov had come of age politically. At the turn of the new century, he was twenty-seven. Hitherto, as an inexperienced young monarch, he had been content to leave routine administration and much of the formulation of policy in the hands of relatives and older advisers. Gradually he had assembled his own court of chosen companions as a rival body to the traditional institutions. Now he emerged as entirely his own man. In the wake of the *strel'tsy* revolt, he challenged the networks of political influence. The boyar council ceased to be an effective body. Even friends to whom he had previously looked for guidance no longer played an important part in his deliberations. His two closest foreign advisers, Lefort and Gordon, both died in 1699. Thereafter, Peter certainly had favourites whom he placed in positions of considerable authority, but he stood alone at the pinnacle of power, imposing his own will, selecting and rejecting confidants, secure in the knowledge that he knew what was best for Russia.

Military and naval matters, as ever, consumed most of the Tsar's time and energy. He visited Voronezh and Archangel to supervise the continuing development of the navy and the dockyards. Most importantly of all, he provided Russia with its first standing army. He was by now determined to take on Sweden in open warfare, and knew that antiquated methods of recruitment would not give him the large professional fighting force that would be necessary. The *strel'tsy* part-timers had proved their inadequacy, and the traditional practice of bolstering the army with peasant levies under the command of their aristocratic masters was positively medieval. Peter could never attract sufficient experienced foreigners to fill all the senior army positions (and being 'foreign' did not necessarily imply top quality; mercenary officers were, after all, only in it for money), and the nobility continued to provide most of his officer corps. But he could ensure that the rank and file owed him their prior loyalty. In 1699, he called for the creation of eighteen new infantry regiments and two of mounted dragoons. Some of these were made up of volunteers, attracted by reasonable pay and rations. They did not have to augment their income with other business activities, like the *strel'tsy*. But there were not enough serfs ready to come forward or enough masters ready to manumit their serfs. Peter's regiments always had to be topped up by conscription and by new edicts embracing categories of men, such as clerical workers, hitherto exempt. The three characteristics of the Russian armies that served in the coming wars were: they were large; they had to be constantly augmented as the result of casualties and desertion; they were not hugely efficient. Peter's military achievements over the next twenty years were not the result of having the best army in Europe. For all his studying of up-to-the-minute technology and strategy, he lacked the time and the expert personnel to train his large fighting force. What he did have was an inexhaustible supply of troops, a large taxable population able to keep them supplied and an indomitable will that refused to entertain the possibility of ultimate defeat.

It was clear from the Tsar's intense concentration on military and naval matters that he was preparing for a major war. Rumours abounded as to where that war would be fought. Any war was going to be generally unpopular. Even members of Peter's inner circle, such as Lefort, opposed it. This was why he did not show his hand until the last possible moment. He did not discuss the coming conflict with the boyar council or any of his cronies, except Fedor Golovin, one of the diplomatic leaders of the Grand Embassy. Peter was, naturally, concerned to prevent news of his plans reaching Sweden before he was ready to announce them and knew that the Moscow political community leaked like a sieve. But his secrecy may also have reflected his own uncertainty. He was about to make what was (certainly in retrospect, at least) the most important decision of his reign. Sweden was a formidable military power. Many observers regarded the Swedish army as the finest in Europe. It was not to be confronted without very careful thought. In Poland, Augustus had yet to stamp his authority on the nobility, most of whom were opposed to war, and there was a question mark over how effective the King would be as an ally in a major conflict. On the other hand, the accession of a teenage king in Stockholm and the unstable situation in Livonia made for a now-or-never situation. If ever a ruler was confronted with the Shakespearean 'tide in the affairs of men' consideration, this was it. Peter must have reflected, long and hard, that to take it 'on the flood' might, indeed, 'lead on to fortune', while to let the opportunity slip would condemn him to the 'shallows and miseries' of mediocrity.

Everything depended on diplomatic and military news from Saxony, relayed by the envoy Georg Carlowitz, and the winding up of the Turkish war. In February 1700, Augustus, encouraged by a treaty with Christian V of Denmark and by the assurance of support from Johann von Patkul, leader of the local dissidents, invaded Livonia. Peter dispatched troops to the Polish frontier to dissuade anti-Saxon elements from making trouble in the King's absence. Meanwhile, Peter's agents were engaged in exhaustive and exhausting negotiations at Constantinople. At last, in July, the terms of a thirty-year truce were agreed. Peter was now free to turn all his attention northwards. The Turkish agreement was announced with firework celebrations on 18 August and Russia declared war on Sweden the very next day. The Great Northern War had begun.

From the very beginning, things began to go disastrously wrong. The loss of Lefort and Gordon had left Peter drastically short of good generals whose mettle had been proved in battle. In January 1700, Shein also died. In Livonia, Patkul failed to deliver the support he had promised. As a result, Augustus' campaign scarcely got off the ground. His army laid siege to Riga in February but failed to take the port. The alliance with Denmark had begun to unravel the previous autumn when King Christian was killed in a hunting accident. His successor, Frederick IV, was another young ruler, days short of his eighteenth birthday and unskilled in matters military. Then, Russian logistics unravelled when a supply train including part of Peter's artillery became hopelessly bogged down in marshy terrain. But the main reason for the failure of the Russo-Saxon initiative was the allies' underestimation of Charles XII. The young Swedish king soon showed himself to have just as much courage, determination and self-will as the Russian tsar. He had had a military upbringing, was inured to personal hardship, and bolstered a steely obduracy with the arrogance and self-belief of youth. In his eccentricities he was not dissimilar to Peter. Charles was given to wild and violent escapades such as flailing his advisers with his bare fists, hunting animals through the rooms and corridors of his palace and roistering through the streets of his capital clad only in a shirt. Where he was superior to Peter was in strategic thinking.

Charles turned his attention first to Denmark. The Danes had opened their offensive by laying siege to the disputed fortress of Rendsburg in the duchy of Holstein-Gottorp. Rather than march to the defence of the castle, the Swedish king aimed his attack at Copenhagen, which he proceeded to bombard. The shocked Frederick IV had no option but to sue immediately for peace. Ominously, the treaty was signed on the same day as Russia's formal declaration of war. By the time the news reached Moscow, Peter's army of 40,000 was on its way to invest the port of Narva. The decision to make this his first objective reveals that Peter's claim to be recovering territory that was rightfully Russian was merely a front; at no time had Narva been a part of the Tsar's patrimony. What followed in the snowy autumn of 1700 was, from the Russian point of view, a shambles. Peter made the fatal assumptions that Charles could not reach Narva before the city fell, and that even if he did, numerical supremacy would tell in Russia's favour. In fact, the Swedish king landed on the Estonian coast in late October and force-marched his 9,000-strong army to Narva within a few days. Meanwhile, the Russians were in a poor state – badly led, badly fed and badly supplied. Peter had repeatedly changed the leadership structure, eventually demoting Sheremetev from supreme command to general of cavalry and replacing him with Charles Eugene, Duke of Croy, an out-of-work imperial mercenary.

The siege stalled because the troops were poorly trained to handle artillery and because arrangements to keep such a large force fed and equipped were inadequate.

Belatedly appreciating the situation, Peter went off to drum up reinforcements from Novgorod. At least, that was the official explanation for his quitting Narva. But was he really motivated by cowardly self-preservation? Some historians have certainly drawn that obvious conclusion. But if he did distance himself from the action in order to avoid capture, it was because there was much more invested in his survival than the preservation of his person. Losing a battle would be bad for Russia, but losing the Tsar (even if only temporarily, while humiliating peace terms were discussed) would be disastrous. Peter's will was the rock on which the new nation was being built. Take that away and the factionalism that had so recently been suppressed would rear up again. Reaction would rule. Cowardice would have been so uncharacteristic of Peter that we can acquit him of the charge. But that is not to say that his decision was a cool one based on political calculation. He was in a state of considerable shock at the extent of his crushing defeat at the hands of a young novice monarch. He needed time to assess the situation and his response. There can be no doubt that his 'desertion' was the last straw for his army. The Russians were left with no focus for their loyalty and no heart for the fray. At the initial Swedish assault they crumpled and delivered to Charles XII an overwhelming victory in his first pitched battle. His exploits grabbed the imagination of many throughout Europe, where he soon became something of a living legend: '... his Swedish majesty in the late battle had his horse's head shot off with a cannon bullet, but forthwith mounted another, and animated his men, without seeming to be anyways daunted; upon which victory the Saxons quartered in Courland are very uneasy, and many of them daily desert'.[9]

Europe had a new celebrity, and one who pushed Tsar Peter into the shade. Charles captured Croy, a bevy of generals, thousands of soldiers and all the artillery, and left more than 8,000 Russians dead in the snow or swept away in the icy waters of the Narva river in their panic to escape. Only Sheremetev's cavalry and the Preobrazhensky and Semenovsky guards made a reasonable showing. Tsar Peter's first foray into Western warfare was an unmitigated disaster. To hammer home the point, Charles XII had a medal struck showing his adversary fleeing the field in tears. Peter was distraught. He had been humiliated. The army on whose modernisation he had lavished so much attention had been exposed as an ineffectual rabble. His dreams of a secure Baltic base were in ruins. The Moscow 'I told you so' brigade were in the ascendant. In foreign chancelleries there was a sense of satisfaction that the presumptuous Tsar had got his comeuppance.

If Peter's stock had collapsed internationally, he only had himself to blame. Western diplomats had viewed with alarm the escalation of war in the Baltic lands. It was in the interests of the maritime powers to keep the northern sea lanes open, and they had responded with alacrity when Sweden and Denmark had commenced hostilities. The previous spring, an Anglo-Dutch squadron had been dispatched to Danish waters in an attempt to keep the belligerents apart. Louis XIV, meanwhile, had offered his mediation between Augustus and Charles, only to be rebuffed by the Polish king. The Western nations had kept a close watch on Russia throughout 1700. They had every reason to feel aggrieved with Peter, whose diplomats had repeatedly denied rumours that their tsar had any intention of taking up arms against Sweden. Even before news of the Tsar's declaration of war reached London, the likelihood of this event was accepted and the consequences considered inevitable: ''Tis now generally believed the tsar of Muscovy will join the King of Poland against the Swedes and endeavour to retake Narva … but in case he should, 'tis supposed England, France and Holland will assist Sweden.'[10] Peter had responded to this news with angry threats: ' … the tsar's ambassador has declared in Holland, if the English and Dutch assist Sweden, his master will seize all their merchants' effects in Russia, Archangel, etc.'.[11] After the Riga debacle there was no place for such hubris. It was generally assumed that Charles XII would follow up his victory with an invasion of Russian territory. In these changed circumstances it was Peter who needed peace and Charles who haughtily refused it. The Russian envoy in Vienna reported an informal meeting with his French, Polish and Swedish counterparts: 'The Frenchman suggested that it would be a good idea for Sweden, Poland and Russia to sign a treaty. The Swede replied that his king was prepared to sign such a treaty with Poland but that between him and the tsar there could be neither treaty nor peace. And he began to laugh.'[12]

But now, in what was undoubtedly Peter's darkest hour, two lights suddenly shone. The first was a strategic miscalculation on the part of Charles XII. Paradoxically, the very extent of Peter's defeat came to his aid. It was Charles' turn to underestimate his adversary. Assuming the Russians to have been 'dealt with', he turned his attention to Augustus, invading Courland and Livonia, then thrusting southwards into Poland. His objective was to make Poland a client state that would act as a permanent buffer against Russia. This allowed the Tsar an invaluable and unexpected breathing space. The other 'light' was the long-expected death of Charles II of Spain, on 1 November 1700. The timing could scarcely have been more opportune for Peter. Within months, the major European powers had plunged into the War of the Spanish Succession. It would keep them busy for twelve years and leave them no leisure to intervene in the squabbles of the Baltic states.

Indeed, they were generally content to see Swedes, Russians and Poles fighting among themselves and not providing material or diplomatic assistance to France or Austria and their respective allies.

Peter Romanov is one of the great exemplars of Abraham Lincoln's famous dictum, 'Success is going from failure to failure without losing your enthusiasm.' Charles XII and many members of the diplomatic community who had not met the Tsar assumed that they had heard the last of this barbaric potentate from the land of rivers and marsh beyond the pale of civilisation. Those who did know him realised what a mistake it would be to write him off: '[The tsar] is, without doubt, imbued by Nature with genius and remarkable gifts ... as all right-thinking men are bound to agree, quite without flattery. However ... everything changes here from day to day and it is advisable for the European powers to deal constantly with this country and not reject it because they do not know what it will become in time.'[13] So the Danish ambassador sagely (perhaps prophetically) advised his home government in March 1701. His imperial opposite number, though disparaging about the Russian army, identified what has always been one of the nation's two enormous assets: 'None but the Tatars fear the armies of the tsar ... It is an easy matter for them to call out several thousand men against the enemy; but they are a mere uncouth mob, which, overcome by its own size, loses the victory it has but just gained.'[14]

As Peter took stock of his situation he realised that he could, indeed, call out 'several thousand men'. The supply of Russian serfs was, to all intents and purposes, inexhaustible. He could always outnumber any enemy who came against him, and if his army was an incompetent rabble, he could step up the training and equipment programme – given time. And time was what Charles XII had just given him. Russia's other asset was its thousands of kilometres of poor land, under snow for several months of the year and swept by bitter winds. It was as much a 'moat defensive' as the English Channel was to William III's subjects. It had foiled invaders in the past and would do so in the future. Peter took the long view. He could sanguinely contemplate the sacrifice of unnumbered thousands of his fellow countrymen in pursuit of a simple goal – victory. 'The Swedes will go on beating us for a long time,' he observed, 'but eventually they will teach us how to beat them.' Interestingly, Charles XII assessed the situation in almost identical words: 'We shall be fighting this side of the water for many a year to come.'

Peter might not have grasped in 1701 that the other leaders engaged in what would come to be known as the Great Northern War were his match in stubbornness and determination. Charles, convinced of his own invincibility, pursued Augustus from pillar to post, in quest of the decisive engagement that would make him master of Poland. Augustus was determined to hang on to his crown. Militarily, the Polish king was no match for his young adversary, but no one told him so, or if they did, he did not listen. He confronted the Swedes over and over again. Every time he was defeated, he withdrew and set up camp somewhere else. For seven campaigning seasons Charles pursued his troublesome enemy through Poland and Saxony, before eventually forcing Augustus to abdicate the Polish throne in favour of a candidate of his choosing. Even then Augustus planned a comeback. As a result of the intractability of the combatants, what might have been a brief conflict dragged on for twenty-one years.

'He has, I believe ... travelled twenty times more than any prince in the world did before him and which in no country, but by sled way, could be performed – his usual method of travelling in the winter, being after the rate of more than a hundred English miles a day.'[15] So wrote John Perry, one of the engineers Peter had recruited in England, about the immense energy with which the Tsar set about putting his country on a war footing. The task was urgent. The obstacles to be overcome were immense. Untrained serf-soldiers and squabbling generals were the least of his problems. Russia had vast natural resources but lacked the infrastructure to exploit them and channel their proceeds into government projects. The upper echelons of society constituted an immovable monolith with no experience of or interest in technical innovation, the employment of capital, international commerce or scientific enquiry. As if that was not problem enough, the blessing of the Orthodox hierarchy turned this obscurantism into what one observer called 'the cult of immobility'. All this was, of course, nothing new to Peter. He was accustomed to having his reforming efforts confronted by suspicion, resentment and wilful ignorance. But he now tackled these demons of stubborn traditionalism with an ardour and energy that were, even by his standards, truly remarkable. All his initiatives were far from being successful. The opposition could still frustrate him, and his own inadequate grasp of the mysteries of state economics meant that some of his ideas were impracticable. Given the conditions, reform was inevitably grindingly slow. Yet what Peter achieved for Russia internally and internationally during two decades of warfare places him firmly in the top rank of European leaders.

The army and navy, as Perry explained, became Peter's overmastering priority after the Battle of Narva. '[He] spent the greatest part of his time in the effectually giving his order for the raising of his recruits and in the placing his officers, the seeing his regiments exercised and providing all things whatsoever that were necessary for his army, the care of which he would not trust to many of his lords, but saw it all done himself, even to the minutest particular.'[16] This period did not witness any startling reforms of the Russian military machine. The arrangements for recruitment were already in place, as were the tactical initiatives taken by Peter's European officers in the 1690s. It was largely a question of getting the army, and particularly the Russian officer corps, to embrace the new ideas. Despite allocating junior military rank to himself, and by this demonstrating to his aristocrats that they should not suppose that high birth would guarantee them senior military command, the Tsar frequently subjected his generals to verbal and even physical abuse. Sheremetov, despite his achievements in the field, often suffered the rough edge of Peter's tongue. Nor was disagreement only on tactical matters. Because there was no established military commissariat, mishandling of funds and supplies was endemic. There were several examples of officers being cashiered for corruption. On the positive side, Peter dispatched an increasing number of noblemen's sons abroad to learn the techniques of modern warfare, and his own Academy of Mathematics and Navigation provided education for a further two hundred students.

But an army is not made up of officers alone. Transforming tens of thousands of draftees into a recognisable fighting force with a sense of identity and pride in their work was a different kind of challenge. One answer was to provide the rank and file with decent uniforms. The large quantities of woollen cloth needed for this had to be imported from Holland and England – until someone had the bright idea of developing Russia's own textile industry. The necessary artisans were recruited in Holland:

> A large square for this purpose was projected and built with brick on the side of the Moscow river, with workhouses for employing several hundred persons … the charge of doing which amounted to several hundred thousand roubles before … one yard of cloth was produced and when it came to be fully tried, it was found that the Russ wool, which is very short and as coarse almost as dog's hair, would not make any thread for cloth, so that afterwards they were obliged to send to Holland for wool to mix with it …[17]

Flax was a commodity Russia was well supplied with, but once again, resistance to change stood in the way of producing linen suitable for making soldiers' shirts. 'The Russes still obstinately persist in their own way and will make their cloth too narrow for any use.'[18]

One success story – though again, only gradual – was metalworking. Russia desperately needed its own independent supplies of iron and copper to provide the army and navy with cannon, small arms, anchors and a multitude of fittings for ships and wagons. The country was rich in ore but poor in the technology to extract it and turn it into manufactured goods. In 1700, Peter set up a government department to exploit the natural resources. Mines and factories were established, mostly in the far north between Lake Onega and the White Sea coast. But what would develop into a major Russian industry was slow to come on stream. Perry reported:

> ... there are a great many iron mines and works in the tsar's country, particularly near Voronezh and near Moscow and on the side of the Onega Lake, at each of which very great quantities of iron-work are made for all manner of occasions in Russia, with all sorts of arms for supplying the tsar's army, the making of which is now brought to pretty good perfection and it is even pretended that, by reason of the price of provision being less and labour cheaper than in other parts, they will supply other nations with arms and other iron manufacture ...[19]

Production had, indeed, outstripped that of other countries by the time Perry wrote, but that was in 1716. By then Russia was self-sufficient in military weapons and gunpowder. It was a remarkable achievement, inspired by the exigencies of war. But the reform was too slow to enable Peter to turn the tables on Sweden. In the immediate aftermath of Narva, the Tsar was in a hurry. He ordered the requisitioning of metal objects such as church bells. Fortunately for him, the Orthodox patriarch had just died. By declining to appoint a successor and by ruling the church through his own yes-man, Ivan Musin-Pushkin, Peter minimised the effect of the inevitable outcry.

Peter's worst headache was how to fund the army and navy, and he turned first to the church, which was sitting on vast assets. The religious reforms that, as we have seen, he instigated at this time undoubtedly had a basically financial motivation. Other ways of improving government revenue in the short term included making tax collection more efficient and tinkering with the coinage. A variety of taxes were payable throughout the Tsar's realm – market tolls, poll tax, property tax, customs duties, purchase taxes on items such as salt and alcohol, etc. – but they were collected on a regional basis and passed on to different central departments. In the process, numerous pockets were lined at the expense of both the Tsar and his exploited people. Even among Peter's entourage there were individuals who added their own charges to market commodities that were never passed on to the state. The most notorious example was the favourite Menshikov's tax on timber and coffins, which netted him millions and for which he was never brought to book. Peter set in hand the rationalisation of the system on a model he had observed in Holland. This reform, like others, was long term and, largely due to the opposition of vested interests, it only moved by fits and starts. The temptation was, therefore, to devise new exactions to repair the holes in government income. Import duties were increased, often without notice.

State monopolies were established in such products as tar and potash. The most bizarre of Peter's new impositions (though not devised primarily for financial reasons) was a tax on beards. Well-to-do Russians were obliged to pay a hundred roubles a year for the privilege of remaining hirsute. Even poorer men were stopped at town gates and requested to hand over a kopek. Perry derived great amusement from the objection of traditionalists to this interference with their religious 'rights'. He recorded a conversation with one man who had become newly shorn rather than pay a fine: 'I asked him what he had done with his beard. Upon which he put his hand in his bosom and pulled it out and showed it to me, further telling me that, when he came home, he would lay it up to have it put in his coffin and buried along with him, that he might be able to give an account of it to St Nicholas when he came to the other world.'[20]

The lessons Peter had learned, or thought he had learned, from his visits to the Tower of London mint encouraged him to experiment with the Russian coinage. He called in all existing specie and replaced it with coins that were either smaller or debased by the use of alloys. The inflationary impact was immediate: 'The exchange, on which trade particularly depends, after this, soon fell to between 30 and 40 per cent and the price of everything ... was soon advanced in proportion to the exchange.'[21]

Overall improvement was thus frustratingly slow for Peter, but this did not prevent him from prosecuting the war with every resource at his disposal. He provided Augustus with auxiliaries to keep Charles XII busy in Poland, and sent fresh recruits into Livonia, which the Swedish king had left poorly guarded. But it was at sea that Peter enjoyed his first victory over the Swedes. In May, Charles sent seven well-armed ships to attack Archangel, with the objective of cutting Russia off from all Western supplies. The flotilla reached the estuary of the Severnaya Dvina at the end of June and was but a few kilometres from its objective. It was only the courage of two local seamen that prevented what would have been a devastating blow. They had been captured by the Swedes and pressed into service as pilots. Instead of steering two of the ships through the narrow channels, they deliberately ran them aground close to the fortress of Novodvinsk. The invaders took fright from the ensuing bombardment and retreated, leaving their two stranded vessels behind. If Peter had any doubt about the importance of gaining a Baltic presence, this aborted assault must have dispelled it.

Six months later, Sheremetev delivered to the Tsar his first Western land victory, at Erestfer (near Dorpat, modern Tartu). After a run of indecisive skirmishes, the Russian general pursued his opposite number, Major General W. A. von Schlippenbach, to his winter quarters. The two forces were closely matched numerically, but Sheremetev had equipped his army with sledge-mounted cannon, and these were to prove decisive. During the engagement, the Swedes lost more than two thousand men. Russian casualties were half that number. Schlippenbach fell back towards Dorpat, and it was only deteriorating weather that prevented Sheremetev from pursuing him and finishing the job. At last Peter had something to celebrate, and he made sure that all Moscow, especially his critics, knew about the victory of Erestfer. He ordered extravagant celebrations, including, inevitably, a firework display, decorated Sheremetev with the Order of St Andrew and had Swedish prisoners put up for public auction. As a Dutch diplomat sourly observed, the Russians made so much fuss over one fairly small-scale battle that one would think they had turned the whole world upside down.

That wry comment may not have been so far from the truth. Erestfer was an important turning point in both Russian and Swedish fortunes. The year 1702 was an *annus mirabilis* for Russian arms. The strategy was to thrust northwards by land and water, using Lake Ladoga (the largest in Europe) and the River Neva, which flows from it, as a highway to the Gulf of Finland. Peter had lightweight galleys built and launched on the lake. On 7 May, he had the pleasure of commanding one of his ships in a successful engagement with two Swedish vessels. Meanwhile, Sheremetev had cleared the ground of Swedish garrisons in preparation for a major combined assault. The target was Nöteborg, the island fortress at the outfall of the lake. After a two-week bombardment, the stronghold capitulated. The way now lay open to the sea, but Peter deferred the final push until the following year. In the spring of 1703, he assembled an impressive army to invest Nyenkans, at the mouth of the river.

The capture of this small citadel marked the final expulsion of the Swedes from the far eastern end of the Baltic. It was the fulfilment of Peter's great dream. But the success would need to be consolidated. The place had to be mightily fortified to make it a safe haven for the ships of Russia and all its trading partners. It only remained to find the right location for Peter's northern headquarters. On 16 May 1703, having toured the cluster of islands at the mouth of the river, the Tsar reached Hare Island and decided that it would be the ideal site. Here he would create a port and a city that would be Russia's gateway to the West. He called it St Petersburg.

5

'An army of veterans beaten by a mob'

There, by the billows desolate,
He stood, with mighty thoughts elate,
And gazed, but in the distance only
A sorry skiff on the broad spate
Of Neva drifted seaward, lonely.
The moss-grown miry banks with rare
Hovels were dotted here and there
Where wretched Finns for shelter crowded;
The murmuring woodlands had no share
Of sunshine, all in mist beshrouded.

And thus he mused: 'From here, indeed,
Shall we strike terror in the Swede,
And here a city, by our labour
Founded, shall gall our haughty neighbour.
Here cut – so Nature gives command –
Your window through on Europe. Stand
Firm-footed by the sea unchanging!
Ay, ships of every flag shall come
By waters they had never swum,
And we shall revel, freely ranging.'[1]

If taking on the military might of Sweden was audacious and brave, taking on the forces of nature, as many of Peter's advisers pointed out, was sheer folly. As it became clear that the Tsar was enraptured with the location of his new fortified camp and had the vision of developing it into a city, it seemed to those around him that he must have taken leave of his senses. When Alexander Pushkin wrote his eulogy, *The Bronze Horseman*, a hundred and thirty years later, St Petersburg had blossomed into a beautiful city, the 'Venice of the North', and its foundation had become a legend. But when Peter's contemporaries gazed around at the bleak landscape of rain- and snow-swept marsh and forest, it seemed inconceivable (and pointless to conceive) that streets of stone-built mansions, shops and government buildings could spring up along the banks of the Neva (which took its name from the Finnish word for mud).

Although it would be another nine years before St Petersburg was officially designated as Russia's new capital, the Tsar was already referring to it as such as early as 1704, and it was not long after that that he began poring over elaborate plans for the city, which would be the first in the modern world to be built from scratch. Breathtakingly revolutionary though this project was, it is not difficult to trace the logic of Peter's thinking. St Petersburg was the key to Russia's existence as a maritime nation. Through it would flow the commerce of trading partners. From it would sail ships bearing troops and Russian exports. Peter had always appreciated that trade was the lifeblood of a prosperous nation – the more so since his return from the West. In October 1699 he had issued a ukase of startling and impractical naïveté:

> Moscow and provincial merchants of all ranks shall trade [with foreign countries] as the merchants of other states do, that is, they shall form trading companies and shall deliver their merchandise for the account of their company to the city of Archangel, to Astrakhan, and a smaller amount to Novgorod. Let all the merchants establish, in a general council among themselves, fitting rules in order to expand their trade – which will result in increased revenue for the great sovereign's treasury.[2]

Peter seems not to have appreciated that enterprises like the Dutch East India Company and the English Muscovy Company could not spring up without a sound financial infrastructure and years of commercial experience. However, replacing Archangel with St Petersburg as the country's principal trading port was a bold and essential move towards achieving the objective he ardently desired.

The new city had to have a harbour capable of accommodating scores of ships, warehouses for the storage of trade goods and military and naval supplies, shipyards for building and repairing Russia's growing navy, houses for officials, tradesmen and artisans and an infrastructure capable of supporting a large population. More than that, it had to have *status*. St Petersburg would be the first glimpse most foreign visitors would have of Peter's empire. He wanted them to see not just an unimpressive, functional port, but a city that compared favourably with any other in Europe; a city of broad streets lined with fine houses built in the latest style and occupied by elegant men and women as cultured and refined as any to be found in Vienna, London or Amsterdam. Peter had been impressed by the palaces, boulevards and squares being created by William III, Leopold I, and Frederick III of Brandenburg-Prussia. But it was Amsterdam, with its canals, bridges, cobbled urban thoroughfares and merchants' premises stocked with goods from every part of the world that provided his main inspiration. If the Dutch could defy nature and create a maritime capital on soggy, flood-prone ground, so could he.

Peter identified wholly with this place that, in his letters to Menshikov, he called 'Paradise'. There was a strongly personal dimension to this grand undertaking. The new city reached out towards the sea, which he loved, and was conceptually and geographically far removed from Moscow, which he hated. It symbolised his own and his people's escape from all that was represented by the old capital, with its claustrophobic dwellings and wretched memories. Peter visited the building site as often as possible and had a log cabin built from which he directed all the works. Visitors can still see it, encased, shrine-like, in brick by Catherine the Great. When he was elsewhere, the Tsar kept in touch with engineers, architects and builders by a constant stream of letters. Frequently, after explaining in detail what he wanted, he would end these missives with the injunction, 'but don't do anything till I get there'. Control freak that he was, Peter was determined to leave nothing to chance or to the whim of underlings. His precise instructions covered every aspect of the works, from the type of paint to be used on external walls to exotic plants for gracing gardens and parks, from the purchase of Dutch pictures (mostly marine subjects) to the transportation of decorative stone from the Urals, from the importation of classical statuary to the siting of public latrines.

Just as he ordered objects for his capital, so Peter commanded people to build it and to populate it. St Petersburg is sometimes described as a city built on bones, and this remarkable metropolis was constructed at enormous human cost. Every year, during the summer season, thirty or forty thousand serfs and prisoners of war were drafted in. Most of them were marched for long distances by armed guards, to prevent their escape. Backbreaking work and damp, unhealthy conditions took a terrible toll. Peter's response when construction fell behind schedule was to order fresh levies of what were, in effect, slaves. It is no surprise to learn that well-to-do Muscovites hated St Petersburg as much as Peter loved it. He was not concerned about what they thought of it; he simply ordered them to come. As the city grew, so he gradually moved his government and court there. This meant that Moscow society had to relocate. Its leading members were ordered to build substantial houses in the new capital and to take up residence with their families. They resented it, and with reason.

> ... all manner of provisions are usually three or four times as dear and forage for their horses, etc. at least six or eight times as dear as it is at Moscow, which happens from the small quantity which the country thereabouts produces, being more than two thirds woods and bogs ... not only the nobility, but merchants and tradesmen of all sorts are obliged to go and live there and to trade with such things as they are ordered, which crowd of people enhances the price of provisions and makes a scarcity for those men who are absolutely necessary to live there on account of the land and sea service and in carrying on those buildings and works which the tsar has already and further designs to make there.[3]

Nothing better illustrates the power exercised by this autocrat than his ability to uproot men, women and children from their families, friends and familiar haunts. Not only were they obliged to build substantial houses in the unfinished northern city, they were not even permitted a free hand in designing them. For the sake of uniformity, Peter designated the external style of all St Petersburg's domestic buildings. Only the interiors were left for their owners to decorate and furnish as they wished. The creation of Tsar Peter's magnificent omelette involved the breaking of an enormous number of eggs. No one could complain; not just because Peter was all-powerful, but because, as a German diplomat observed, everyone accepted as a fact of life that 'everything belongs to God and the tsar'. Doubtless, it also occurred to Peter that by physically distancing Moscow's leaders from their relatives and friends, he was disrupting the formation of anti-government cliques.

All this town planning would have fully occupied any ordinary ruler, but Peter was also constantly working on a wide-ranging programme of reform – and fighting a long war as well. The conflicts of the first decades of the eighteenth century, in which Peter played an increasingly prominent part, drastically changed the face of Europe. France was prevented from achieving union with Spain, and Prussia emerged as a dominant nation. But what was happening in the east and north of what men thought of as Europe was equally important. The once-great powers of Sweden and Poland-Lithuania went into permanent decline. The long process of partitioning Poland between Russia, Prussia and Austria began. Baltic trade revived because the sea lanes were no longer dominated by a single nation. And the Tsar of Russia, whom other crowned heads had regarded with intrigued condescension in 1697–8, pulled up his chair to the top table.

The Great Northern War raged for eighteen of Peter's remaining twenty-two years, but the first phase, up to 1709, was the most crucial. It was dominated by the characters of Peter and Charles XII. The latter was a brilliant tactician and charismatic field commander, who invariably preferred bold, unexpected initiatives to considered long-term planning and who seldom sought or followed counsel. His adversary was a man who knew his limitations as a strategist, gradually promoted himself through the military and naval ranks, entrusting overall command to his generals, and kept his eyes fixed on the end game. Charles spent almost all his time with the army, moving round eastern Europe from camp to battlefield to winter quarters. Peter, when not actively campaigning, was to be found in St Petersburg or Moscow, getting on with the thousand and one tasks of government. Charles always put his faith in pitched battles. Peter became increasingly cautious over the years. While concentrating enormous efforts on the training of his army and navy, he understood that his great advantages were the size of his recruitable male population and the difficult terrain that any adversary would have to cross to reach the heart of his empire.

Charles XII was, as we have seen, fixated on disposing of Augustus, and that done, forcing Peter away from his Baltic foothold. No one could deflect him from these objectives. His officials pointed out the strain that Sweden was experiencing in financing the war. His generals suggested that more might be gained from negotiation than unremitting conflict. More importantly, Charles' obduracy lost him the support of his potential allies. Britain and Holland were eager to have Sweden's support against France. They were annoyed by the disruption of Baltic trade. As long as the King was set on pursuing his 'private' war, they could not factor him into their own plans. Another problem for the Swedish king was the unreliability of the Polish nobility. Not only were they hopelessly divided into factions pursuing their own agendas, they were no more enthusiastic about a Swedish overlord than they were about a Saxon one.

At the time that Peter was preparing his assault on Nyenkans, Charles imposed yet another defeat on Augustus at the Battle of Pultusk. He now judged that the time was right for establishing a new, pro-Swedish Poland. In January 1704, the King was solemnly deposed. The most obvious replacement was Jacob Sobieski, the son of the previous ruler. The only difficulty was that Augustus' faction had kidnapped him. Charles therefore put up as his own puppet one of the Polish nobles, Stanislaw Leszczynski. On 2 July, in a field outside Warsaw ringed with Swedish steel, Stanislaw was proclaimed by a cowed Polish diet, the first of two unfortunate kings to bear the same name. No one was fooled by this 'settlement' of the Polish question. The nation's leaders remained divided between the pro-Swedish Confederation of Warsaw and the Confederation of Sandomierz, which continued to support Augustus. As long as Russian and Saxon armies were in the field, and as long as Poland's aristocracy remained at loggerheads, Charles' objective would remain impossible. A month after the hollow coronation, depressing news arrived from Livonia and Ingria. Russian armies had captured Dorpat and Narva. The loss of the latter was a particularly bitter pill for Charles to swallow. The Tsar had reversed his humiliating defeat of 1700 and, enraged by the refusal of surrender terms, had slaughtered the garrison.

Peter's confidence grew from month to month. He knew that he could afford to wait while his adversary rushed his armies to and fro in a vain attempt to make a reality of his occupation of Poland. He continued to keep Augustus supplied with levies and he moved an army under the leadership of the Scottish-German general George Ogilvie into Lithuania, where it could menace the Swedes. At the same time, Sheremetev occupied the duchy of Courland, Lithuania's Baltic region (taken by Sweden in 1701), to cut off Charles from Livonia. His strategy was sound and would be proved in the manoeuvring round Grodno in the winter of 1706 (see below). But we must avoid the temptations of hindsight. In the critical days of war and intensely unpopular reform, matters did not seem at all clear-cut. The Tsar had his own problems with generals, who were forever squabbling and dissident elements at home who took advantage of his frequent absences at the front. The focus of discontent was Menshikov, to whom Peter entrusted the conduct of several affairs both military and administrative. A report from the Prussian envoy, Georg Keyserling, of April 1705 gives a good impression of just how delicately everything seemed to be balanced:

> Just as the King of Sweden puts himself to such great risk in the present situation, so the tsar would also stand exposed to no less danger if the King of Sweden should be the victor in a main battle, for in that case it would be to suppose that the King of Sweden would not go to Livonia and busy himself with the recovery of the fortresses but would invade the interior of the Muscovite state, which could happen most easily towards Smolensk, for this city is not at all secure and would be able to offer little resistance and nothing could later prevent the King of Sweden from pushing through right to the residence of Moscow where there is also no defensive works, and to cause the Muscovite state so much more dangerous a disaster because all the best families are cooking poison, gall and revenge in their hearts because of the dishonourable

execution some years back of their nearest relatives, whose corpses they still see daily on stakes and wheels before their eyes, also because they secretly and passionately demand a change under the hard oppression and daily exercised insolence and cruelty against them on the part of the favourite … the whole country is inclined to revolution because of their abolished customs, shorn beards, forbidden clothing, confiscated monastery property, their divine service which has been altered in some places and the new heavy taxes that are invented daily and whose names they did not even know before. Therefore, this so very vexed nation could well come to meet the King of Sweden with a welcome … In so far that the tsar has a victorious army in the field, he need fear no revolt in his country, for although the clergy in the monasteries leave little undone to foment sedition, and might well dispose the ordinary man to it, but the great are so very intimidated by the terrifying traces of their executed relatives that they will provide no leaders.[4]

Menshikov's influence in military matters also occasioned resentment. He was outranked by Sheremetev and Ogilvie, but his intimacy with the Tsar meant that the generals often struggled, not always successfully, to carry their point of view. The situation was not helped by the fact that Sheremetev, as Russia's most successful home-grown general, was a popular hero. Some dissidents even looked on him as a potential replacement for the Tsar. There is nothing to suggest that Sheremetev was anything other than loyal, but his relations with the Tsar were never warm, and Peter was so suspicious of him that he even posted spies in the general's camp to watch for any signs of disaffection. As for Ogilvie, as well as being foreign, he was a newcomer, a prickly customer and highly critical of the Russian army and its leaders. Were it not for Peter's dominant personality, it is difficult to see how the military command could have held together at all. In the summer of 1705, Ogilvie was all for pressing forward from the Niemen in order to link up with Augustus' army. Peter's other advisers, among whom Menshikov was prominent, were in favour of digging in along the river. Ogilvie was, accordingly, ordered to establish his base at Grodno and there sit out the winter. It was as well that he did so, because in January, Charles launched a surprise attack on his eastern front. He invested Grodno and tried to draw the Russians into a pitched battle. Peter declined the invitation. He ordered Ogilvie to fall back, even though it meant sacrificing his artillery and baggage train. If the Swede wanted to advance into the winter-wasted land to the east, he was welcome to try. Charles pursued the retreating Russians for two hundred kilometres before deciding better of it.

But Peter had another reason for bringing his troops nearer home. In July

1705, he was stunned to receive news of a revolt at Astrakhan on the distant Volga delta. Once again it was *strel'tsy* elements who were at the heart of the trouble. They made common cause with men who had left or been exiled from Moscow because of their opposition to Peter's policies. Their complaints were the old ones – dislike of all the government's 'foreign' and 'heretical' innovations. Their proposed course of action was the usual one – a march to Moscow to present their grievances to the Tsar and purge his councils of all 'Germans'. And as ever, they cloaked their rebellion in religious garb as a crusade for Christian truth against demonic error. The only differences from previous revolts were twofold. This time there was no connection with Sophia, who had died in 1704. And this time the complainers had a specific target: they blamed the Tsar's evil genius, Alexander Menshikov, for the novel policies corroding Russia's identity. Peter's response was also twofold: he sent messages to the rebels assuring them that he would consider their grievances, and he dispatched Sheremetev to Astrakhan with four regiments and instructions to use whatever methods were necessary to restore order. Swift and draconian suppression was important, not because unrest in a distant town of itself posed a threat to the security of the state, but because any success on the part of rebel elements would encourage outbreaks elsewhere. Peter's policies were so universally unpopular that he had left himself no room for manoeuvre. Negotiation with or mercy shown to rebels would have been seen as a sign of weakness. In March 1706, Sheremetev put down the rebellion. In addition to those killed in the fighting, hundreds were marched back to Moscow for trial and interrogation. The general was careful not to make Shein's mistake of executing offenders the Tsar might want to examine. Once securely incarcerated in Moscow, the captives were subjected to the same exhaustive regime of investigation as the 1698 rebels had endured. Over the next two years, more than 320 were put to death in Moscow and their rotting corpses added to those already on display. Others failed to survive interrogation.

In the summer, Peter returned to the western front. One of the first problems to be dealt with was the squabbling of the generals. This had become more intense during the withdrawal from Grodno. Peter was devoted to Menshikov and showered remunerative offices on him. However, he was not so besotted that he would not listen to contrary advice from his military experts. He also knew how unpopular the favourite was and that some complaints were abundantly justified. Sheremetev he still did not like, but the general had once again proved his loyalty in Astrakhan. Ogilvie was a good field commander but he got on everyone's nerves. He was the one who had to go. He received the black spot in September and departed within weeks. But as one personnel difficulty was resolved, another appeared. Fedor

Golovin, who had headed the Grand Embassy, was the Tsar's leading expert on foreign affairs, and the nearest thing Peter had to a prime minister. He died suddenly in July. As well as creating a hole in the administration, this was a considerable personal loss to Peter. He never found a suitable successor and divided Golovin's responsibilities among other ministers.

At about the same time, Charles XII had, as he thought, disposed of the Augustus problem. Having realised the unwisdom of pursuing the Russians into their own territory, he had decided to deal once and for all with the deposed King of Poland. He marched his army fifteen hundred kilometres across Poland, through Austrian Silesia into the Saxon heartland. It was a prodigious feat and it alarmed the whole of Europe. Augustus' government in Dresden wilted in the Swedish heat. At the castle of Altranstädt, near Leipzig, they signed a treaty (26 September 1706) by the terms of which Augustus renounced the Polish crown and his alliance with Russia. This left Peter alone to face the enemy while weakened by recent events at home and the unpopularity of the war. He put out diplomatic feelers to Charles, offering restoration of some of the conquered Baltic lands but rejecting any suggestion of relinquishing St Petersburg. However, Peter was very far from being resigned to allowing Swedish power to reign supreme in Poland. He spent several months of 1706–7 in the country meeting with members of the Sandomierz Confederation in an attempt to set up a credible rival government to that of Stanislaw. The discussions did not go well. The proud Polish nobles were not disposed to be overawed by Peter's presence or undermined by his bribes. When he gave them expensive gifts to ensure their support, they responded by offering him even more lavish ones. They made it clear that their determination to cast off the shackles of Charles XII did not indicate a willingness to chain themselves to Tsar Peter. He assuaged his frustration with their independent spirit by removing large quantities of valuable items from several Polish castles.

It was at this point that the headstrong twenty-four-year-old Charles made his biggest mistake. For a brief moment he was the pivotal figure in the fate of the continent. It is conventional to think of the Great Northern War as a sideshow to the War of the Spanish Succession, which was engulfing most of the rest of Europe. The reality is not so simple. If we seek a helpful metaphor, we might think of the continental nations as so many cogs, some of which were continuously interlocked while others were only engaged occasionally. All were important in their various ways, and their interaction influenced the direction in which the whole continent moved. The period 1706–7 marked the turning point of the war in the west. The Duke of Marlborough inflicted a crushing defeat on the French at Ramilles and forced France out of the Spanish Netherlands. Prince Eugene of Savoy, the Austrian general, cleared the enemy out of northern Italy. Louis XIV's regime was reeling from these blows, but it was far from being crushed. The French king needed allies, especially allies with supplies of fresh, well-trained troops, under the command of one of the age's great military leaders. He had been subsidising Charles XII for some time, and now, he believed, was the moment to call in favours. In the spring of 1707 he sent envoys to the Swedish camp at Altranstädt to negotiate for Charles' assistance. The British–Dutch–Austrian alliance was equally concerned to keep Sweden out of the war. So important was this that the man they sent to talk with Charles was none other than the Duke of Marlborough. His task was not so straightforward, for although the main objective was to keep Sweden neutral (by focusing Charles' attention on Poland), the commercial security of the Baltic could best be served by encouraging Sweden and Russia to reach a negotiated settlement. Charles, however, was not moved by the flattering attentions of the diplomats. He thought only in terms of maintaining his northern empire and crushing by military might any who threatened it. Thus, for example, though he was induced to sign a defensive treaty with Brandenburg-Prussia (Marlborough's invaluable military ally), he refused to discuss Frederick I's ambitions with regard to Pomerania. And he irritated the Western diplomats by his haughty disinclination to entertain the merest possibility of doing a deal with the Russian tsar. Had Charles agreed to negotiate, he would have safeguarded his position in the north, pleased the major powers and could have sold his sword to one of the contending parties in the western war. The subsequent history of Sweden and Europe would have been very different. Unfortunately, Charles was not intellectually equipped to see the bigger picture.

On the contrary, he made it clear that he was not interested in the war in the west. Having, as he thought, disposed of one of his enemies, he now turned all his attention to delivering the knock-out blow to Peter. He thus became the first of a hapless succession of dictators who believed that military invasion of Russia was a viable option. Charles was, of course, well informed about Russia's internal divisions. He did not lack for dissidents who had come over to his camp with stories that incipient rebellion was simmering throughout Peter's domain. It may well have been such intelligence that persuaded the Swedish king to strike, not against Ingria, but at the heart of the empire, via Smolensk and Moscow. Thus was developed the grand vision of Charles XII as the liberator who would free Russia from its barbarian tyranny and replace the oppressive Tsar Peter with an enlightened ruler – and one who would dance to whatever tune Charles chose to play. Charles always gambled for the highest stakes. A campaign in the north would win back lost territory and expel Russia from the Baltic, but deposing Peter would push Russia back to where it belonged – beyond the pale of European civilisation.

Charles was encouraged, in October 1707, by news that Peter had yet another rebellion on his hands. Cossacks in the Don valley, led by Konraty Bulavin, fell upon officials from Moscow and massacred them. This was the signal for what would be the most dangerous and widespread rising of the reign. It was not suppressed until the following July. The causes of this revolt differed from those that had fuelled the *strel'tsy* uprisings (see p. 172 below). They related more to local grievances, but that afforded no comfort to the government. In the tense wartime situation, any dislocation threatened to ignite discontent elsewhere and lead to military resources being diverted from the Swedish war.

That war was now moving towards its crisis. Charles made his winter camp near Grodno. From there he issued his orders for the convergence of his military forces. His own army consisted of 35,000 men. At Riga there were 12,500 under the command of Count Adam Löwenhaupt, and in Swedish Finland a further 14,000 troops stood ready for deployment. Charles intended to leave the Finnish army for a strike against St Petersburg and to summon Löwenhaupt to join him with fresh soldiers and supplies as soon as he had decided where and when to begin his advance into Russia. In June he made his move, advancing five hundred kilometres to the Dnieper. At the same time he had leaflets distributed by his agents in Russia urging the people to rise up against the Tsar. Peter's response was the tried tactic of withdrawal, leaving scorched earth behind him and carrying out harassing attacks on the enemy's line of march. He avoided a pitched battle, but in the skirmishes that could not be evaded, his forces fared badly. At Mogilev, on the Dnieper, Charles paused, waiting for the supply train from Riga. Here he received two pieces of news, one welcome, one not. The bad news was that Löwenhaupt, having experienced difficulties commandeering horses and wagons, had not even started out. He did not begin his 650-kilometre journey until the end of July. This disappointment was somewhat relieved by an embassy from the Ukraine. The military commander, Ivan Mazepa, offered to desert his Russian overlord and bring 30,000 Cossacks over to the Swedish side.

In fact, these two developments confronted Charles with a difficult choice. His men were tired from long marching and weakened by scarcity of food. Should he sit it out at Mogilev, wait for Löwenhaupt and then move into secure winter quarters, or demand a further effort from his troops by moving them to the Ukraine, where they would find supplies as well as Mazepa's welcome addition to the army? It was an urgent entreaty from the Cossack leader that made up his mind. Having betrayed Peter, Mazepa was anxious to link up with the Swedes before his treason was discovered. Charles made the fateful decision to march south.

Now, for the first time, Peter began to outgeneral his adversary. He immediately sent Menshikov to the Ukraine to reassert Russian authority and replace the traitor with a loyal officer. As a result, few of the Ukrainian Cossacks followed Mazepa to the Swedish camp. The tide of war was beginning to turn against Charles, but at least he could comfort himself with the news that Löwenhaupt was finally on the move. However, all was not going well for the lumbering supply train of thousands of wagons. It struggled through the morass of the wet Lithuanian autumn, and by mid-September had only reached Mogilev. It was hopelessly exposed and offered a tempting target to the Russians. Peter decided to deal with it in person. Leaving a disgruntled Sheremetev in charge of the main army, and with Menshikov as his cavalry commander, he led a force of 14,500 to intercept the supply train at Lesnaya on the Dnieper. The battle raged all day. Löwenhaupt and his soldiers put up a fierce resistance but their position was untenable. Under cover of darkness, the general and less than half his army escaped from the field, leaving his precious wagons to be captured by Peter's elated troops. The Swedes had fared no better in the north. An attack on St Petersburg had been driven off with severe losses, thus proving Peter's wisdom in heavily fortifying his new capital.

When Fortune changes sides, she often does so dramatically. Charles, deprived of his food supplies and with his army swollen by the men from Livonia and the Ukraine, commandeered billets for his weary troops in an area east of Kiev, around Romny, Priluki and Lochvika, and hoped to wait there until the next campaign season. He knew that he would have to face harassment from Russian and Cossack raiding parties. What he was not prepared for was one of the six worst winters in modern European history. The brutal winter of 1708–9 produced record low temperatures and lasted much longer than usual. As hypothermia and famine, accompanied by a virulent outbreak of plague, hit the continent, countless people died. Ten thousand Germans fled for refuge to Britain. The Baltic was still frozen in May. Venetians beheld the astonishing spectacle of their lagoon covered by a sheet of ice. Charles' soldiers, huddled in barns and sheds, were frequently called out to see off enemy hit-and-run attacks. Such attacks often resulted in more of their shelters being burned to the ground. Many Swedish soldiers were reduced to living cringed against walls or in shallow trenches gouged out of the iron earth. Surgeons were kept busy amputating frostbitten fingers, toes and even limbs. The men who survived spent much of their time collecting up and disposing of the bodies of their comrades. By the end of the winter, the Swedish army had been reduced by almost half. A Lutheran pastor with the army was one of those who left a vivid record of the appalling suffering: 'We experienced such cold as I shall never forget. The spittle from mouths turned to ice before it reached the ground, sparrows fell frozen from the roofs to the ground. You could see some men without hands, others without hands and feet, others deprived of fingers, face, ears and noses, others crawling like quadrupeds.'[5] The climatic conditions were, of course, just as bad for the Russian army, and it too suffered losses during that dreadful winter. But the Russian supply lines were intact and they were able to enjoy quarters that, though spartan, were not hemmed in by the enemy. And Peter had the overall advantage that he could always top up his numbers with new conscripts.

During these fearful months, the multi-tasking Tsar was constantly on the move. He inspected the shipyards at Voronezh and the fortifications at Azov. He toured St Petersburg to direct and energise the construction activity there. Everywhere he observed at first hand the progress (or lack of it) being made in implementing his various reforms. His most pressing concern was to ensure that all parts of the country were serving the war effort by efficiently collecting taxes, recruiting troops and providing their quotas of food for the army. It was to improve these activities that he inaugurated a new system of central and regional government. He replaced the ancient, creaking arrangement of chancelleries whose areas of authority often overlapped with an administration based on nine regions (gubernias). He appointed officials from Moscow or confirmed local agents in office with augmented powers. This time, he was careful not to stir up fresh resentment by staffing the bureaucracy with new men. Most of the local governors were drawn from ancient families. The reasoning behind the administrative reform was sound, but the problem of creating in such a large territory with a poor communication network a system that was both efficient and corruption-free was too great even for Peter. No organisation is better than the men who run it, and the Tsar devoted hours to visiting and dictating letters to his officials in order to deal with petty objections, local rivalries and deliberate obstruction of his plans. Gradually, between 1707 and 1711, a new system evolved, which, though it depended hugely on his own energetic participation, worked as well for the time being as could have been hoped.

In April 1709, winter began to loosen its grip on the Ukraine. It was obvious to both sides that the next campaign season would be crucial. Desperately in need of some kind – any kind – of 'seventh cavalry', Charles appealed to the Ottoman sultan to send him some Tatar levies from the Crimea. However, Ahmed III preferred to see which way the wind was blowing and forbade any of his subordinate governors to commit themselves. Charles' main hope of reinforcements now lay in fresh levies raised by his puppet king Stanislaw in Poland. He also negotiated with groups of Cossacks coming up from the south. Some of his officers urged him to withdraw westwards in order to link up with the expected new contingents, but 'retreat' was not a word in the Swedish king's vocabulary. He decided, instead, to establish control of the main road running eastwards from Kiev to Kharkov, the best route from Poland, so as to secure his supply line. With this in view, he brought his army up to the small fortified town of Poltava, located at the point where the Kharkov road crossed the River Vorskla. It was situated on a wooded ridge and was garrisoned by 4,000 Russians, well provided with artillery. For the siege to be successful, it needed to take effect quickly, before the main Russian army arrived. Somewhat surprisingly, Charles failed to achieve this. Perhaps he was more accustomed to pitched battles that provided rapid results rather than plodding siege warfare. Perhaps his success had customarily depended on his tactical ability in manoeuvring in open terrain. Perhaps he simply lacked the firepower to create the necessary breach. Whatever the reason, the bombardment that began on 1 May was still in progress on 15 June, despite the fact that the Russians were by then so short of ammunition that they were firing any missiles that came to hand into the Swedish ranks. Charles was even hit by a dead cat hurled from one of the Russian cannons. By this time the entire Russian army, some 40,000 strong, had assembled on the eastern side of the Vorskla north of Poltava. From this position Peter, still hesitant about facing the formidable Swedes in open battle, contented himself with more harassing jabs at small units of the enemy. He may have hoped that news just arrived from Poland might oblige the Swedes to withdraw. King Stanislaw had proved to be a broken reed. Concerned about his own insecure position, he had sent a message to Charles that he could not spare any troops to aid his ally. Peter would have loved to see the Swedes strike camp and retire westwards. His cavalry could then have harried their retreat just as they had harried the Swedish advance. But true to form, Charles decided that the best form of defence was attack. He would force the reluctant Tsar to face him in open combat. Thus the stage was set for one of the most momentous battles in the modern history of Europe.

Peter's first objective was to bring his army across the river. To divert the enemy, he sent a detachment of cavalry to make a feint across the Vorskla south of Poltava. Charles rode out from his camp to see what the enemy was up to. Then occurred one of those chance minor events that sometimes decide the fate of nations. A musket ball struck the King in the left foot and opened up a long gash, which began to bleed profusely. He refused to have it attended to immediately, and only when he was on the point of toppling from his horse was he carried, half conscious, to the surgeon's station. It was 17 June, Charles' twenty-seventh birthday – not a good omen.

For three days, while the Swedish king lay in a fever and his generals, paralysed by their unwillingness to take any initiative, did nothing, Peter established a new camp west of the Vorskla. He spent a week preparing his strategy and choosing the field of battle. On the night of 26 June, he advanced his men a couple of kilometres to the south and set up a forward camp with hastily constructed timber walls and outworks or redoubts extending forward into the plain. To the rear, the camp was protected by the river and marshy ground. If this precluded the possibility of attack from behind, it would also deter any faint-hearted Russians from fleeing. This was essentially a defensive position. Peter was challenging his adversary either to attack or to abandon the invasion. By this time he knew Charles well enough to guess what his decision would be. He must also have known that the Swedes would be denied the presence of their charismatic king on the field of battle. On paper, everything was in his favour. The Russians outnumbered the enemy two to one. They had chosen the site for the battle. The Swedes were weakened by the privations of the winter and were desperately short of food. They were going into battle without their supreme commander. Above all, the Russian army was very different from the one that had been defeated at Narva eight and a half years earlier. Improved training and equipment, together with experience in the field, had transformed Peter's peasant levies into a credible fighting machine. Nevertheless, he must have been nervous. It was his first head-to-head encounter with one of Europe's most successful generals and the first trial of his army in a set battle with the legendary Swedes.

Before fighting commenced, Peter made a speech to his senior officers and any others close enough to hear. Its sentiments were meant to be passed on down the line:

> Let the Russian troops know that the hour has come which has placed the fate of the fatherland in their hands, to decide whether Russia will be lost or will be reborn in a better condition. Do not think of yourselves as armed and drawn up to fight for Peter but for the state which has been entrusted to Peter, for your kin and for the people of all Russia, which has until now been your defence and now awaits the final decision of fortune. Do not be confused by the enemy's reputation for invincibility which themselves have shown to be false on many occasions. Keep before your eyes in this action that God and truth are fighting with us, which the Lord strong in battle has already testified by his aid in many military actions, think of this alone. Of Peter know only that he sets no value on his life if only Russia lives and Russian piety, glory and well-being.[6]

These stirring words were written down years later by the hagiographer Archbishop Feofan Prokopovich, and are no more likely to be correct in detail than any other remembered or attributed speech made at a moment of high drama. They represent the rhetoric the writer thought Peter *ought* to have uttered. That does not mean to say that they are not intrinsically true. Indeed, they fit well with the character of Peter the Great as we know it. He *was* more concerned for his country than for his own reputation. For all his moral peccadilloes, he *was* conventionally pious (and almost Protestant in his devotion to the Bible). And he *did* understand that at Poltava, Russia was facing a crossroads, that the outcome of this single battle would determine how the new Russia would be received both at home and abroad. That day, 28 June 1709, would also change the world's perception of Peter Romanov. Before, men had thought of him as a brutal autocrat or an enlightened despot, a far-sighted reformer or a heretical traitor to all that Russians held dear, a visionary or an eccentric. Henceforth he would be regarded, even if reluctantly by some, as a hero.

The word 'hero' does not, strictly speaking, fit Peter's behaviour in the field. The famous representation of the dashing cavalry commander on the prancing steed is an iconic image and does not represent his calm and cautious reactions to the unfolding changes and chances of the fateful day. That is not because he was not a brave leader of men; it is because Poltava was not that kind of battle. Charles XII responded to the challenge his opposite number had thrown down. He was a master of the bold and the unexpected. He understood well that the way to defeat a numerically superior enemy was to take it by surprise, to hit it when and where it was vulnerable. He studied the Russian position, and what Peter thought of as his strength, Charles believed was a weakness. The Tsar had used the soggy terrain on the east to guard his left flank. This would severely limit his freedom of movement, restricting his ability to retreat or regroup. If Charles, by means of a sudden strike at the front and right of the enemy position, could cause panic, the only direction in which retreating Russians could go would be north, and his cavalry could hack them down before they could get back across the river.

Charles ordered a pre-dawn all-out attack. His cavalry would smash through the redoubts, opening the way for the infantry to scale the Russians' wooden walls and engage them in hand-to-hand fighting. He was brought on a litter to a place where he could overlook the battle. Long before first light, his foot-soldiers were in position. But where was the cavalry? Charles had been forced to delegate command to officers who, though experienced, lacked his flair. It took them too long to prepare. Only at around four a.m., when the sun began to outline sharply the eastern ridge, were Generals Rehnskjöld and Löwenhaupt ready with their mounted troops.

Peter, meanwhile, had not been idle. Correctly anticipating Charles' tactics, he had used the hours of darkness to strengthen his position. He had sent men out in front of the camp to construct yet more redoubts. These were not finished before daylight, but they did present the attackers with a further line of obstacles. At the same time, the Tsar had his entire army ready and at their posts well before dawn. This diligence robbed the Swedes of that element of surprise that was vital to their success. Charles threw his infantry against the redoubts to clear a path for the cavalry. Despite a murderous fire from seventy cannon positioned to defend the centre, some were quickly successful, but others became bogged down in hand-to-hand fighting. The Swedes were discovering that their opponents were not the same as those who had faced them at Narva and been easily intimidated. The centre ground became a heaving melee, but on the Russian right things appeared to be going better for the attackers. This was Menshikov's wing, and seeing the foot-soldiers falling back, he charged out at the head of his mounted dragoons. Charles ordered some of his cavalry in to engage them. For more than an hour, the mounted troops hacked at each other amidst the choking dust thrown up by their horses' hooves. When the situation became critical, Menshikov sent for Peter to bring up his main army. The Tsar's reply was, 'Fall back.'

This was not a failure of nerve on Peter's part. From his vantage point he could see that his position was being assailed on three fronts. The centre and the right were holding their own, but to the left Löwenhaupt had worked around the outworks and was approaching the camp with a small but determined force. Now was not the time for Peter to throw all his fresh troops into battle at the request of his headstrong friend. What mattered was holding his ground. The Swedes were losing men fast. Peter knew that time was on his side. He could afford to be patient.

On the left, Rehnskjöld had not pursued Menshikov from the field. He paused to take stock and was joined by Charles, who had been brought forward despite the protests of his officers. What they saw was a well-disciplined Swedish army that, despite its rapidly thinning ranks, was heroically sticking to its task. The problem was that it was too divided to be effective. The Swedes urgently needed to regroup. Charles sent messages to Löwenhaupt and Major General Roos, commanding the centre, to break off their engagements and reassemble in the open field. It was now almost seven o'clock. Anxiously Charles waited. And waited. It was two hours before Löwenhaupt was able to extricate his battalions and march them to the rendezvous point. Roos' men never made it. Watching from the camp wall, Peter saw them struggling to disengage. The Tsar acted promptly. He sent fresh troops against the Swedes, and in the hot engagement that followed, all but four hundred of Roos' men were killed or wounded.

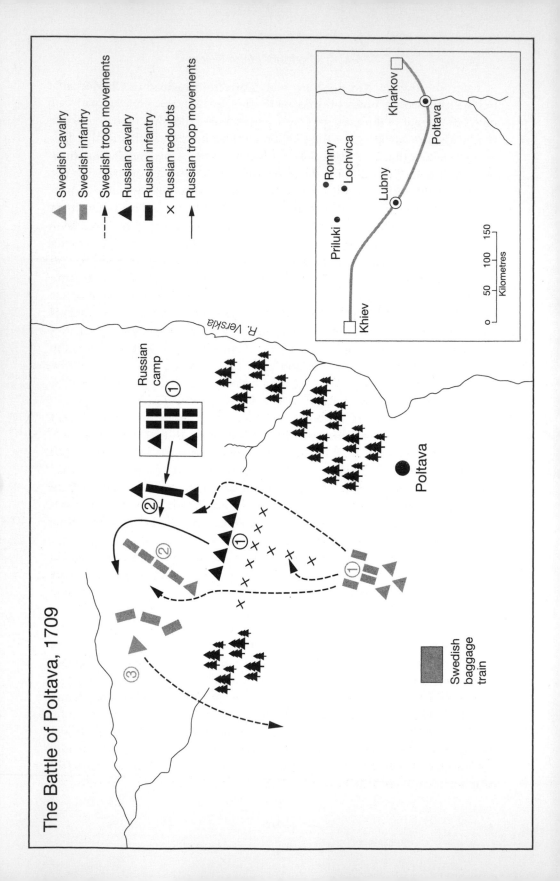

The Battle of Poltava, 1709

Swedish cavalry
Swedish infantry
Swedish troop movements
Russian cavalry
Russian infantry
Russian redoubts
Russian troop movements

Russian camp
①
②

①
②
③

Poltava

R. Verskla

Swedish baggage train

Khiev
Priluki
Romny
Lochvica
Lubny
Poltava
Kharkov

Kilometres
0 50 100 150

Charles had now no option but to retreat. Rehnskjöld drew up the remnants of the Swedish army in column of march. This was the moment Peter had been waiting for. Now he would give the Swedish king his open battle, but on his own terms. He threw down the camp walls and emerged with 30,000 troops who were still fresh. They formed up in battle line, infantry in the centre, cavalry on the wings, artillery to the rear, firing over their heads. It was now mid-morning and the Swedish army had already been decimated. Yet astonishingly, the issue was still undecided. Defeat was something Charles did not acknowledge and most of his men had not experienced. The defiant Swedes showed to the last what a magnificent army they were. Rehnskjöld did not wait for the battle to come to him. He ordered an infantry attack. The blue-coated troops marched steadily forward. Rank upon rank were cut down by an unremitting hail of cannon balls and grapeshot, but nothing stopped their advance. Almost miraculously, the Swedish right wing reached the Russian lines. Elsewhere, it was a different story. To the left, the infantry was halted by the devastating artillery barrage. Peter now ordered a counter-charge, splitting the buckling Swedish line in two. The enemy infantry at last began to throw down their arms and flee the field. Yet still the day was not won. Swedish cavalry tried to turn the tide of battle with an attack on the Russian left. With calm discipline, Peter's officers called the infantry and field artillery into a square formation. Against this human rock the waves of Swedish horsemen thundered in vain until Menshikov's cavalry came to its relief.

By midday it was all over. The shreds of Charles' army were hurrying southwards. The King himself only narrowly avoided capture. His litter was smashed by a cannon ball and several of his bearers were killed. His personal guard was wiped out. Only when some of the cavalry got him on to a horse and escorted him from the field was he able to make his escape. He left behind almost 7,000 dead and wounded and 2,760 prisoners. Russian losses amounted to 4,500 dead and wounded.

Daniel Defoe described the outcome of the Battle of Poltava as 'an army of veterans beaten by a mob, a crowd, a mere militia; an army of the bravest fellows in the world, beaten by scoundrels'.[7] It was unjust denigration. Peter had created an army based on Western models that for courage, discipline and organisation proved on the day to be a match for a celebrated, awesome military machine. The caveat 'on the day' is important. The circumstances were predominantly in the Russians' favour, and it would be more accurate to say that Charles lost the battle than that Peter won it. Had the two armies met on more equal terms, there can be little doubt that the outcome would have been different. But to Peter must go the credit for dictating the terms on which Poltava was fought. His strategy of denying the Swedes a pitched battle, of keeping his Polish allies in the field, of drawing Charles farther and farther away from his supplies, of daring the Swede to advance into inhospitable territory paid off.

What is beyond doubt is the impact the Russian victory made throughout Europe. In London, Defoe deplored the defeat of Charles, a 'Protestant champion', by the Muscovite leader, 'whose power no good man wishes to see greater than it is'. But the essayist and politician Richard Steele pronounced Louis of France and Peter of Russia to be the two greatest men in Europe. There was considerable sympathy in Britain for the unfortunate King Charles, but another political pamphleteer, William Benson, who had travelled in Sweden, berated the King as the worst kind of tyrant, a man who had reduced his country to beggary in his insane pursuit of conquest and glory. An anonymous contributor to the literary debate put his finger on the widespread bewilderment among those who followed events in the distant parts of the continent. Sweden, Muscovy, Hungary and Turkey might be, technically, he admitted, 'in Europe', but they should not be allowed to impact on what he referred to grandly as 'the governing part of Europe'.[8]

Rulers and statesmen were well aware that the Russian victory did not permit them to maintain such an aloof attitude. Peter's diplomats were immediately busy establishing their master as a member of 'the governing part of Europe'. They worked to draw Prussia, Denmark and neighbouring German lands into an alliance against 'Swedish expansionism'. They explained Russia's pacific intentions to the anxious major powers. Queen Anne hastened to offer her congratulations to the hero of Poltava. Britain was concerned to keep the northern seaways open. But it was the nations closer to the Baltic that had the more pressing reasons for establishing good relations with Russia. Peter had badly mauled the Swedish empire, and the birds of prey were soon circling the stricken body. Charles' possessions on the southern Baltic coastline were marked out by his ambitious neighbours. Frederick I of Prussia signed a treaty with the Tsar that promised him the important port of Elbing (Elblag) at the mouth of the Vistula in return for closing his territory to Swedish troops. Denmark's hopes of grabbing territory were revived and Frederick IV renewed the Russo-Danish treaty and his country's war against Sweden.

Other events in 1710 signalled Peter's emergence as a major player in European politics. In October, he secured the first alliance of the house of Romanov with another ruling dynasty. After his troops had occupied Courland, a vassal state of Poland–Lithuania, he opened negotiations with the Regent, Duke Ferdinand, for the marriage of the sixteen-year-old Duke Frederick William to his own niece, Anna Ivanova. The wedding celebrations, like so much in the life of this extraordinary man, had elements of the innovative, the controversial and the downright bizarre. Because the bridegroom was a Catholic, no Orthodox priest was, by church law, permitted to perform the ritual. Peter got round this by finding an officiant whose scruples were amenable to royal pressure. The ceremony was held in the most luxurious house in St Petersburg, the first palace to be built in the new capital and finished before the Tsar's own residence. It belonged, needless to say, to Alexander Menshikov. The service was a hotchpotch of Orthodox and Catholic elements and was truncated when Peter grew bored and told the priest to 'get on with it'. The subsequent celebrations included a serenade by waterborne musicians and the inevitable firework display. Days later, in the same chapel and under identical circumstances, another wedding was celebrated. Peter kept a court dwarf and it was this diminutive man who was united with his dwarf bride. Every dwarf in the city was rounded up, dressed in elaborate finery and ordered to attend. Anna and Frederick were guests of honour and obliged to join in the amusement provided by the unfortunate couple. They might well have wondered which wedding was the reality and which the parody. Sadly, their own married life was destined to be extremely short. In January they set off for Courland. Within hours of their departure, Frederick died, the result, it was said, of his excesses at the Tsar's court. Anna took up residence in her new home and 'ruled' Courland with the aid of advisers chosen by her uncle. The duchy was now a Russian satrapy.

Augustus of Saxony was, theoretically, a prime beneficiary of Poltava. His supporters in Poland had helped the Russian cause in the recent conflict by creating so many problems for Stanislaw I that he was unable to offer the Swedes any military support. In 1710, a triumphant Augustus returned to power. His rival fled to asylum in Alsace, his only real solace being the marriage of his daughter to Louis XV in 1725. But before resuming his throne, Augustus was obliged to consume a large portion of humble pie. By the terms of a new treaty solemnised at Thorn, he acknowledged that he held his position only by the good graces of the Tsar of Russia. Peter demanded the right to station his troops in Poland and added Estonia to his possessions. Augustus' holding of Livonia and even Saxony were made dependent on his continued allegiance to the alliance. He had traded away his independence – and also the independence of Poland.

Preoccupied though they were with the War of the Spanish Succession, the major powers had to revise their attitude to Russia after Poltava. They watched with growing alarm as Peter tightened his grip on the southern Baltic coast. In July 1710, Riga surrendered to Sheremetev. Within weeks, the few remaining enemy strongholds, weakened as much by plague as by hostile action, capitulated. Peter had now established, by military and diplomatic activity, effective control over the southern Baltic coastline from St

Petersburg to the Prussian border, a stretch of territory far in excess of any-thing formerly ruled directly by Sweden. Moreover, he was rapidly building a sizeable fleet in shipyards on Lake Ladoga. He no longer needed his ally and conveniently forgot all about allowing Augustus to rule Livonia. The maritime nations were in a weak position in any negotiations with Russian diplomats. Their two concerns were maintaining the balance of power in the north and restoring trade. Holding these objectives together was dif-ficult, if not impossible. Peace in the region was essential. Since they were in no position to make demands backed by the threat of naval intervention, they could only accept Peter's conquests. He hastened to assure them that peaceful commerce was also his primary objective – as indeed it was. He was careful not to antagonise the political elements in the lands that now came under his sway by a programme of 'Russification'. Local officials were, for the most part, confirmed in their responsibilities. The customs of the people were respected. Religious toleration prevailed. Peter set about organising the recovery of the large tracts of land that had been devastated by a decade of war.

Louis XIV recognised the increased international standing of the Russian tsar. He was reluctantly facing the unpleasant truth that France was running out of options. The humiliating military defeats of 1707 had been followed in the next year by yet more reverses. At Oudenarde he had lost another 15,000 men, killed, wounded and captured. Minorca and Sardinia fell to his enemies. On top of this came the vile winter of 1709. The suffering of the French people during the great freeze was well beyond anything experienced in living memory, and the luxuries of the royal court could not keep the icy fingers of despair from clamping themselves on the morale of the King and his advisers. Louis was desperate to find some way of ending the war. He sent out diplomats to foreign rulers who might act as intermediaries – Frederick IV of Denmark, Augustus of Poland and Peter of Russia. Nothing came of these overtures, and the war continued for another four years. Meanwhile, Britain, Holland and their allies were treating the Tsar with kid gloves. They were obliged to accept the fait accompli in the north but wanted to make it clear that this did not imply a willingness to wink at further Russian expan-sion. Charles had one more army left in the region: 8,000 men under General Krassow had retreated into Pomerania. Peter was anxious to remove this threat, but this would have involved pushing the conflict further westwards and possibly spilling into German lands. This the major powers would not entertain. In March 1710, they obliged the two belligerents to accede to the Convention of The Hague, by which they accepted the neutrality of the Empire and bound themselves not to carry their quarrel on to German soil. It could only be a damage-limitation exercise. The Baltic rivals were too deep in conflict to abandon their own military plans. Although the convention was endorsed by the government in Stockholm, the ever-stubborn Charles XII refused to accept an arrangement that would have locked up Krassow's army in Pomerania. For their part, the Danes were determined, with Russian help, to extract maximum advantage from Sweden's weakness. Peter had become the arbiter of northern European affairs. But he was about to discover that those who make a meteoric ascent to power and prestige cannot resist the gravitational pull that can, just as suddenly, drag them down again.

The Great Northern War was very far from being over. Charles XII had not been brought to the point of suing for peace. He had by no means abandoned his hope of staging a recovery and his optimism was not wholly without foundation. After Poltava, what was left of the Swedish army had retreated southwards to the Dnieper. Had they been able to commandeer enough boats, they might have made good their escape. But the Russians caught up with them on the wrong side of the river. Here, Charles deserted 12,000 troops, who surrendered to the enemy, while he crossed over with a 1,000–strong bodyguard and made his way to Turkish territory. Ahmed III saw the political potential of the refugees and allowed them to set up their camp at Bendery, between Odessa and Kisinov. Here the Swedish king recuperated from his wound and doggedly planned the next stage in the war. This involved urging the Sultan to take to the field against Peter and to provide Charles with an escort to enable him to return to Swedish territory. Ahmed had unfinished business with the Russian tsar, but was not easily persuaded. Only when Charles' energetic entreaties received diplomatic support from the Christian nations was he stirred to action. Britain and France both had their own reasons for wanting to pluck feathers from the Russian eagle's wings. Urged by Charles and encouraged by covert aid from the Western powers, the Ottoman sultan declared war at the end of 1710.

With so much to do at home and in the newly acquired territories, the last thing Peter wanted was the prospect of war on two fronts. His military capability had been considerably reduced by the recent campaigns and by the plague. Despite his reform of the regional administration, recruitment was sluggish. His initial reaction was to offer Charles peace terms so that he could concentrate all his military forces on the Turkish menace. The Swedish king, quite unchastened by his reverses, was not prepared to contemplate the slightest degree of compromise. He was set on wiping out the disgrace of Poltava by humiliating the Russian tsar. Since he could not do this personally, he was relying on his Muslim protector to do it for him.

There is little doubt that he would have succeeded had it not been for the reluctance of both the major combatants to press the issue to a military conclusion. There is something odd about the Russo-Turkish War of 1711.

Neither side fought it with passion or conviction. For neither was it part of an ongoing strategy. The victor did not follow up his success. The vanquished was not crushed by his failure. Peter and Ahmed both had priorities elsewhere: the Tsar on the Baltic shore and the Sultan on the Mediterranean. Both rulers were concerned not to agitate the notoriously unstable Balkan region. In 1709, Peter had sent lavish gifts to the Sultan and even burned part of his own Azov fleet to demonstrate that he had no territorial ambitions in the area. He was genuinely angry and worried about the undermining of relations with the Porte, and his preparations for war had about them an air of bad-tempered panic. He knew that he was going to have to face a large Ottoman horde on its home territory with a smaller army, force-marched southwards over more than 2,000 kilometres of barren terrain. He harangued his officials about their failure to recruit troops and his generals about their failure to assemble and move their forces rapidly enough. He ranted that he would punish them as 'traitors and betrayers of the fatherland'. When he set off for the war zone, it was almost with an air of doom. On his arrival, he sent back instructions about what was to happen were he to be killed in battle.

However, the urgency of the situation did lead to an important constitutional innovation. Peter set up an instrument of government called the Senate, which was to be in control during his absence and to manage routine affairs at all times. The new body had much more authority than the old boyar council, and its routine was well regulated. The ten members were to meet regularly and had a wide brief including oversight of the courts, collection of state finances, recruitment and provisioning of the army, finding and transporting construction gangs for St Petersburg and regulation of commerce. To Peter it seemed like 'a good idea at the time', but the delegation of powers by autocrats seldom works. The ruler, whatever his original intentions, finds it difficult to keep his hands off the reins of power, and his appointees are usually nervous about exceeding their remit. This can produce a recipe for confusion and delay. Within weeks Peter was writing angry letters to the Senate for not keeping him fully informed. With such a heavy burden of responsibility, it is not surprising that the Senate found little time to write reports. When Peter learned what his appointees were doing, he frequently told them that they should not be doing it. It was unreasonable of him to expect the senators to second-guess his intentions, especially as he was a ruler passionate about change, whose mind constantly hopped from one new idea to the next. All that being said, the institution of the Senate was an important step in the transfer of administration from omnicompetent tsar to a hierarchical bureaucracy. For the rest of his life Peter tinkered with this institution, but it survived.

He also decided to put his personal affairs in order on the eve of his departure for the war. The event that took place at Preobrazhenskoe in early March 1711 reads like something from a fairy tale, a tale that has its beginning in Sheremetev's siege of Marienburg in 1702. Among the hundreds of Lithuanian prisoners he took was Martha Skavronska, an eighteen-year-old servant girl in the household of a Lutheran pastor. Technically she was married, having been briefly the wife of a Swedish soldier, long since departed from the area. The general appropriated for himself this prize of war, but soon afterwards Menshikov took a fancy to her and, not being in the habit of denying himself anything he wanted, demanded that Sheremetev sell the girl to him. Martha was not only pretty, she was an extremely strong character. She and Menshikov became close friends, though whether they were anything more is not known. When she was introduced to Peter, he was immediately attracted. Menshikov made a present of her to the Tsar, probably with the intention of having an agent who would be close to the monarch at all times. He can scarcely have known how successful his plan would be. The relationship of Peter and Martha is one of the great love stories. She became his constant and dearest companion. She shared his drinking bouts. She accompanied him on military campaigns. She was a buffer between him and the world and the only person who could calm his towering rages. On several occasions she intervened to save men who had provoked the Tsar's wrath. Perhaps the greatest reason for their close bond was that Martha was able to share Peter's love of the simple life. While St Petersburg was being constructed, they lived together in the famous log cabin, where Martha performed the duties of an ordinary housewife and Peter tended the garden. In 1705, she converted to the Orthodox faith and took the baptismal name of Catherine. Two years later, according to legend, the couple were married in a ceremony that had to be kept secret because many Russians refused to accept the legality of Peter's separation from Eudoxia and would have been scandalised anyway by his marriage to a foreigner – and a peasant at that! During the early years of their relationship, Catherine was almost constantly pregnant, though only two of her children, Anna and Elizabeth, survived infancy.

Days before Peter set off to join the army, he summoned his two nieces and his sister to Preobrazhenskoe, and told them that they were to regard Catherine as his lawful wife and consort. Should he fail to return from the Turkish front, she and her daughters were to be treated honourably. If all went well in the war, he proposed to marry Catherine in a new ceremony as soon as possible. On 6 March a public statement was made to the same effect.

The Russian objective in the 1711 campaign was to cut off a Turkish army marching along the Danube valley towards the Ukraine and Poland. Peter wanted a quick victory leading to a renewed peace treaty. It was vital to him to return northwards before Krassow, whose army, swelled by fresh recruitment, now numbered 26,000, could break out of Pomerania. Knowing that the odds were heavily against him, Peter tried to give the conflict the aura of a crusade by appealing to Orthodox rulers throughout the region to join him in chastising the infidel. He assured the Cossack and Tatar rulers, 'I am taking upon myself a heavy burden for the sake of the love of God,' and he urged loyal Christians to join him in taking revenge on the Turks, who had 'trampled on our faith, taken our churches and lands by cunning, pillaged and destroyed many of our churches and monasteries'.[9] In other words, a desperate Peter was now deliberately trying to stir up trouble in the borderlands for his own purposes. Unfortunately, most of the Tatar and Cossack chieftains could see little to choose between rule from St Petersburg and rule from Constantinople. Only one *hospodar*, Dmitri Cantemir, came to Peter's assistance, with a mere 5,000 men from Moldavia.

Once more the weather became a major player in the conflicts of Peter and his enemies. This time it was not numbing cold that debilitated his soldiers, but enervating heat. The harvest of 1710 had been poor and spring crops had been stripped by locusts. The army stumbled their way through a scorched, dusty landscape of arid fields and dried-up watercourses. With his men growing weaker by the day, it became obvious to Peter that there would have to be a change of plan. Instead of going in search of the enemy, he now reverted to those tactics that came more naturally to him. He would withdraw, forcing the Turks to pursue him to a place where he could defend himself more effectively, while detaching part of the cavalry to threaten the enemy's supply lines. General Rönne was sent to attack the Danube fort of Braila, and Sheremetev did his best to extricate the bulk of the army from the trap into which it had plunged.

By 7 July, the lumbering retreat had reached a point on the River Pruth somewhere to the south-east of Iasi. There it came to a halt, confronted by an enormous Turkish force firmly established on both sides of the river. Peter's army of 38,000 men was surrounded by 140,000 Ottomans under the leadership of Grand Vizier Azem Mehmet Pasha. The Turks went about their siege in a leisurely, businesslike way. On the landward side of the Russian army, they set up batteries of 300 cannon. From across the river they bombarded at will any who ventured outside the enemy encampment. The Russians returned fire with their own artillery but could make little real impression on the Ottoman host. It should all have been over quickly. It should have been a slaughter. According to some authorities, Peter sent the following message to the Senate:

I inform you that I with all my army, through no fault or mistake, but through false information, being surrounded by forces four times as strong and cut off from all lines of supply, look forward – unless with the special help of God – to nothing but complete destruction or captivity amongst the Turks. In the latter case you are no longer to look upon me as your tsar and ruler and are to do nothing which I tell you, even if I write it with my own hand, until I reappear amongst you in my own person. Should I perish and authentic news of my death reach you, choose amongst yourselves the one most worthy to be my successor.[10]

The authenticity of this letter has been questioned, but there can be little doubt that its mood represented Peter's depression and sense of foreboding. Yet instead of swift destruction, he and his men had to endure three days of uncertainty. Three times Sheremetev, at Peter's instruction, asked for a truce, but there was no response. Azem Mehmet, it seems, could not make up his mind how best to exploit the situation.

His hesitation had much to do with political realities in Constantinople. Factions and personal rivalries held sway in the court of the Sultan. The Vizier had to weigh up the merits of returning as a popular military hero (and, therefore, perceived as a potential threat by Ahmed) or as a wise negotiator who had cowed the victor of Poltava (and, more to the point, still had an unscathed army at his back). If he tried to batter the Russians into oblivion, he would himself lose more men in the process. His return to Constantinople would be hampered by Rönne, who had by now captured Braila. While Azem Mehmet deliberated where his own best interests lay, intervention came from an unexpected quarter. The wily and devoted Catherine took the initiative – or so legend has it. Having received no response from the enemy, Peter decided that it would be better to die fighting than to be starved into abject surrender. He gave the order to strike camp and retreat. His generals counselled that this would result in certain annihilation. It was at this point that the royal mistress suggested that Peter should send once more to the Vizier but this time making him a present of all her jewellery. This was done and Azem Mehmet agreed to open talks. There seems little reason to doubt the truth of this story. It is wholly in keeping with what we know of this brave and sagacious woman. She understood that the way to a man's heart is through his purse, and by her action she saved her lover and her country.

Peter instructed his negotiating team to give the Turks whatever they wanted in order for him to get home with his troops. The list of demands was fairly humiliating. Russia had to surrender Azov, destroy all the fortifications they had built to guard the Don delta and burn all its ships. Peter promised to withdraw all the forces stationed in Poland–Lithuania and to allow Charles XII to return home. The loss of his first major prize of war was something he felt deeply. He had nursed the great ambition of making Azov a southern St Petersburg, linked by new waterways to the heart of the country and giving access to the Mediterranean. These grand plans now had to be abandoned. But the other terms of the Treaty of Pruth were vague in the extreme and incapable of enforcement. As Peter took a roundabout way home, he dispatched messages ahead, reporting on the outcome of the campaign and virtually congratulating himself at having restored peace in the south. Now, he said, there was nothing to distract Russia and her allies from the war against Sweden. His next objective was the invasion of Pomerania. He was particularly pleased that he was able to put all his country's resources into the northern war before the War of the Spanish Succession reached its conclusion. When the major powers were free from their own squabbles, he knew they would start to put pressure on Russia.

All interested parties acknowledged that Peter had got off remarkably lightly. He certainly fared better personally than his adversaries. Charles XII was furious that the Tsar had not been effectively forced to yield all his conquests of recent years. When he received news of the treaty, he immediately took to horse and rushed off to confront the Grand Vizier. Azem Mehmet brushed his protests aside laconically. 'I have fought the Russians,' he said. 'If you want to do so, do it with your own men.' It would be another three years before Charles was able to get back to Swedish territory, and then it would be not at the head of an army nor even with a Turkish escort, but travelling in disguise by back roads with only a handful of companions. Fate had even worse in store for the Grand Vizier. On his return to Constantinople, he fell foul of court intrigue, was deposed for taking bribes and dispatched to a distant corner of the empire, where he died (probably violently).

And so the crisis passed. Peter travelled by way of Poland to Carlsbad, where he took the waters of the warm springs. But there was little time to relax. His head was already full of new plans – weddings to be celebrated and more lands to be conquered.

6

Unhappy Families

For the next seven years, two men frustrated the designs of the reformist Tsar. Charles XII obstinately refused to come to the negotiating table and Tsarevich Alexis declined to accept the role Peter wished to thrust upon him. The Swedish king and the Russian prince both stood in the way of Peter's plans for his country. Alexis became the focus of all those reactionary elements within Russian society that Peter most despised. Charles forced Peter to go on pouring into the northern war resources that could have been used to build up the nation's infrastructure. The workaholic Tsar continued with his modernising programme but always against the backdrop of the problems caused by his old enemy and his own son.

After his physically, mentally and emotionally draining conflict with the Turks, Peter made straight for Carlsbad, already a pilgrimage centre for wealthy and fashionable invalids. He was, by eighteenth-century standards, approaching middle age and was beginning to be preoccupied with his health. The robust frame he had mindlessly abused for so long was beginning to rebel. In St Petersburg in 1708, he had been laid up with a fever that he insisted he must have contracted in Poland (it being impossible that his earthly paradise could harbour harmful contagions). 'God sees when you have no strength,' he grumbled to Menshikov, 'because without health and strength it's impossible to do your duty.' He had received a course of mercury treatment, probably for venereal disease, which left him 'as weak as a baby'. His journey southwards in the next year was slowed down by another bout of illness, which depressed his spirits as much as the prospect of the coming war. 'I am sick and in despair,' he wrote to Menshikov, 'and do not know what to do for the best.' For someone of such manic energy any restricting ailment was particularly frustrating. This did not mean that he changed his habits. It was of his very nature to indulge his appetites to the full. Nor was it just wine, spirits and women that he took in immoderate quantities. His food intake was prodigious. In his earlier years, excess calories were rapidly burned up by his restless physical and mental energy, but now overindulgence began to tell. The sulphurous springs at Carlsbad were believed to be efficacious for digestive disorders, and from this time on Peter paid frequent visits to this and other spas. In 1716, mineral springs were discovered at Martsial'nye, near Olonets, and the Tsar personally organised the development there of Russia's own spa. Thereafter he visited it often with his court.

Matters medical and surgical fascinated him increasingly as the years passed. He was accompanied everywhere by a personal physician, the most important of whom was the Scot, Robert Erskine, who served from 1705 to his death in 1718. As well as being constantly available to the royal family, Erskine fostered the Tsar's interest in medical science, and organised the Apothecaries' Chancery and the Imperial Dispensary. The former consisted of laboratories, library and herb gardens and was responsible for accumulating information and conducting experiments on a variety of remedies. The dispensary was a considerable undertaking. It was a royal monopoly for the manufacture and distribution of drugs to the nation and especially to the army and navy. Peter took a very close interest in Erskine's work, providing him with premises in the summer palace, and in 1718 giving him the town residence of Alexander Kikin, recently executed for treason, as his business headquarters. It goes almost without saying that Erskine's curatorship had to embrace the more bizarre aspects of Peter's 'scientific' activities. The collecting of curios was a prevailing fashion among wealthy European culture vultures, who displayed their finds in their 'cabinets' to publicise their pursuit of knowledge. Peter joined the trend. He picked up numerous natural history specimens during his travels, and even bought complete collections. His personal museum was not restricted to geological rarities, stuffed animals and bird skeletons; it included deformed creatures such as animals with extra limbs, and, most sought after of all, human freaks. Peter became the proud owner of two-headed babies, Siamese twins and bearded ladies. The list of his acquisitions includes items that are reminiscent of pre-Reformation holy relic collections made by the gullibly devout: e.g. a child with a fish's tail, and two dogs born of a human virgin mother. Orders were sent to regional governors to be on the lookout for new additions to the royal collection. Erskine and his successors had to store and display this ever-growing accumulation of oddities.

The royal physician's primary task of keeping the Tsar healthy was no sinecure. Peter, as we might well suspect, was a difficult patient. When Erskine diagnosed 'a relaxation of the fibres of the stomach, with a swelling of the legs and bilious colics', he prescribed a course of spa waters preceded by a more abstemious regime. Not only did Peter refuse to deny himself, he increased his food intake in order to 'build up his strength' for the forthcoming spa ordeal. He considered himself to be, if not as well qualified as his doctor, at least a considerable medical expert in his own right. Sometimes he did his own bloodletting. He carried out post-mortems. More terrifyingly, he performed operations, from tooth-pulling to minor surgery, on living people.

From Carlsbad, Peter travelled on to Torgau. Here he attended the wedding of the Tsarevich Alexis to Princess Charlotte-Christina-Sophia of Brunswick-Wolfenbüttel. Neither the bride nor the groom was happy at their union – but in reality, their happiness was of little consequence. Tsar Peter might marry a peasant girl for love, but his son was obliged to sacrifice himself on the altar of dynastic alliance. Peter was continuing his campaign of intermeshing his family with those of the princely clans of Europe. The sixteen-year-old Charlotte might come from one of the minor German dukedoms, but her sister was married to the Emperor Charles VI. No longer could the ruler of Russia be regarded as the master of a remote, barbarian fastness. He had achieved parity with the leaders of 'the governing part of Europe'. More to the point, he had forged one more link in the chain of his anti-Swedish alliance.

The price he paid was the further alienation of his own heir. One of the saddest misfortunes that can befall a man is to be born the son of a great father, particularly if he is expected to follow in that father's footsteps. Peter sired thirteen children; three by his first wife, Eudoxia, and ten by Catherine. Alexis, born in 1690, was the only boy to survive infancy. In his early years he was brought up by his mother and saw little of his father. There was nothing unusual about that in the upper echelons of Russian society. Nor was it strange that as Alexis grew to understand something of the estrangement of his parents, he should side with his mother and be irrevocably influenced by the ideas, beliefs and prejudices prevailing among the traditionalist priests, ladies and gentlemen who made up her household. What is surprising is that for many years Peter made no effort to counteract these hostile attitudes and to train Alexis to inherit the crown of a new, reformed Russia. In a post-Freudian world, we know how formative are those influences that dominate a child's earliest years. Peter lacked that information. He assumed that he could wipe clean the blackboard of his son's mind and write upon it those messages he wanted. The results were distressing and, ultimately, fatal.

That Peter never felt any affection for his son is quite clear from all the evidence, but it is strange that a ruler who planned in detail every aspect of civil and military administration should have neglected to pay much attention to the succession. The arrangements for Alexis' early education seem to have been muddled. The Tsar was concerned to counteract the reactionary influence of Eudoxia and her entourage. When Peter dispatched his ex-wife to a monastery, he forcibly separated her from her son. He contemplated sending the boy abroad, but nothing came of that. Instead he employed German tutors, and from 1701 gave Menshikov overall responsibility for the Tsarevich's upbringing. This must have had the effect of tugging Alexis in two different directions. Small wonder that he was confused. He was too young to cope intellectually with the competing visions of reformers and reactionaries, and could do little more than be led by his emotions to follow those principles and ideals espoused by his mother. It was in the following year that Peter began associating his son with him in national affairs. He took the twelve-year-old to the naval base at Archangel and to the military camps engaged in the Baltic campaign. In 1704 Alexis watched, from a safe distance, the siege of Narva. It became readily apparent that the Tsarevich had no taste for military matters. Peter's reaction was not simply that of disappointment; he was disgusted with Alexis' lack of interest in the war. 'You must love everything that contributes to the glory and honour of the fatherland,' he chided. 'If my advice is lost in the wind and you do not do as I wish, I do not recognise you as my son.'[1]

The tragedy of Alexis Petrovich lies not simply in his total estrangement from his father but in the inner turmoil resulting from the conflict between being the sort of son his father wanted and the sort of prince he believed his country needed. The young man did make some effort to follow his father – at least in small things. One of Peter's lifelong hobbies was wood-turning, and he carried a portable lathe with him wherever he went. Alexis too took up this craft and acquired some skill in it. He also tried to emulate Peter's capacity for strong drink, but only succeeded in becoming an alcoholic. For his part, the Tsar did, belatedly, take in hand the training of his teenage son. In 1707–8, when the threat of Swedish invasion was at its height and Peter was away with the army, he left Alexis in nominal control of Moscow to oversee the fortification of the city and to deal with enemy agents who were distributing seditious pamphlets. He also sent the Prince to Smolensk to ensure the efficient gathering of provisions for the army. Judging by the reports Alexis sent to his father, it would seem that he did his best to shoulder these responsibilities. Yet Peter was seldom satisfied. His letters to Alexis were either brusque demands for action or accusations that the Tsarevich was lazy and incompetent.

The question must be asked whether the heir to the Russian empire was really useless and unworthy of the responsibility or whether Peter was setting an impossibly high standard. A father-to-son letter written when their

relationship was approaching its crisis point goes to the heart of the answer: 'you criticise everything I do at the risk of my person and the undermining of my health for the sake of my people and their wellbeing and I have all the reason in the world to believe you will overthrow it all if you outlive me ... I cannot agree to let you continue in your own way, like some amphibian, neither fish nor mammal. So, amend your behaviour; prove yourself worthy of the succession or go off and become a monk.'[2] Peter demanded of Alexis the level of devotion and industry to which he subjected himself. That was a frightening standard to impose on anybody. As he grew older, Peter frequently held himself up as an example to all servants of the Russian state, as well he might do. The claim that he did his duty quite regardless of his own comfort and health was one that he could make in all honesty. By the same token it was unreasonable to expect of ordinary mortals the same degree of dedication. Not only did Alexis not possess the mental and physical stamina to partner his father in the work of reform, his heart was not in it. This was intensely frustrating to Peter. He had no other direct male heir. Therefore, it seemed that everything Peter had worked for was destined to be swept away eventually by Tsar Alexis and his traditionalist advisers. That was something he refused to contemplate. By 1715 at the latest he had determined to exclude the Tsarevich from the succession if he could not force him into an acceptable mould. In an argument with the Danish ambassador, he made his position quite clear. 'According to your hypothesis,' he protested,

> a prince who, to form for himself a state that is prosperous and redoubtable, has exposed his life a hundred times, sacrificed his health and brought to a conclusion by his application, by his care and by his skill, his affairs to such a point as to make himself and his state respected and feared by all his neighbours would then be absolutely obliged to ... pass the fruits of his labours into the hands of a fool [who] would begin the destruction of them ... I would call it committing the greatest of cruelties to immolate the safety of the state to the simple established law of succession. I suppose that he who proclaims this law has not the qualities required to rule. The monasteries are the right places to house weak princes and to cover up their stupidity but the throne is not their business.[3]

This was not the way the majority of Russians saw things. After the Bulavin rebellion of 1708–9, few of the Tsar's subjects risked plotting revolt. Over the years, Peter's painstaking and ruthless interrogation of all who might be remotely involved in disloyal acts proved to be an effective deterrent. But disaffection had not decreased. On the contrary, the longer the Swedish war

dragged on and the more wealth and power the Tsar's creatures, particularly Menshikov, accumulated, the louder became the murmurings against the regime. However, most dissidents were prepared to wait for better days rather than take direct action. Alexis' love for traditional customs and beliefs was well known, and it could only be a matter of time before the good old days returned. The Tsarevich became the focus of all reactionary hopes – *malgré lui*.

This very fact put him in danger. Just as Sophia had been suspected of collusion in earlier revolts, so Alexis could be, and was, rumoured to be encouraging and supporting those who might hasten the end of Peter's reign. In 1707, a French diplomat had reported that many Russians hoped that Charles XII would win the war and place Alexis on the throne. He suggested that 'the peoples will not refuse from his hand a prince who is already dear to them both by the danger in which he is of losing his life by the cruelty of his father and by the aversion and contempt which he has for foreigners'.[4] The Austrian envoy believed that if Peter were not killed or deposed, Russia might descend into civil war when he died: 'A secret party which is coming together in favour of the tsarevitch against the favourite [Menshikov], can be detected here, for it seems that the uncommon inclination of the tsar for the latter could make great confusion for the tsarevitch [on his father's death], since the favourite is making the entire army dependent on him and inclined towards him.'[5] All manner of speculation was rife, all of it focused on the demise or removal of Peter and the reversal of his policies. This could not but affect relations between ruler and heir. It was not necessary for Alexis to be guilty of any disloyalty for him to arouse the enmity of his father.

The marriage of Alexis to a German princess was dictated by dynastic considerations, but it was also part of Peter's plan to convert his son to a Western mindset. After Poltava, when the threat of Swedish invasion had receded, the young man had been sent to Dresden to complete his education. It was, of course, too late. Instead of spending his time studying manuals of military strategy, Alexis plunged into abstruse theological treatises and seemed set on finding 'proofs' that his father's reforms were contraventions of divine law: in medieval Europe, he discovered, long robes had been the norm and Charlemagne had forbidden the wearing of short coats; the Frankish King Chilperic I had come to a sticky end because of his rapacity towards the church. Instead of inspecting fortifications and arsenals, Alexis toured monasteries and churches.

Peter later insisted that he had allowed Alexis to decline the proposed marriage to the scrawny Princess Charlotte. This may have been technically true, but the Tsarevich would have been too frightened to go against his father's wishes. So the wedding duly took place in the Torgau palace of the

bride's grandmother, the Queen of Poland, in October 1711. The ceremony seems to have been a religious mishmash, with segments in Russian, Latin and German. Charlotte was allowed to keep her Lutheran faith, and days later, Peter took the opportunity to visit the arch-heretic's home town of Wittenberg, a few kilometres down the Elbe. There, he demonstrated that his objection to superstitious practices was not confined to Orthodoxy. When he was solemnly shown the stain on the wall reputedly caused by the reformer throwing his inkpot at the devil, he took pleasure in pointing out that the ink had been freshly applied. The amalgamating of cultures in the newlyweds' household would have been difficult under any normal circumstances, but there was nothing normal about these circumstances and no possibility of the couple enjoying any domestic happiness. Alexis' health was already being undermined by tuberculosis. He was a depressive who sought relief in drink. The affection he could not find in his father and did not seek in his wife, he discovered in the arms of his vulgar ex-serf mistress, Euphrosyne. The attempt to assert his own intellectual and spiritual identity was supported not by Peter's 'heretical' friends but by the priests of the Moscow churches, whose glowing icons and swirling clouds of incense spoke directly to his soul.

Peter was back in St Petersburg by the end of the year. His major priority was bringing the northern war to a swift and successful conclusion, but there were internal matters that also demanded his attention. He summoned the Senate to meet with him early in the new year and presented them with a long agenda of new business. He was still concerned with the effective governing of the provinces and particularly with the gargantuan task of rooting out corruption. In order to bring the nation's finances under central control, he removed the supervision of tax collectors from regional governors and placed it in the hands of the Senate. This did not stop exploitation and diversion of funds from government to private coffers, but it did cut down the number of hands that could be plunged into the pot. In February, the senators were dispatched back to Moscow with a full schedule of work to do. Peter now fulfilled his promise of regularising his relationship with Catherine. The couple were 'properly' married in the chapel of Menshikov's palace. The low-key ceremony had nothing about it of the pomp and ceremony that normally accompanied the wedding of crowned heads of state. Peter wore the uniform of a rear admiral. Catherine was attended by her two little daughters as bridesmaids. Even the banquet afterwards was extremely modest (and orderly) by Peter's standards.

Then it was off to war again. Peter travelled to Pomerania to join the army led by Menshikov. For the first time Russian troops were involved in a major campaign with their allies, Denmark and Saxony and other neighbouring states. The Tsar was also eager to bring Hanover and Prussia into the coalition. All the northern German princes wanted to share in the rich pickings of the collapsing Swedish empire, but not all were equally equipped or determined to contribute effectively to the military effort involved in wresting it from its Scandinavian master. Bringing his partners to agree on strategy and act collectively, with the major European powers watching anxiously from the wings, was never going to be easy for Peter.

The next stage of the war fell into two parts. The first concluded with the return of Charles XII in November 1714; the second with his death four years later. Events in the north involved directly at one time or another Russia, Sweden, Denmark, Holstein-Gottorp, Hanover, Prussia, Mecklenberg, Holland, Britain, France and even Spain. They threatened the peace of Europe as a whole. They impacted on British dynastic politics. The gradual, though far from inexorable, extension of Russian influence continued to evoke mixed responses in the West. In 1714, the Royal Society of London awarded a fellowship to Menshikov as representative of his master for having advanced the arts and sciences in his own land. But that same progress towards 'civilisation' was seen by other observers as a threat: '... the Russians should be feared more than the Turks. Unlike the latter, they do not remain in their gross ignorance and withdraw once they have completed their ravages but, on the contrary, gain more and more science and experience in matters of war and state, surpassing many nations in calculation and dissimulation and are gradually advancing closer and closer to our lives.'[6] So wrote one of George I's diplomats. Why then did the major Western powers not simply cold-shoulder the pretentious barbarian? Could he not be left to his own devices in the semi-frozen north? The answer was to be found in simple economics, as was pointed out in a Swedish propaganda pamphlet designed to harness the forces of the maritime powers against Russia:

> What better materials are required for a well-furnished [naval] yard than he [Peter] has within his own dominions ...? Does he want timber, planks and masts? His own forests might furnish all the yards in Europe ... Is it iron he wants? He needs not fetch it from the Dutch, for they cannot afford to sell him so cheap as he may have it in the neighbourhood. Is it rigging and sails? His country chiefly supplies all others with hemp. He has got workmen enough from England and Holland to direct his forges and rope yards. Is it pitch and tar? The Dutch themselves are supplied with these commodities from him.[7]

The bitter pill the maritime nations had to swallow was that any nation that aspired to 'rule the waves' could only do so by courtesy of Russia. Britain had experimented with extracting pitch and tar from her American colonies and had tried growing in Ireland hemp and flax in commercial quantities. Neither development was successful. If Peter's Russia was a monster, it was one of the Western world's creating. They had eagerly encouraged the Tsar to develop his military capabilities because their shipyards needed the raw materials his country possessed in abundance. Now they found themselves in the strange and aggravating position of having to deal with him – as an equal. Britain and Holland were not the only states to be nervous of Russian power. The German princes whose territories clustered along the Baltic coast had no desire to exchange domination from St Petersburg for domination from Stockholm. Over the next few years, Peter's strategy had to take account of shifting alliances and support that might evaporate at the first sign of a Swedish revival. During the trials and tribulations of the next couple of years, he more than once asked himself, as he commented to Menshikov, 'What on earth can you do with allies like these?' In fairness, it should be noted that the idiosyncratic ruler of Russia would have found it hard to collaborate with even the most efficient militaristic state on the planet. In all his warlike endeavours so far, he had run his own show.

In 1712, the focus of allied attention was the western Baltic coastal states. A Swedish force, led by Magnus Stenbock, had cleared the seaways of Danish ships and taken possession of the island of Rugen, from which the general planned to cross into and regain Pomerania. He reached the mainland but was then thwarted by the Danes, who destroyed his supply vessels. Orders came from distant Bendery for him to march eastwards in order to place his men at the disposal of Charles XII. This was totally impracticable. To cross Poland with the risk of encountering Russian or pro-Russian opposition was too great a risk. Stenbock did enter into discussion with Augustus II, who was now playing a double game, calculating that he might have more to gain from breaking Tsar Peter's hold over his territory, but prudence persuaded the Swede not to put any weight upon such a bruised reed as Augustus. He headed westwards into Mecklenberg and defeated a Danish–Saxon army at Gadenbusch. But Peter and Menshikov had now arrived. Their forces obliged Stenbock to retreat further until he was offered refuge in the Holstein fortress of Tönningen. The chief minister of Holstein during the minority of its duke was Georg Heinrich von Görtz, a wily politician who acted as protector of Stenbock's army in order to insinuate himself into the forthcoming negotiations and make diplomatic gains for his young master, not to mention financial gains for himself. Meanwhile, Peter had left to Menshikov the task of mopping up the last Swedish outposts. In the summer of 1713 he took Tönningen and Stettin, the Pomeranian capital and port at the mouth of the Oder, which was Sweden's last fortified stronghold in the duchy. At the ensuing peace talks, Menshikov was outwitted (or perhaps bribed) by the one-eyed Görtz, who had reached a secret understanding with Prussia for the handing over of Stettin to Prussia rather than Denmark, in return for support in Holstein's long-running feud with its northern neighbour. Menshikov also acceded to the equal division of captured Swedish troops between Russia, Saxony and Denmark, instead of claiming the lion's share for his own country, which had shouldered the major burden of the recent campaign. It was as well for the general that his master was 1,500 kilometres away in St Petersburg, for the Tsar was furious with his friend's mishandling of the negotiations.

Peter was politically acute. His overmastering objective was to bring Charles XII to his knees as soon as possible. He had no desire to become involved in the political wrangling of the German states, nor did he entertain ambitions to annex territory in the western Baltic. He let it be known that he was prepared to give up several of his conquests in the interests of securing a permanent peace. He knew that anything else would involve hostile reaction from the major European powers. The conference that ended the War of the Spanish Succession began in 1712 and the treaty was signed in April 1713. Britain, Holland and France were now free to direct their diplomatic and, potentially, their military energies to pacifying the Baltic region to their own satisfaction. But matters were not quite that straightforward. In 1714, George Louis, Elector of Hanover, became George I of Great Britain and inevitably involved his new realm in the affairs of northern Germany. At the same time, the Peace of Utrecht was very brittle; Spain and the Empire were at loggerheads over their Italian possessions. Britain, Holland and France were anxious to prevent any resumption of hostilities. But the British government was vulnerable from another direction. Supporters of the exiled Stuarts, driven from the throne in 1688, were assiduously active on the continent in canvassing support in several countries. Having amassed a sizeable war chest and the promise of mercenary forces, their ability to make a nuisance of themselves could not be ignored in the corridors of European diplomacy. These tangled strands in international politics meant that Peter could not simply acquire the quick peace settlement with Sweden that he desired.

But his military-backed diplomacy did not rely solely on the land campaign in the western Baltic. Sweden itself was vulnerable to attack from the sea, and with this in mind, Peter had been building up his navy. The extent of Russian shipbuilding in these years was truly prodigious, and outstripped that of Europe's traditional maritime powers. Peter had been obliged by the terms of the Treaty of Pruth to destroy his Azov fleet, but he more than made up for this loss by the output of his yards on Lake Ladoga. Between 1710 and

1712, eight capital ships, each carrying more than fifty guns, were launched. In addition the Russians commanded a fleet of a hundred scampavias, swift, highly manoeuvrable Mediterranean-style galleys. Peter calculated that such vessels held the key to naval warfare in the difficult Swedish and Finnish coastal waters hitherto dominated by Charles XII's powerful fleet. The navy was, of course, Peter's pride and joy, and he now used it to pave the way for delivering the *coup de grâce* to the Swedish empire. His objective was the Åland peninsula, between Finland and Sweden. With control of these islands and the surrounding sea, he would be able to muster his forces for an invasion of the Swedish mainland. This, he believed, would, as he wrote to Admiral Fedor Apraksin, 'bend the Swedish neck' and force Charles to come to terms. Just as Charles had done before the showdown at Poltava, Peter had his agents distribute pamphlets in the enemy capital protesting his desire to end the long and debilitating war. Unlike Charles, he did not attempt to interfere in his adversary's internal politics by encouraging rebellion against the King.

As soon as his ports were unfrozen in the spring of 1714, Peter led his entire galley force to Helsinki, landed with 16,000 troops and captured the town with little difficulty. Leaving his galleys there, he assumed command of nine capital ships and five frigates and sailed across the Gulf of Finland to Tallinn, where he rendezvoused with more vessels. However, Rear Admiral Peter Mikhailov was thwarted in his plan to link up with his galleys and sail his formidable combined fleet into Swedish home waters. A serious outbreak of plague decimated his crews at Tallinn. The galleys, commanded by Admiral Apraksin, had to begin the offensive alone. They successfully established a forward base on the eastern side of the Gangut peninsula. It was July before Peter's squadron could rejoin them there. The delay had given the Swedish navy, under Admiral Wattrang, plenty of time to assemble and position itself to defend the islands. Peter, ever cautious, did not want to encounter Wattrang's entire fleet in open battle if he could avoid it. The geography of the region came to his aid. The maze of islands and channels separating the Gulf of Bothnia from the Baltic offered a wide choice for an attacking force. In order to confuse the enemy, Peter had some of the galleys dismantled and ferried across the Gangut peninsula. The ruse worked. Wattrang divided his fleet in order to keep an eye on Russian movements. He sent a strong detachment to attack the Russian base, while keeping his main force in reserve. Unfortunately the ships he sent to do battle were becalmed; Apraksin's galleys rowed past them and trapped the main Swedish contingent in a fjord near Hangö. In the ensuing engagement, Peter's ships, though outgunned, won a convincing victory. They captured ten Swedish vessels and the vice admiral commanding. The way was thus open to Åbo and the Åland islands. To Peter, this triumph was sweeter than Poltava, as he exultantly explained in a message to St Petersburg:

> We beg to report the manner in which the Almighty Lord God was pleased to glorify Russia. For, after granting us many victories on land, now we have been crowned with victory at sea, for on the 27th day of this month by Hangö, near the haven of Rilax-Figl, we captured the Swedish rear-admiral, Nilson Erenschild, with one frigate, six galleys and two sloops, after much and very fierce fire ... in this war, as with our allies in the war with France, many Generals and even field marshals have been taken, but not one Flag-officer.[8]

Peter returned to the capital, had a celebratory medal struck and ordered lavish celebrations. One ceremony was his own promotion to the rank of vice-admiral. So that Catherine should share in the honours, the Tsar decorated his wife with the newly created Order of St Catherine, for her bravery and steadfastness in sharing the dangers faced by the Russian army at the Battle of the Pruth.

At about the same time, news reached Peter that Charles XII was back. His continued presence in Bendery had proved to be a growing embarrassment to Sultan Ahmed. The Swedish king had failed to keep the Russo-Turkish War on the boil, and after much tense negotiation, the Treaty of Adrianople had been signed between the two nations in June 1713. At one point, Ahmed even ordered that his unwelcome guest should be abducted and hustled aboard a French ship. The resulting skirmish, known as the Kalabalik, failed in its intent. Charles remained in Ottoman territory until the autumn of 1714, hoping for an honourable escort back to his own land. When it became obvious even to the pig-headed Charles that this was not going to happen, he made his own perilous and adventurous way home, arriving in Pomeranian Stralsund (under siege by Prussian, Saxon and Danish forces) in November. Still he remained committed to a military solution, but it was obvious that in the short term he would have to rely on diplomacy while mustering his forces to continue the war. Thus 1715 was something of an oasis in the desert of armed conflict that European affairs had been for so long.

The restless Tsar, who seldom spent more than three months in any one place, was now able to enjoy an extended stay in St Petersburg and to give daily attention to its continuing construction. A dozen years of unremitting building work, constantly driven on by Peter's personal visits and his steady flow of instructions, had transformed the marshy islands of the Neva delta into a city with a grid plan of wide, straight streets, linked by bridges, lined with stone-built houses and dotted with squares, gardens and churches. From the massive Peter and Paul fortress, which guarded the harbour, rows of other buildings had spread out, providing government offices, commercial warehouses and the stock exchange. Across the river, the Admiralty shipyard launched its first vessel in 1706. Nearby, Peter laid out his summer palace, which was finally completed in 1715. The palace garden, which was open to the public, covered twenty-five acres, and to create it, Peter lured to Russia none other than Jean-Baptiste-Alexandre Le Blond. Le Blond, *architecte du roi* to Louis XIV, was largely responsible for the new fashion of French formal gardens that was sweeping Europe. His *La théorie et la pratique du jardinage* was the Bible of avant-garde garden designers. Peter bestowed upon him the title of Architect-General and an enormous pension of 5,000 roubles, which was more than he was paying any other foreign craftsman. The Frenchman earned his money. The Summer Garden boasted trees and plants collected by horticultural scavengers in many lands, as well as hothouses, aviaries and gravelled walks decorated with classical statuary. Le Blond also set up work-shops for the production of tapestries, stucco decoration, wood carving and sculpture, whose output graced the city's new palaces. Before his sudden death from smallpox in 1719, he even perfected a system of oil-fired street lighting. St Petersburg's main thoroughfare, Nevsky Prospekt, ran twenty-five kilometres, from the impressive Admiralty Building to the Alexander Nevsky Monastery (named after a thirteenth-century military hero), which Peter founded in 1710. Its straightness was marred by a 'kink' due, as modern tour guides delight to point out, to the employment of foreign labour. The story is that Finnish and Swedish prisoner work gangs started from opposite ends. Only when it was too late did anyone discover that they were laying out the street on different trajectories.

As we have seen, Peter's instruction to the great families to build town mansions in the new capital aroused considerable resentment, but his conflict with the boyars was as nothing to the war he waged on the forces of nature. Peter was not going to allow his modern model city to be made up of ram-shackle, fire-prone streets. In the early days, houses, shops and offices were, of necessity, erected hastily of timber. This invited disaster but did provide the opportunity for citizens to see another side of their tsar. According to one ambassador, Peter relished the challenge of fire:

> He takes part in all the rescue operations and since he has an extraordin-arily quick mind he sees at once what has to be done to extinguish the fire. He climbs up to the roof. He goes to the points where the danger is greatest, he urges the nobles, like the common people, to take part in the struggle and he does not stop until the fire is out ... But when the

sovereign is not present, it is another thing entirely. The people look on indifferent and do nothing to extinguish the fire ... they only wait for an opportunity to steal something.[9]

But prevention was better than cure. The Tsar's earthly paradise would be built of stone. The problem was that no stone was to be had anywhere near the site. It was tackled in true Petrine fashion. Every wagon, boat and ship coming into the city was obliged to carry a consignment of stone in addition to its other cargo. The use of stone anywhere else in the country was forbidden.

However, the main threat to the Tsar's grand design was not the occasional conflagration. It was water (the modern city has sixty-three canals and rivers). To support the weight of buildings, pine piles had to be driven into the low-lying ground. Even then, some constructions collapsed before builders had mastered techniques for coping with the difficult conditions. Every autumn brought storms that uprooted trees and tore the roofs from houses. In bad years the Neva overflowed its banks: 1703, 1706, 1715, 1717 and 1721 witnessed particularly severe inundations. Few buildings escaped being under a metre or more of water, and there was significant loss of life. There was no lack of ill-wishers ready to draw the moral from such disasters. Priests denounced St Petersburg as a latter-day Sodom, suffering visitations of divine wrath, and prophesied its total destruction. One such was dealt with in a way that let the punishment fit the crime: he was sentenced to three years' hard labour in the construction gangs building the city. Peter's determination to drive forward the creation of his urban masterpiece was more than matched by the widespread resentment of those who would cheerfully have seen the wilderness return to recapture its conquered territory.

But Peter won. With a speed unmatched by the growth of any modern city, St Petersburg spread to encompass an ever-wider area. Much of the credit must go to the first governor, Menshikov, for although he used the grand project to enrich himself, he did expend enormous energy in realising the vision of his friend and monarch. That vision extended to almost every aspect of urban life, from the colours to be used for all external façades (bright, to offset the lack of sunshine) to regulations against begging; from refuse disposal to the variety of trees that were to line the streets; from setting up craft workshops to bringing in cartloads of soil and manure for the gardens; from establishing a police force (an innovation imported from Paris in 1718) to issuing edicts about the type of moss to be used for stuffing the joins in timber buildings. Yet, paradoxically, the end result was not uniformity. Peter's enthusiasms lacked precise focus. New ideas excited and fascinated him. His mind was like a sponge with an enormous absorptive capacity. His admiration for men of talent was unbounded. And he wanted to funnel everything into St Petersburg – works of art, architectural styles, exotic plants, technical innovations, and the craftsmen capable of producing them and teaching his own people how to reproduce them. Peter was the most lavish royal patron in Europe, and hundreds of skilled workers came to St Petersburg for longer or shorter periods of time. The city was a Mecca for genius, a place where established masters could win fresh laurels and where aspiring newcomers could make their reputations. Thus, for example, Domenico Trezzini already had a well-known architectural practice and influenced building styles in Holland and Denmark, but spent the second half of his life (1703–34) in St Petersburg, where his most dramatic contribution was the Peter and Paul Church with its needle-like spire, still a prominent feature of the city's skyline. By contrast, his fellow countryman, Gaetano Chiaveri, arrived as a young architect full of enthusiasm for rococo ornamentation, which was all the rage, and worked on several of Peter's buildings before moving on to greater things in Dresden (the Hofkirche), Warsaw and Rome. The mushrooming capital became, in the words of art historian Igor Grabar, 'a theatre of architectural experiment' in which Dutch neoclassicism, Italian baroque and its more restrained German relative stood shoulder to shoulder. It would be later in the century before a distinctive Russian baroque style evolved.

Peter was not only introducing revolutionary new buildings inside the city limits. Well-to-do Russians maintained country estates within easy reach of Moscow, and the royal family was no exception. The Tsar intended that the pattern of summer and winter houses should be replicated by residents of the new capital, and he set in hand construction of his own upmarket dacha. Inevitably, it was situated on the coast of the Gulf of Finland. As soon as he had secured his foothold on the Baltic, he built lodges or rest houses where he could break his journey when travelling to and from St Petersburg. They would certainly have been simple log cabins like the one preserved on the Petrovsky Embankment. The most important of these was the one that became known as Peterhof (Peter's Court), some thirty kilometres from the centre of the city. The site was on rising ground opposite the island of Kotlin, which guards the approach to St Petersburg and where the Tsar created the fortified naval base of Kronslot. Since Peter was seldom separated from his ships, he needed a nearby residence. In 1704, he began the construction of a palace that would develop in the hands of himself and his successors into one of the most spectacular royal residences in Europe.

Peterhof provides the modern visitor with what is perhaps the most tangible evidence of the contrasting – almost contradictory – sides of Peter's personality. On the one hand, he was impressed with the splendours with which European monarchs surrounded themselves. Since he needed to convince the world that Russia was no cultural backwater, he was obliged to build and decorate his palaces without counting the cost. Cartloads and shiploads of rare, beautiful artefacts – paintings, tapestries, sculptures, silverware, gold and jewelled ornaments (including what came to be known as the Siberian Collection of archaeological antiquities excavated from ancient burial sites), furniture, clocks, porcelain, bronzes, marbles, chandeliers, carved panelling – were constantly arriving in St Petersburg for the adornment of the Tsar's residences. But on the other hand, Peter took little personal pride in these acquisitions. He still preferred to live in modest surroundings. He found the compact houses of Dutch towns most to his taste and replicated many of their features in his own residential quarters. Today, it is the hilltop palace Peterhof, with its gilt-panelled rooms and stunning fountains and cascades, that impresses visitors. This building was begun by Peter, but it was not where he elected to stay during his visits. His initial vision for the site was as a holiday home for himself and his young family. With this in mind, he brought the internationally famed Andreas Schluter to Russia in 1713. Unfortunately, the architect died a year later and the task of completing the work was taken up by his young assistant, Johann Braunstein. He supervised the creation of a pavilion, dubbed by the Tsar Monplaisir, set amidst gardens and fountains created by Le Blond. Sometimes called 'the little Dutch house', Monplaisir was modelled closely on the summer residences beloved of Amsterdam's merchant princes. Here Peter would come with Catherine and the girls to enjoy domestic harmony amidst the gravelled walks, flower beds, grottoes and elaborate fountains – and, of course, the sea views. A little to the west, he had an even more private building constructed. The Hermitage was a small two-storey house surrounded by a moat with a drawbridge. Its first-floor dining hall was equipped with an ingenious device that allowed the table to be lowered to the kitchen below, where the required dishes would be placed upon it. Then it would be hauled back to where Peter and his guests were waiting. Here the Tsar could hold important conferences in complete security and well away from prying ears.

But the modest pavilions were inadequate for the needs of the court. From the beginning, Peter had grander designs for Peterhof, designs that were expanded after his visit to Versailles in 1716 (see p. 138 below). When the Holstein nobleman Friedrich von Bergholz visited the palace complex in 1721, he was able to approach it along ' a very jolly road ... through groves of trees and past many dachas that were constructed by the noblest grandees to please the tsar and make the road most pleasant'. He admired the collection of Dutch paintings with which Peter had decorated Monplaisir, and reported that the Tsar still usually elected to stay there whenever he visited Peterhof, because 'he feels completely at ease there'. Bergholz admired the Upper Chambers, still under construction, but noted that, in contrast to the intricately decorated state rooms, Peter's study was a much more intimate oak-lined chamber. Two years later Bergholz was back again as part of a large assemblage of guests invited by Peter for an official 'house-warming'. They arrived by sea, which was the most impressive way to approach the palace. A straight canal sufficiently wide to accommodate three sailing boats abreast ran 500 metres inland and led directly to the base of the stunning cascade and fountains fronting the palace. Having disembarked, the guests enjoyed a guided tour of the lower grounds led by the Tsar in person before climbing the steps beside the watercourse to reach the Upper Chambers. They took lunch in the large, ornate Italian Salon but were not joined there by their host. Peter and Catherine retired to Monplaisir to eat in private. Although Peterhof was extended and beautified by future Romanov generations, the palace and grounds still bear the stamp of their original designer. Every aspect of the work was carried out to detailed plans agreed between Peter and his architects. Thousands of trees were imported for the gardens. An army of workmen was employed for more than ten years. The fountain system, which remains the most memorable aspect of Peterhof for most visitors, was a creation of engineering genius. It was fed by a reservoir thirteen kilometres away. Four thousand labourers were employed to dig the canal that brought water down to the palace. The pressure was sufficient to feed (eventually) 144 fountains without the aid of mechanical pumps. The gilded statuary depicted figures from classical legend but were replete with contemporary significance. Peter was portrayed as one of the heroes of old, and the statue of the Gorgon was given the face of Charles XII.

Peter needed the solace of this rural retreat. Life elsewhere was seldom free from stress. While he worked with his usual industry and imposed his iron will on the country, he felt himself increasingly isolated. 'Saint of God, protect your namesake, our only hope'; so the Orthodox metropolitan had prayed to St Alexis in March 1712, in the peroration of a swingeing sermon attacking government corruption and, obliquely, the morals of the Tsar. Such public denunciations severely dented any obedient patriotism stirred up by military triumphs and lavish public celebrations. They certainly went to Alexis' head. When he was in his cups (an increasingly common state), he spoke openly about the different regime he would institute when he became tsar. Heads would roll. The navy would be burned. St Petersburg would be abandoned. There was no sign of a reconciliation between father and son. Peter persisted in demanding that the Tsarevich continue his studies and prepare himself to take on the burdens of state, but it became increasingly obvious that the young man was not merely lazy; he lacked the intellectual capacity to undertake the work of government. On one occasion when his father asked for evidence of his progress in drawing up military plans, Alexis was so frightened of revealing his lack of study that he deliberately fired a pistol across his right hand, inflicting severe powder burns. It was a painful way to avoid the examination. His abominable treatment of his wife certainly did nothing to improve relations with the German princes and her brother-in-law, the Emperor. Apart from getting her pregnant, he largely ignored her. When the wretched Charlotte fled to her parents, the task of fetching her back to court fell to Peter. When she presented him with a daughter in the summer of 1714, the Tsarevich saw no reason to return from Carlsbad, where he was taking the waters. In December, he eventually arrived back in St Petersburg and installed his mistress under the conjugal roof.

Yet what exercised Peter even more throughout the winter was the behaviour of his favourite, Alexander Menshikov. Complaints about the corrupt methods Menshikov was using to build up his immense fortune and his state within a state could no longer be ignored. And he was not the only one who was enriching himself at the government's expense. Bribery and extortion, like oil slicks on water, spread wide their deadly influence. Underlings were drawn into the mire of backhanders and unofficial 'commissions'. Leading members of the government and senior officials, seeing that the favourite got away with blatant malfeasance, followed his example. It would have seemed foolish not to do so. By 1714, irregularity had become the norm. A typical example of the kind of scandal that was prevalent was the engrossing of grain for the capital. Merchants were prevented from bringing their supplies into the city but were forced to sell it to Menshikov's agents at a low price. Not only was it then sold in St Petersburg at a huge profit, the cost of transport was charged to the government. A more sinister example of cynical profiteering was the pocketing of money scheduled for food for the thousands of workers brought in for the construction of St Petersburg. While labourers went hungry, and in very many cases died, Menshikov and his cronies were lining their pockets at the government's expense. The favourite's arrogant reliance on Peter's friendship had long since lured him into dangerous overconfidence. He was almost reckless in providing his rivals with ammunition they might use against him if ever they were given a chance. That chance was provided by Menshikov's mishandling of the diplomatic exchanges with Saxony and Denmark.

Peter now began to pay more attention to complaints against his old friend. Indeed, he canvassed comment. It may well have been the sheer splendour in which Menshikov lived in the capital that was the last straw.

The favourite's baroque palace on Vasilevsky Island was by far the most magnificent building in St Petersburg. It was completed before the Tsar's own winter palace and was built to a grander specification. Some time in 1714 Peter learned that workmen designated for the construction of the royal building had been diverted by Menshikov to his own project. It is significant that the showdown between ruler and favourite occurred after one of the many lavish celebrations staged at Menshikov's palace, where he had thrown an extravagant birthday party to show off the latest additions to the mansion. Later that day, Peter gave his host a dressing-down in front of several people, including foreign diplomats. Various versions exist of the Tsar's harangue, which apparently went on for a couple of hours. One recorder made a point of stating that Peter had, uncharacteristically, refrained from strong drink at the banquet in order to keep a clear head for the task before him. Peter pointed out the disparity in the public display of wealth between the sovereign and his subject. If Menshikov was richer than his master, there could be only one reason why. 'Today I see the marks of your faithlessness,' Peter declared. 'I raised you up from nothing but you are raising yourself above me. I knew well that you were robbing me and I permitted it but now I am well informed that you have not only stolen hundreds of thousands but millions and just this year you have stolen more than a million.' The outraged Tsar itemised the complaints that were pouring in on every hand, from humble subjects right up to the Holy Roman Emperor, and he issued a stark warning: 'If you think you have taken everything away from me, remember that I still have axe and block and I can have all thieves executed.'[10] Menshikov fell to his knees, begging for mercy and promising restitution, as well he might, but the Tsar was not to be placated. Even when Catherine ventured a word in her friend's defence, she was silenced.

The examination Peter now set in hand lasted well into the spring of 1715. By the standards of the inquisitions that followed the *strel'tsy* and Astrakhan revolts, it was neither exhaustive nor ruthless. This was inevitable, since the corruption was endemic and involved many of the most powerful men in the land. It was more a question of finding scapegoats than of rooting out every vestige of wrongdoing. To have done so would have been to decimate the entire administration, both central and regional. Dismissals, fines and public floggings were the punishments meted out to the unfortunate underlings selected to suffer in the place of their superiors. Menshikov got off with a heavy fine, but he never regained the degree of intimacy with the Tsar that he had once enjoyed. In the shuffling of personalities at the top, it is not surprising to note that Sheremetev's rise was attendant on Menshikov's fall. As for Peter, he knew that it was not enough to punish offenders. As long as there were loopholes in the operation of government, grasping and unscrupulous officials would take advantage of them. Once more, therefore, he bent his mind to an overhaul of the administration.

In January 1715, one of those bizarre events occurred that illustrate the multifaceted personality of this remarkable man. Peter was in the middle of fighting a war, dealing with critical events touching his relations with those closest to him, continuing to plan and build his new capital, struggling with the administrative organisation of his empire and overseeing complex diplomatic negotiations. Yet he found time to organise one of those grotesque events that punctuated his reign. He had maintained the elaborate fiction of the parallel court of the Prince-Caesar and the Prince-Pope, the presence of which constantly mocked the more pretentious aspects of royal life. When he was absent from Moscow and St Petersburg, Peter seldom failed to send reports to the Prince-Caesar, Fedor Romodanovsky. This rough-and-ready, bibulous, outspoken apparent buffoon of a man did not share all Peter's reforming ideals. Many Russians recognised in him a supporter of traditional values. But whatever his own views were on a variety of subjects, Romodanovsky's master virtue was personal loyalty to the Tsar. Peter knew he could rely on the Prince-Caesar, under his satirical camouflage, to keep a close eye on affairs and personalities at the centre and to undertake any actions that might be necessary, whether open or clandestine. The same was partially true of the Prince-Pope, Nikita Zotov. This elderly dignitary had been the young Peter's tutor and was subsequently raised to various important state offices. Although he appeared in public ceremonies and processions as a pantomime figure, mocking religious rituals (and may, for that reason, have been underestimated by some of the Tsar's opponents), he was extremely astute, and Peter knew that he could rely on him implicitly.

When the day of the septuagenarian's retirement drew near, Peter resolved that it should be marked with a particularly spectacular masquerade. The week-long celebrations in January 1715 involved over a thousand invitees appearing in fancy dress and parading around the city, with Peter in the guise of a Dutch sailor leading the column beating a drum. Everyone was, of course, expected to drink copiously and to join enthusiastically in the various diversions arranged for them. The centre point was Zotov's wedding to a bride many years his junior (what better way of parodying the head of the Catholic church than, in jest, marrying him off?). No element was omitted that might add to the absurdity of the proceedings: '... invitations to guests were delivered by stammerers, the bridesmen were cripples, the runners were fat men with gout, the priest was allegedly almost 100 years old. The mock tsar was carried in a sledge drawn by bears.'[11] After the feasting, the ill-matched couple were conveyed to the bridal chamber and their subsequent behaviour observed secretly through holes in the walls.

Militarily, 1715 was a quiet year. Back in his capital, Charles XII was struggling to raise the necessary funds and manpower to continue the war. Russia was poised to carry the offensive into the Swedish homeland if the King still refused to come to terms. Wismar and Stralsund, the remaining Swedish forts on the southern Baltic coast, were under siege and fell before the end of the year. Other interested parties had their own problems. Britain had a new monarch and had to deal with a rebellion of Scottish Jacobites led by the Old Pretender (son of James II). He was financed by French supporters, and it was by no means certain that the Protestant succession would survive. In the autumn, Louis XIV died, leaving the government of France in the hands of the Duc d'Orléans during the minority of the late king's infant great-grandson. The five-year-old Louis XV was a sickly child, and the prospect existed of another succession crisis because Philip V of Spain coveted the French crown. To confound matters still further, the Spanish king also supported the Jacobite challenger to the British throne. In northern Germany, Denmark, Prussia, Saxony and Holstein carved up the former Swedish territories. Everyone had a vested interest in the peaceful settlement of the region along the lines of the new territorial divisions. Everyone except Charles XII. And he now had a new ally, Georg von Görtz. The former Holstein minister had transferred his allegiance to the Swedish crown and was busy trying to raise funds for the continuance of the war. His negotiations in Spain involved a £60,000 loan in return for Swedish naval support in transporting a Jacobite army to northern England. These convoluted activities acted in Peter's favour, in that the maritime powers, Britain and Holland, exasperated with Sweden's potential involvement in destabilising activities, looked with favour on Russia and the establishment of good trading relations. In the summer, a merchant fleet was sent to St Petersburg under a strong Anglo-Dutch escort to protect it against possible Swedish attack.

Later in the year, the tragedy that was the life of Alexis took a step towards its doleful conclusion. In October, his wife was delivered of a son. Days later, Tsaritsa Catherine also gave birth to a boy. Both children were christened Peter. Suddenly the whole dynastic picture was changed. Russia now had three potential heirs to the throne. The Tsar had already, when particularly enraged, threatened to disinherit Alexis. Now that could be done without creating constitutional difficulties. Father–son relations were continuing to decline. Alexis, at twenty-five, was still behaving like a petulant adolescent who could not discover his own identity and hid from his problems behind alternate bouts of debauchery and piety. Peter tried to avoid facing the reality that, as his successor, Alexis would dismantle everything he had been at great pains to build. But his attitude towards his son was based on duty, not paternal affection. On the very day before the birth of his grandson, Peter wrote: 'I have not spared and do not spare my own life for my country and my people, so why should I spare you who are so unworthy? Better a worthy stranger than my own unworthy son.'[12] Nine days after giving birth, Charlotte died. Her life had been little more than imprisonment in a loveless cage, but Alexis gave every sign of being distraught. Whether this was an expression of belated affection or of a guilty conscience, we cannot know. What is known is that Alexis now wrote to the Tsar expressing his wish to relinquish the throne. If this gesture was made to appease his father, it did not succeed. Peter had hoped his son would rise to the challenge. Instead Alexis had given further proof of his own spinelessness. In January, Peter sent yet another bitter letter. He gave his son six months to choose between accepting his royal destiny or being incarcerated for life in a monastery.

If the Tsarevich was failing in his duty, the same could not be said of other young members of his family. In February, Peter travelled to Danzig for the wedding of his niece, Catherine, to Duke Carl Leopold of Mecklenburg. The Tsarevna was quite a catch for the autocratic princeling, who needed a powerful ally in his internal struggle with the landowning class. Previously he had tied his fortunes to the Swedish crown and was referred to contemptuously as 'Charles XII's monkey'. In reality, he was an arrogant boor with a penchant for mindless brutality who had no interest in the international situation and was concerned only with enhancing his own power. It probably did not occur to him that by signing a treaty that included the stationing of Russian troops on his territory, he was giving away a sizeable portion of his independence and fuelling the hostility of his own subjects and also of neighbouring German rulers. Such a bridegroom can scarcely have appealed to poor Catherine, but, of course, her happiness was of no account. The real gainer from this contract was Peter, who would be able to bring the small state firmly within the Russian sphere of influence, station troops there and, if all went according to plan, acquire Wismar as a fortified Russian base. There was even some talk of linking Wismar and the Elbe by canal, which would have given Russia all-year-round access to the western Baltic and the North Sea.

Peter's trip to Danzig was the first leg of another major European tour, which would keep him out of Russia until October 1717. This was a very different journey to the Grand Embassy. There was no pretence at travelling incognito. Nor was the Russian ruler any longer a curiosity to be regarded with amused condescension by other monarchs. The man who had dismantled the Swedish empire was a force to be reckoned with. The man who had intruded himself into the political life of the German states could no longer be discounted as an Oriental despot holding sway beyond Europe's eastern boundaries. At every stage of his tour, Peter of Russia was courted by diplomats eager to discover his intentions, secure his friendship or thwart his ambitions.

In the summer of 1716, having visited the kings of Prussia and Denmark to discuss strategy, Peter gathered his forces for a naval assault on the Skåne region of the Swedish mainland. This set alarm bells ringing in several European chancelleries. George I, ruler of Britain and Hanover, was already concerned about Russian activity in Mecklenburg. Now he faced the prospect of the 'balance of the north' being seriously and permanently weighted in Russia's favour by the conquest and total humiliation of Sweden. With control of the seaways, Peter would be in a position to dictate terms to his trading partners. George was also alarmed by rumours that the Tsar was in communication with Jacobite agents planning another military coup. There was an element of truth in such suspicions. Peter's physician, Robert Erskine, currently travelling with his master, was a younger brother of Sir John Erskine of Alva, who was deep in the intrigues of the exiled Stuarts. One of the Jacobite schemes was the securing of a Russian alliance based on the marriage of the Pretender to one of Peter's female relatives. Robert Erskine certainly acted as a go-between in these extremely tentative negotiations. Letters were discovered and indignantly published by the government in London. Peter disavowed all knowledge of the affair and stood by his doctor, but that did not satisfy George I. He favoured an ultimatum to the Tsar backed by the threat of military action. It was only divisions among his own ministers that prevented him pursuing this course. In fact, the Baltic situation contributed to a major political crisis in Britain leading to the resignation of cabinet leaders Viscount Townsend and Sir Robert Walpole. In October 1716, Britain and France patched up their ancient quarrels in a treaty by which, in return for British opposition to Spanish dynastic pretensions, the French agreed to stop supporting the Jacobites. Three months later, Holland joined what became the Triple Alliance. One objective of this coming together of major powers was the protection of Swedish rights in the north. Further opposition to Russian expansion came from Vienna, where the Emperor was nervous about the Tsar's growing influence within the Holy Roman Empire. Peter, for the first time in his life, was experiencing a build-up of diplomatic opposition to his policies among those very states whose friendship he most coveted.

In the event, however, it was logistical rather than political difficulties that called a halt to the Swedish invasion plan. Back in St Petersburg, the Senate dragged its heels over financing and dispatching the supplies for which the army and navy were waiting. Throughout the summer, Peter and Admiral Apraksin bombarded the capital with letters demanding urgent attention to their needs. Menshikov, who had been left behind and was desperate to re-establish himself in the Tsar's favour, personally confronted the Senate on several occasions, but to little effect. The officials simply blamed the field commanders for trying to pass on the responsibility for their own shortcomings. In July, Apraksin, who was charged with launching a diversionary raid from Åbo, was forced to withdraw to the Finnish mainland; his troops were dropping like flies from disease and malnutrition. Charles XII took advantage of the situation to divide his enemies. He marched his army into Danish-owned Norway. Frederick IV was obliged to divert his forces to defend his territory, and the grand combined-fleet invasion was called off.

It was at this low point in Peter's fortunes that he received from home embarrassing news that sent him into a towering rage. Alexis had disappeared. Recently Peter had written to his son telling him that he had had quite long enough to respond to the ultimatum he had delivered before leaving the capital, and demanding to know which monastery the Tsarevich had decided to join. If, in fact, he had decided to withdraw his renunciation of the throne, he was to repair immediately to Denmark to rendezvous with his father. Within weeks, Alexis left St Petersburg – but not en route for Copenhagen. He put into operation a well-prepared plan to seek support from his late wife's relatives. Accompanied by Euphrosyne and four attendants, he made his way to Vienna to cast himself on the charity of the Emperor Charles VI.

7

'The horizon is clear'

Whatever ends an insatiate desire of opulency and a boundless thirst for dominion can ever put him upon, to satisfy their craving and voracious appetites, those must assuredly be his … he is grown too formidable for the repose, not only of his neighbours, but also of Europe in general … [If] incredulous people look narrowly into the nature and the ends and the designs of this great monarch, they will find they are laid very deep and that his plans carry in them a prodigious deal of prudence and foresight … Will they not … own that we ought to fear everything from him?[1]

So wrote an alarmist and hostile pamphleteer in 1716 about the career and ambitions of Tsar Peter. Informed public opinion in Britain was turning against the Russian ruler, but he still had his champions, who continued to regard him as a hero and standard-bearer of enlightenment.

> Unmeasured realms lay hid in noiseless reign
> And Russia covered half the world in vain!
> Till ripening time this giant-genius sent:
> Divinely-sized – to suit his crown's extent!
> He breathed prolific soul, inspired the land
> And called forth order with directive hand.[2]

The mixed perceptions of this new international phenomenon mirror fairly closely those that greeted the rise of Hitler in the early 1930s. A growing anxiety about his spreading influence and unchallenged power was offset by admiration for his reforms at home and the national pride he inspired in his people. The prevailing attitude among the political leaders of the Western powers, however, tended towards suspicion and alarm. While they had been preoccupied with their own concerns, marching their armies to and fro throughout the War of the Spanish Succession, Peter had been securing for himself a dominant role in northern Europe that looked alarmingly as though it might become permanent. His conquered and satellite territories stretched like a long arm along the southern Baltic. After aborting the Swedish invasion, he had a large land and sea force at his disposal. Where might he be planning to employ it next? If he continued expanding his navy at the current rate, his maritime power would soon exceed that of Sweden and Denmark combined. Then he would be in a position to challenge the British and the Dutch in their home waters. He must be checked – and checked without delay. Most of this scaremongering was groundless. For example, British ministers were so conscious of the Jacobite threat that they were ready to believe any rumour about the Pretender's activities, including his plans to bring a Russian army across the Channel. Why else, they asked, was the Tsar eagerly offering employment to English naval officers dismissed from the service for Jacobite sympathies (seven in the year 1717 alone, including one rear-admiral). In fact, Peter never had any intention of interfering in Britain's dynastic arrangements. But fear and prejudice, not for the first or last time in international affairs (it is only a few years since American and British governments convinced themselves that Iraq was poised to launch nuclear mayhem within forty-eight hours), had more impact than hard evidence. For the next couple of years, diplomatic activity vis-à-vis Russia centred on reaching diplomatic agreement with it while at the same time forming potential alliances against it.

From Peter's viewpoint, the need was to dispel the anxieties of his western neighbours while yet exploiting the advantage his military and diplomatic achievements had gained him. This was why he spent months travelling to and fro between European courts. The cornerstone of his policy was peace with Sweden, and by the spring of 1717, he seemed to have found an influential ally. Georg von Görtz had by now so insinuated himself into the confidence of Charles XII as to be entrusted with negotiations. The envoy suggested calling a peace conference. At last it seemed that the Swedish king was coming to his senses. What Peter did not know was that Charles had been in correspondence with Tsarevich Alexis with a view to his being placed on the throne with the backing of foreign troops. Alexis was desperate to revive this scheme, which had first been proposed before Poltava. Charles seems to have been convinced that Peter's deposition by his disaffected people was only a matter of time and that Alexis was now ready to put himself at the head of a rebellion. He knew that the Tsarevich was seeking help from the Emperor and he was anxious to get a step ahead of imperial diplomats.

The activities of his son were an extreme embarrassment to Peter, but they did not deflect him from his primary objective of securing peace. He certainly did not contemplate rushing back to St Petersburg. Until some time in late October 1716, he had no inkling of Alexis' defection. The runaway had sent letters ahead intimating that he was on his way to join his father. At the port of Libau (Liepaja) he had bumped into his aunt, Maria Alexeyevna, and told her that he was, with all filial obedience, bound for Copenhagen. In fact, it was only when he had reached Danzig that he burned his boats irrevocably by turning south. The fateful decision was influenced by his meeting up with Alexander Kikin. Alexis was, as ever, in two minds (or more than two), and had it not been for senior officials and courtiers with a grudge against the Tsar, who intended to use the Tsarevich as the figurehead for a coup, he would never have plucked up the courage to defy his father. Kikin, an admiralty official and close companion of Menshikov, was described by a foreign observer as 'one of the shrewdest and craftiest of the Russians'. He had been caught up in the anti-corruption investigation of 1715 and been so severely interrogated that he had suffered a minor stroke. Following this, he had been dismissed from his post, deprived of his fine house in St Petersburg and sent into exile. But he had been speedily pardoned and restored to some of his former prominence. These experiences, far from inspiring him to greater loyalty, left him deeply resentful. He helped Alexis to screw his courage to the sticking place and travelled on ahead to spy out the land. At Danzig he was able to convince the young truant that the Emperor was well disposed towards him, that there were elements in the army in Mecklenburg ready to mutiny and that a change of regime in Russia would be looked on favourably by several foreign governments.

Charles VI was not averse to receiving his late sister-in-law's husband in Vienna, but he was far from clear how he could turn Peter's discomfiture to his advantage. He favoured anything that might distract the Tsar from his activities in Germany, but he was nervous about giving Peter cause for military action. As soon as Peter learned that his son was on the loose, he set his bloodhounds on the trail. Chief among them was the veteran politico Peter Tolstoy (an ancestor of the novelist Leo Tolstoy), a cunning operator who had once been deep in the councils of Tsarevna Sophia and had become adept in the arts of self-preservation. Peter had the measure of the man and had once commented, touching Tolstoy's forehead, 'Oh head, head, if I didn't know you were so clever, I'd have had you cut off long ago.' Autocrats need servants who are sufficiently unscrupulous and amoral to do their dirty work for them while also being totally trustworthy. Tolstoy was a member of that rare breed. As Alexis and Euphrosyne made their way incognito through Europe, Tolstoy was on their trail.

By mid–November 1716, the runaways were in Vienna, Alexis sporting a moustache and Euphrosyne dressed as a man. The vice chancellor, Frederick von Schönborn, was detailed to look after the unexpected guests, while the Emperor and his council decided what to do with them. After much discussion, it was resolved to hide the Tsarevich and his companions until it became clear what diplomatic use might be made of them. They were, accordingly, conveyed to Ehrenberg, a mountaintop castle in the Tyrol. As soon as Peter heard from Tolstoy that the fugitives were on Austrian soil, he politely requested the Emperor to send them back to Russia. Charles replied that he had no knowledge of Alexis' whereabouts. But he could not outwit Tolstoy's agents. By questioning and bribing servants, prominent citizens and courtiers, they took little time to discover the truth. Schönborn sent messages to Alexis pointing out the embarrassment in which his imperial majesty found himself. The distraught young man begged the Emperor not to abandon him to his father's fury. After much anguished negotiation a compromise was reached: Charles would continue to protect the Tsarevich but only if he removed himself as far as possible from the centre of the empire. That meant the distant imperial city of Naples. In the spring of 1717, Alexis and Euphrosyne were back on the road, and by mid-May they were lodged in the fortress of St Elmo, overlooking the bay. It was July before the Tsar was fully informed of his son's new refuge. Now he took a firmer line with the Emperor. The situation, he declared was 'unacceptable'. He insisted on the immediate return of Alexis and backed his request with threats that were scarcely veiled: 'We cannot allow Your Imperial Majesty to oppose our demands ... [We await] your final decision, which will determine the measures we will have to take.'

Charles and his advisers weighed their choices very carefully. It was intolerable that the Holy Roman Emperor should be dictated to by a half-barbarian monarch (news of whose latest antics was currently going the rounds of Western courts – see pp. 137–8 below). Charles had extended his protection to Alexis and was honour bound to stand by his word. On the other hand, Peter did have impressive armies in Pomerania and Mecklenburg and could make a real nuisance of himself. Was the Tsar bluffing, or was he really willing to make a *casus belli* of the Alexis affair? Charles was already at war with Turkey and his relations with Spain were unstable. He had no desire to add military confrontation with Russia to his list of commitments, unless it could prove profitable. For there was a more fundamental issue to be considered: how secure was the Russian monarch on his throne? He was unpopular at home and also with the international diplomatic community. If the Emperor were to give the Tsarevich his backing, would Alexis be in a position to grab the throne? If so, there could be little doubt that Russia would once more turn in on itself and cease to be a problem to its Western neighbours. That outcome would be a great prize. Everything hinged on the personality of Alexis. Was he a big enough man to bear the burden of so great a destiny? While Charles mulled over this question, he bought time by agreeing to allow Tolstoy to travel to Naples and interview the Tsarevich.

By this time, Peter's travels had brought him to Spa, where he spent a month taking the waters. His digestive disorders had been no whit improved by weeks of overindulgence in Paris, where he spent most of the early summer. His primary objectives were to persuade the French to abandon their traditional support of Sweden and also to weaken the Triple Alliance. But if he wanted to win friends and influence people, he certainly did not set about it the right way. It was with some reluctance that the French regent, the Duc d'Orléans, had agreed to receive the Russian party at court. He understood the purpose of the visit and was determined not to allow the friendly relations he had established with Britain and Holland to be upset. He was also forewarned about the Tsar's rough and ready manners and was concerned about how the visitor would behave in the sophisticated court of a child king where decorum and strict etiquette reigned. For his part, Peter was determined not to be overawed by Parisian society, which set the tone for European culture. He abhorred pretentiousness. Not only would he not go out of his way to tone down his behaviour; he seems from the outset to have courted conflict. His belligerent attitude may very well have had something to do with French reluctance to welcome Catherine. Peter's wife had accompanied him throughout the tour, but it seems he was not prepared to expose her unpolished behaviour to the scrutiny and sniggers of Louis XV's courtiers, and left her in Holland when he sailed for Dunkirk.

During the journey to Paris, he repeatedly found fault with the arrangements made for him and his suite. The carriages provided for his transport were not good enough. The lodgings allocated were, by contrast, overelaborate. When towns en route prepared welcomes for him, he simply drove on through. He turned his nose up at the exquisite dishes prepared for his consumption and complained about the beer (though that did not stop him drinking copious quantities of it). Once at court, the Tsar's demeanour, as had been foreseen, clashed with the highly ritualised conventions surrounding the French monarchy. Peter, the hail-fellow-well-met monarch who genuinely despised the mystique of sovereignty, made no allowance whatsoever for the sensibilities of the royal family and their outraged attendants. One French aristocrat deplored what he considered the Tsar's lack of respect when the Regent arrived to pay a courtesy call on his guest. Peter, he claimed, adopted an air of superiority, walking before Orléans into the study, taking the more important seat and insisting on speaking through an interpreter, even though his own command of French was equal to the task of exchanging civilities. Later, when the Tsar was introduced to the seven-year-old king, he alarmed the royal attendants by whisking his majesty off his feet and clasping him in avuncular embrace. But it was his meeting with Madame de Maintenon that most shocked observers. Peter was eager to meet the eighty-two-year-old widow of Louis XIV, but she did not share his enthusiasm and retired to her bedchamber when he came to call. Undeterred, he marched up to the room, flung open the door, drew back the bed curtains and sat down beside the old lady. The fastidious French stared wide-eyed at Peter's unrestrained eating, drinking and wenching. On one occasion he stuffed himself so full that on his way back to his lodgings, he soiled the cushions of his coach.

Peter's unbounded curiosity had not diminished with the passing of the years. He visited the Académie Française and the Académie des Sciences and enjoyed watching experiments and discussing the latest advances in technology. A high point of his stay was his exploration of the palace and grounds of Versailles. He wandered, notebook in hand, among the splendours of Europe's most magnificent royal residence and made memos of features that might be installed in his palaces at Peterhof and Strelna. He met several of the gardeners, architects and engineers responsible for such dramatic and elegant delights, and offered inducements to them to come to Russia in order to create buildings and gardens that, he promised, would put Louis XIV's achievements in the shade.

Personal reactions to the ill-regulated embassy undoubtedly coloured diplomatic relations. Opinion at the French court was divided between those who supported the Triple Alliance and those for whom friendly relations with the old enemies of Britain and Holland were still unthinkable. Peter, therefore, had some hope of securing a Franco-Russian treaty, perhaps cemented by a royal marriage. However, the Regent was not to be swayed from his policy, and Peter's representatives made little progress. The Tsar left France at the end of June, spent the next month taking a cure at Spa and was reunited with Catherine in Amsterdam. Towards the end of the summer, the couple visited Berlin, to spend a few weeks as guests of Frederick William I. They were graciously received, though the Queen, Sophia Dorothea (daughter of George I of Britain), did take the precaution of removing everything breakable from the houses where the Russians were lodged. Meanwhile, the Alexis saga continued.

The Emperor detained Tolstoy and his colleagues as long as possible, and it was September before they were on the road to Naples. Charles sent ahead of them strict orders to his viceroy, Wirich, Count Daun. He was to be present at all interviews between the parties and to ensure that the Tsar's untrustworthy envoys behaved themselves. However, he was also to urge Alexis to be reconciled with his father. Charles had decided that the weak and irresolute Tsarevich was unlikely to be a useful pawn in Imperial–Russian relations. That being the case, Alexis was an embarrassment. All that mattered now was that he should suffer no ill treatment while still on imperial soil. In the letter Tolstoy handed to the trembling runaway, Peter flourished the stick and the carrot. Having berated his son yet again for his unfilial and unpatriotic behaviour, the writer instructed him to entrust himself to his messengers and carry out their instructions to the letter. If he did so, Peter solemnly promised, 'Before God and his judgement ... I will not punish you and if you submit to my will by obeying me and if you return, I will love you better than ever. But, if you do not, I, as a father, and in accordance with the authority I hold from God, will curse you eternally for your contempt and for the crimes you have committed against your father, and as your sovereign I will pronounce you traitor and you may be sure that I will find a way to punish you as such ...'[3]

It is not difficult to imagine the turmoil into which this cast Alexis. Could he trust the offer of forgiveness? Was it just a trick? Was his destruction already planned? If he refused the apparent olive branch, how long could he avoid his father's long reach? In fact, all the questions were irrelevant. Alexis was not and probably never had been in charge of his own destiny. Tolstoy, Daun and, eventually, even Euphrosyne persuaded the wretched young man that he had no alternative but to return to Russia. The Tsarevich had been manoeuvred into a corner, but even now he tried to strike a bargain with his father's agents. He would agree to go back, he said, on condition that he was allowed to marry his mistress and live in quiet retirement. Tolstoy was instructed to promise that Alexis' wishes would be taken into consideration. Peter, of course, had no intention of allowing his son to spend the rest of his days anywhere where he might be persuaded or forced by malcontents into heading a rebellion.

There were still many men in the upper echelons of Russian society who were resentful of the Tsar's increasing power and who were prepared, if the opportunity presented itself, to back a coup. Alexander Kikin was one such. The prospect of his plan unravelling drove him to fresh intrigues. He contacted Augustus II of Poland-Saxony with a proposal to persuade Alexis to evade his guards and find a new haven where he could hide until the opportunity arose to be inaugurated as the new tsar after his father's death or deposition. Nothing came of this initiative. Alexis was, by now, a thoroughly broken reed. From the point of view of any would-be conspirators, the less the Tsarevich knew the better. Once Peter's interrogators had got to work, they would have little difficulty in extracting names and details from him. As Alexis drew near to the Russian border, he was not alone in feeling apprehensive.

The Tsarevich reached Moscow in January 1718. Peter had returned to the capital three months earlier. He found the place awash with rumour. A multitude of stories were circulating about himself, about the fate of his son and about the behaviour of senior members of the government. The uncertainties and anxieties that wild tales and shrewd political assessments had generated form the background to the dark events of the next few months. Those events cannot be understood without taking into account the ferment of suspicion, fear and personal animosities that was current in St Petersburg between October 1717 and June 1718. It would be an exaggeration to suggest that Peter was gripped by paranoia, but as the problem of the succession loomed progressively larger in his thinking, he took ever more extreme precautions to ensure that Russia would not slip back into its old ways after his death. Peter Tyrholm, a member of the Danish legation, assessed the arrangements the Tsar had made for the government during his recent absence:

> ... since the tsar intended that his will would be executed after his death, and seeing that there would be almost insurmountable difficulties to achieve that, he considered it proper to put Prince Menshikov, the admiral [Fedor Apraksin] and his brother, Count [Peter] Apraksin in singular favour, and that is the better founded since the first has the command of the land armies, the second the sea, and the third as a member of the Senate spies on the actions of his colleagues and obstructs them even when he considers them proper, which is why I have called these three lords ... the Triumvirate ...[4]

However, Peter was far from happy with the government he had left in place during his absence. The Senate had not proved to be the efficient administrative tool he had hoped for. He was furious at having his military and naval campaigns jeopardised by the incompetence and personal rivalries that held up vital supplies. Even while he was away from Russia, he received reports of continuing corruption at all levels of government. Soon after his return, his frustration burst out in a public display of anger. Brandishing his sword at a group of senators and officials, he shouted, 'I did poorly the last time to fine you with money. If I had taken your heads off I would have [kept my] money. I don't know whom I can trust now. Everything is conceived for my ruin. I have only traitors around me!'[5] This was the outburst of a frustrated man who had grandiose plans for his country but was dependent on underlings who did not share his vision and whose behaviour was shaped by personal ambition and the peculation that had been endemic in public life for generations. The Tsar's administrators were scarcely to blame. The system they had to operate was medieval. It had failed to keep pace with the monumental growth of Muscovy and with the demands of a modern expansionist state. There was confusion of territorial authority and technical proficiency. Tax collection was the responsibility of regional governors but was organised by centrally appointed officials. The equitable operation of local law courts was supposedly ensured by fiscals answerable to the Senate, but in practice, these agents were notoriously corrupt. Peter now embarked on a further round of administrative reforms based on models developed in Europe.

The collegiate system he inaugurated was the first major step in Russia towards a modern bureaucracy. Peter set up eight 'colleges' or special-ist government departments, dealing with foreign affairs, justice, revenue, military affairs, audit, treasury, commerce and industry. He personally drew up detailed regulations for the operation of each college, and these were brought together in the General Regulation (1719–24), a codebook of almost military precision, which set out the aims and objectives of each department and the exact responsibilities of every official. Peter's primary objective in all this was greater efficiency, but he also achieved more direct control by placing trusted favourites in charge of the colleges. Thus, Menshikov and Admiral Apraksin maintained responsibility for military affairs and Tolstoy became president of the commercial college. The Senate remained in being to oversee the new bodies, and several senators were also college presidents (a state of affairs Peter later changed in order to ensure the impartiality of the Senate). Delegation of responsibility theoretically meant that the head of state enjoyed more freedom from administrative minutiae, but a hands-on tsar like Peter could not allow even his most trusted ministers free rein. A 'tidal' pattern of government emerged: when Peter was absent or preoccupied, the tide was out and his senior officials took their own decisions. Then the Tsar returned and the tide came in with a rush as he demanded detailed reports, set up inquiries and berated ministers for their incompetence and corruption. The autumn and winter of 1717–18 were marked by a clutch of intercon-nected investigations. With the passage of time, it became more important than ever for Peter to secure the permanence of his reforms.

Peter's new Russia was still a rickety structure. Had he died during his foreign tour, the Triumvirate would certainly have found if difficult to shore up the country during the regency of little Peter Petrovich, who was, in any case, a sickly child. Whatever passed between the Tsar and his firstborn, most people expected that Alexis would, in one way or another, be brought to the throne. His disappearance gave rise to widespread alarm, and theories about his fate proliferated. Some believed that he had gone away to prepare for a bid for the throne, others that he had been abducted on his father's orders. Some people believed that he had been locked up in a monastery, others that he had gone abroad to raise a foreign army. Everyone knew that the Tsar's bouts of ill health were becoming more frequent and that a change of regime might occur at any time. Speculation was rife. And speculation could take on the colour of treason. In Peter's Russia, criticism of the government was always a risky activity, but the Tsar's absence loosened some tongues. Prominent citizens had grumbled about the burdens Peter was placing on them and declared their impatience to see Alexis on the throne. There was never anything sinister behind such expressions of discontent, but it was not difficult for Peter's inquisitors to claim that they could smell a plot. Thus emerged the so-called 'Suzdal affair'.

Suzdal, some 200 kilometres north-east of Moscow, was the location of the convent where Eudoxia was incarcerated. Relatives and sympathisers were in contact with her and, inevitably, encouraged her to believe that she and her son would be reinstated. In the light of Alexis' flight, such communications could be considered suspicious, and Peter ordered a thorough investigation of Eudoxia's circle. No connection was discovered between friends of the Tsar's hated former wife and the active supporters of Alexis' disobedience, but that did not save the suspects from torture and punishment. Peter was always particularly sensitive about his ex-wife's associates, some of whom now suffered for no other reason than that they had succoured Eudoxia or wished that Peter was dead. For being the erstwhile Tsaritsa's lover and carrying messages for her, Stepan Glebov, a military officer, was impaled on a spike driven through his body from rectum to shoulder and left to die slowly in unimaginable agony. Two of the Suzdal nuns were thrashed with the knout, a traditional Russian flail with a vicious leather thong. The Tsarevna Maria, who had met Alexis in Libau, was imprisoned in Schlüsselburg fortress seemingly for no better reason than that she had carried a letter from the Tsarevich to his mother. Eudoxia herself was moved to a more secure convent, where she was closely guarded and forbidden any contact whatsoever with the outside world. The woman who had presided over a gaudy court lived the rest of her days with a dwarf servant as her only companion.

All this was a sideshow to Peter's investigation of his son. The Tsar had learned from the challenges of Sophia, the *strel'tsy* and other dissidents that there were two vital props for despotism – especially unpopular despotism. One was efficient intelligence-gathering, of which torture formed a necessary part. The other was the demonstration that the regime had a long arm and was determined to bring every last offender to justice. Ruthlessly Peter pursued every one of Alexis' contacts in order to expose whatever network the Prince was part of, but also to probe any pockets of disloyalty in the country. He personally led the inquisition but was ably assisted by the ever-faithful Tolstoy. This reincarnated Torquemada was put in charge of the ominously named Chancellery of Secret Affairs, which was set up specially to track down any connections Alexis might have had with suspected malcontents.

It was not a difficult process. The Tsarevich had been reduced to such a state of terror that he was ready to do anything to avoid the vials of his father's wrath being poured over him. His interrogation began in February 1718 in the great hall of the Kremlin. Alexis was brought to stand before the Tsar's throne in the presence of senators, judges and guards. Peter launched a tirade of abuse and accusation against his son. Alexis threw himself at the Tsar's feet, tearfully begging for pardon. Peter declared his willingness to forgive, on two conditions: that Alexis make a full confession of his crimes, and that he provide a list of all his accomplices. Not a single person was to be omitted. Anyone who had so much as expressed sympathy with the unhappy Tsarevich was to be noted. The grovelling young man poured out a torrent of names. Several of those standing by must have trembled in their shoes lest the panicking prisoner recall an encouraging word or act of kindness that might be construed by the Tsar as traitorous. Private investigation was followed by public declaration. The list of Alexis' crimes was read out in Red Square, together with the Tsar's gracious announcement of pardon. Then – and this was the main point of the exercise – the people were told that the Tsarevich had been debarred from the succession in favour of the infant Peter Petrovich, and that any who disagreed with this decision would be treated as traitors. Alexis was, in effect, being made a surrogate for the nation. Just as the Tsar exercised both a father's love and discipline towards his son, so he cherished and chastised his people.

If Alexis thought his ordeal was now over, he did not understand his father. During the following days, he was pressed for further information about the people he had communicated with concerning his future. Some had declared themselves his supporters against Peter. Some had criticised the Tsar for interfering with the accepted practice of primogeniture. Others, such as Fedor Apraksin, had merely offered to intercede with Peter on his son's behalf. But there were those who had warned the Tsarevich not to trust his father and urged him to make his own plans. It soon became clear that a conspiracy of sorts did exist and that Alexander Kikin was at the heart of it. It was he who had advised Alexis to submit to being sent to a monastery because such a detention could only be temporary. Peter, he said, could not nail the cowl to his son's head. Later it was Kikin who had gone to Vienna to prepare the ground for Alexis' flight. Under torture, Kikin implicated senators and other exalted figures, claiming that they had known of the plan. None had been actively involved, but merely concealing it from the Tsar was a serious offence. When his interrogators decided that Kikin had exhausted his usefulness, he was condemned and sentenced to be broken on the wheel. According to one rumour, the Tsar visited the bleeding traitor when he was in his last extremity. 'How could an intelligent man like you have been guilty of such crimes?' he asked. The dying man replied, 'Intelligence loves the open air but you stifle it.'

The investigations continued through the spring and into the summer. Since the treatment of the heir to the throne had been a major talking point among the Russian elite for several years, there was scarcely anyone who could deny having speculated about, debated or expressed an opinion concerning Peter's dynastic arrangements. For example, Semen Naryshkin, one of Eudoxia's relatives, was brought in to account for a conversation he had had with Alexis on his return from a visit to England. The two men had discussed the attitudes pertaining to primogeniture in various European countries. Naryshkin ventured the opinion that sons denied the succession, for whatever reason, were often discontented. 'What else did you say?' his interrogators demanded. 'I don't know,' Naryshkin replied. 'It was a long time ago and I was drunk.' He was sent into exile. The first clutch of executions took place in March, and Alexis was obliged to watch them, in order to reflect on the dreadful price others were paying for his disobedience. He saw the mangled bodies piled in front of the Kremlin palace surrounded by a ring of impaled heads. Any pity he felt for the victims of Peter's wrath must have been outweighed by relief that his own life had been spared. But such feelings were premature. The Chancellery of Secret Affairs was waiting to question a witness who could be potentially much more dangerous to him.

Euphrosyne had not returned to Russia with her lover. She was pregnant and had been allowed to travel at a more leisurely pace. This kindness was not extended to her entirely out of consideration for her condition. It was imperative that she and Alexis were not reunited until after the birth. Their child would thus be – and known to be – a bastard, and no contender for the throne, even if they were subsequently married. When she reached St Petersburg in mid-April, she was taken to the Peter and Paul fortress for her confinement. It will never be known whether her child died at birth or later of natural causes or was deliberately 'suppressed' within the formidable walls of the castle. The young woman probably did not greatly care. What faced her now was much worse than the ordeal of childbirth. In fact, Peter decided to deal with her differently. He had her brought to him at Peterhof, and there, in the pleasant atmosphere of Monplaisir, asked her about Alexis'

(Right) Tsar Alexei (ruled 1645–1676), Peter's father

(Bottom) The Morning of the Execution of the Strel'tsy in 1698 (1881) by Vasilyi Surikov. Peter took a personal part in the punishment of the Strel'tsy Revolt in 1698.

Catherine I, Peter's peasant wife

The dining room in the
simple cabin where Peter lived while
St. Petersburg was a-building

Bust of Peter and a boat similar to the
one on which he learned to sail

The Battle of Poltava, 1709
(Private Collection / The Bridgeman Art Library)

Peter the Great by Valentin
Serov (1907), a painting
which vividly captures the
tsar's manic energy

A naval engagement in the Baltic, showing
how important Peter's manoeuvrable galleys
were in these waters

The Peter and Paul Fortress, the tsar's first
building in St. Petersburg

Peter and his son Alexei—a relationship doomed
to have tragic consequences

The Summer Gardens, St. Petersburg. Peter
brought plants from many lands to grace his new
northern capital.

Peter's tomb in the
Peter and Paul Cathedral

Statue of Peter by Mikhail Shemiakin,
1991. A controversial modern
take on the tsar

*The Bronze
Horseman* by Etienne
Falconet, erected by
Catherine the Great,
is traditionally
visited by local
newlyweds.

pillow talk. It was his best opportunity to discover what the young man *really* thought of his father and his country, as opposed to what he and others claimed when they were under pressure. The girl did not disappoint him. Whatever her feelings were for Alexis, her sense of self-preservation was stronger. She revealed all the half-crazed Tsarevich's ramblings: his hatred of the new Russia, his delight on hearing that Peter Petrovich was ill and that troops in Mecklenburg were close to mutiny. She told the Tsar about Alexis' faith in the Emperor, his hope for support from the Senate, his conviction that the people would put him on the throne, his determination to abandon St Petersburg, and his drafting of messages to church leaders (undelivered) assuring them that he would return as the nation's leader when it was safe to do so. Euphrosyne was released as a reward for turning state's evidence. Alexis was thrown into the Peter and Paul fortress for further torture and examination.

It was probably at this point that the Tsar decided once and for all that he could not allow Alexis to live. Despite all the efforts of the interrogators, the Tsarevich had not told the truth, the whole truth and nothing but the truth. His repentance had not been sincere. He would always be ready, given different circumstances, to challenge his half-brother for the throne. The investigation, which had slowed down, was re-energised. More names came out. More shreds of apparent conspiracy were revealed. What Alexis now 'remembered' was something much more worrying. According to his new confession, his strategy had centred on an alliance with all the elements hostile to Menshikov. It was assumed that the favourite would be regent during the minority of Peter Petrovich. This arrangement was sure to be very unpopular. Alexis reckoned that he could count on enough political and military leaders who would prefer to see him as tsar or, at least, regent. He had planned to make his base in the Ukraine where his friend, the archimandrite of the Caves Monastery, was held in great esteem. He believed his movement would rapidly gather momentum:

I expected that in Moscow all the bishops and Tsarevna Maria would join me.

And in the Finland corps Prince Mikhail Mikhailovich [Golitsyn] and in Riga, Prince Peter Alekseevich [Golitsyn, Governor of Riga] is also a friend and would not desert his own.

And so all the border with Europe would be mine and all would accept me without any opposition, although not directly as sovereign, certainly as regent.

And in the main army Boris Petrovich [Sheremetev] and many of the officers are friends to me.

And about the simple people, I have heard from many that they love
me.

Also, I expected, though without great confidence, that Tsaritsa
Preskovia would be inclined towards me.

Also, I hoped for the late prince-caesar and [prince] pope, as on
friends.[6]

This devastating information appeared to justify all Peter's fears. It was as he
had said on his return the previous autumn: 'I don't know whom I can trust.'
He was not alone in detecting instability among the political elite. Nervous
diplomats were reporting home that Russia was a tinderbox waiting only for
the striking of a spark.

The problem was what to do about it. The situation was essentially different from the revolts of earlier years. Then, Peter had been dealing with
armed opposition to the government, which justified draconian response. He
had been able to count on the support of loyal troops and officials. In 1718,
he was discovering that several men on whom he hoped he could rely were,
at the very least, ambivalent in their allegiance. Under the circumstances,
to pursue every suspect and round up dozens more leading Russians for
interrogation could well prove counterproductive. On the other hand, he
had to make it clear that he would not tolerate any opposition to his rule or
to his plans for the future of the state. He had only recently supported the
Duke of Mecklenburg against his rebellious nobles and threatened to take
the ringleaders captive back to Russia. It was hard for him to be forced to
admit that he could not stamp his authority firmly on his own family and
ministers.

As the days of the northern summer lengthened, Peter wrestled with the
problem. It aggravated him particularly because it distracted him from more
important business. Peace in the Baltic, at long last, seemed to be within his
grasp. The efforts of Görtz combined with a severe economic crisis in Sweden
had brought the stubborn Charles XII to the point of agreeing to a conference to solve by diplomacy all the issues between the two countries and their
allies. It convened at Åbo in May. The problems involved were complex, and
achieving the necessary compromises, after eighteen years of war, was going
to take time and a great deal of detailed negotiation. Reports and instructions
passed back and forth between Peter and his representatives. Information
about the troubled situation in Russia was also regularly conveyed to foreign
chancelleries. The news reaching London, Vienna, Hanover, Copenhagen
and other capitals was that Russia was teetering on the brink of revolution.
This could only affect adversely the Tsar's negotiating position in Åbo. He
had to bring the Alexis affair to a conclusion as quickly as possible.

Filicide is a terrible crime, and there is no evidence that Peter, even when in the grip of one of his white-hot rages, regarded it simply as a political necessity devoid of moral complications. He turned to the nation's spiritual leaders for guidance, ordering the ecclesiastical establishment to meet and deliberate on the Tsarevich's crimes and advise him on what the church had to say about the punishment of royal sons who rose against their fathers. There were scriptural and historical precedents. Peter likened Alexis to Absalom, who had rebelled against his father, David. David had ordered his generals to suppress the insurrection but spare his son. They ignored his instructions and speared the prince to death. David was grief-stricken but could, at least, claim that his hands were clean. Peter might also have cited the case of Philip II and Don Carlos, which ran remarkably parallel to his own experience with Alexis. The Spanish prince had been estranged from his father and become involved with enemies of the crown. When Philip had his son thrown into prison (where he later died), he felt it necessary to explain his action to the Pope: 'There seemed to be no other remedy for complying with the obligations I have to the service of God and the public welfare of my kingdom.' Peter was certainly aware of the example of Ivan the Terrible, whose reign of terror culminated in the murder of his son and heir, an act that according to legend haunted the Tsar for ever afterwards. That was the story that would be uppermost in people's minds if Alexis were to meet a violent end at his father's instigation.

Was Peter's referral of the case to the metropolitans, archbishops and bishops a cynical instance of buck-passing; an attempt to have someone else shoulder the responsibility of making the fatal decision? He certainly intended to give the church leaders no opportunity to avoid implication in the fate of the Tsarevich. Their decision was to be given in writing and signed by them all, 'to the end that being sufficiently instructed in this affair we may not in anything charge our conscience'.[7] The theologians were more than a match for Peter. They pointed out that the prevailing concern of the Old Testament was God's judgement, and that of the New Testament his mercy. Having proffered that analysis, they neatly sidestepped its application. The church had no jurisdiction in temporal cases. The sword of earthly justice had been entrusted by God to anointed kings. It was for the Tsar alone to decide what should be done with his son. Autocracy had its downside. Peter's dilemma was that he did not shrink from doing what he believed had to be done, but that to safeguard his own reputation at home and abroad, he had to have the very visible support of as many people as possible in deciding the fate of Alexis Petrovich.

In June, Peter convened a court of 126 senators, officials and church dignitaries to try the Tsarevich. He also had Alexis' torture intensified. He wanted to be able to present to the court evidence not merely that the accused had laid plans for a takeover of power after his father's death, but that Alexis had intrigued with the Emperor and with internal enemies of the state to kill and overthrow Russia's lawful sovereign. Repeated lashes with the knout produced the confessions Peter required. They were written down and read out to the court, while the prisoner, scarcely able to stand after his beatings, listened in silence. The windows of the courtroom were opened wide so that the crowd outside could have some inkling of what was going on – the proceedings had to be as public as possible. Foreign diplomats declared that the Tsar presided with tears in his eyes. Throughout his trial, Alexis was too shattered by his ordeal to do anything but mutter his admission that the presented evidence was true. There was, however, one moment when he rallied himself and, in a rare moment of dignity, confronted his father. 'The whole country is on my side,' he said defiantly. 'It is obvious to me now that you desire my death. Well, I will gladly die. Beware of what will happen to you afterwards.'[8] The sessions and the torture continued relentlessly. When all the evidence had been presented, Peter asked the assembled judges for their verdict. They knew what was expected of them. Several of them were on Peter's blacklist of suspects and had only one way of dispelling his suspicion. When Alexis had been declared guilty and the court had announced that the appropriate sentence was death, the prisoner was returned to his cell. Two days later he died there.

The account in the fortress records of Alexis' death is terseness itself. After recording that he had suffered a further beating on the morning of 26 June, it continued: 'That same day in the sixth hour after noon, being under guard in the Trubetskoi bastion in the garrison, tsarevich Alexsei Petrovich departed this life.' The rest is a confusion of rumour and conflicting evidence. Peter's version of events attributed the prisoner's demise to apoplexy and divine intervention. Recording his own mental anguish about whether or not to issue a pardon, he thanked the Almighty for relieving him of the burden and delivering his son from a miserable existence by visiting him with a sudden seizure. Some time on that Friday, when, apparently, it was evident that Alexis was dying, Peter had taken a party of senators and officials to the prison. Was this to confirm that the wretched man's life was all but extinct, or to provide corroborative evidence for a death that he knew was imminent? Inevitably, stories of poison and worse began circulating. According to one macabre story, the Tsarevich had been decapitated – perhaps even by the Tsar in person – and a woman employed to sew the head back on and conceal the join with a cravat. A circumstantially more credible account was, supposedly, written by Alexander Rumiantsev, captain of the castle guard. He described Alexis' last moments in gruesome detail. The villain of this particular piece was Tolstoy, who led a group of assassins to the cell on the morning of the 26th and suffocated the prisoner with pillows. Most historians regard this note as a later forgery, but as is the way with conspiracy theories, it was more readily believed than any more prosaic account. The precipitate death of Alexis blackened Peter's name at the time and has continued to blacken his reputation. And rightly so. Whatever happened in the Peter and Paul fortress on 26 June 1718, the Tsar was responsible for it.

Peter found it difficult to stifle his relief and pleasure. The very next day he celebrated the anniversary of Poltava with the usual party and public rejoicing. He had every reason for satisfaction. The succession issue had been resolved and peace with Sweden seemed to be only a matter of months away. He could call a halt to the investigation of prominent subjects, knowing that no one would dare to cross the ruler whose vengeance had not held back from pursuing his own son. As he declared on a medal struck later in the year, 'The horizon is clear.' Seldom can rejoicing have been more premature. In November, Charles XII was killed, throwing peace negotiations into total confusion. And in the following spring, three-year-old Peter Petrovich suddenly died.

Peter was stunned at the news of the Swedish king's death. He is reported to have been moved to tears by it. The man he had never met face to face but who had dominated his life for almost two decades was no more. The sudden departure of Charles XII did not, of itself, put an end to the hope of peace. The King was defiant to the end. By the autumn of 1718, he had gathered yet another army and marched into Norway at the head of 60,000 men. Although his diplomats were talking with their Russian counterparts at Åbo, Charles probably regarded this as little more than a delaying tactic to buy him time for the next round of his conflict with Peter. The end of the soldier-king came while the Swedes were investing Fredrikshald. Charles rode forward to survey the progress of the siege and was felled by a stray enemy bullet. He was thirty-six.

The King's death left an empty treasury and a succession crisis. Georg von Görtz had done sterling work in pulling the economy round in order to finance Charles' continuing expansionist policies, but the stringent measures he had employed (including savage taxation, devaluation of the coinage and rigid control of imports and exports) were hugely unpopular. Görtz's regime had strengthened royal absolutism at the expense of the nobility and the *riksdag*. Charles' death left him exposed to his enemies. He was arrested, tried on a charge of alienating the crown from the people, and executed in February 1719. His policies, including his peace initiative, died with him. He had based the achievement of northern European peace on agreement between two autocrats. The new government was headed by Ulrika-Eleonora, Charles' younger sister, who almost immediately abdicated in favour of her husband, Frederick of Hesse. He labelled Peter the aggressor and set about forming an alliance of states that would curb the Tsar's activities and drive him back within his own traditional borders. This led to the break-up of the Åbo conference. Frederick had good personal reasons for his hostility to Peter because his claim to the throne was contested by Karl-Frederick of Holstein, Charles XII's nephew, whom Peter was seriously considering as a potential husband for his daughter, Anna.

The year 1719 was a disastrous one for Peter in terms of international relations. He who had so assiduously sought a respected place at the European top table found himself regarded almost universally as a pariah. He was the victim of his own success. Apart from his Baltic conquests, he had built – from scratch – a navy that outshone those of his immediate neighbours and could compete with those of the great maritime powers. It comprised twenty-nine ships of the line of 36–90 guns, and twenty frigates. In addition there was a formidable galley fleet that proved itself extremely effective in shallow coastal waters. When visitors to St Petersburg reported that the Tsar had boasted that his navy would soon outsail and outgun Britain's, the government in London took his claims very seriously. What made matters worse was that other maritime nations were largely dependent on Russia for naval supplies. Concern was accurately, if not succinctly, summarised in the title of a 1719 pamphlet: *Truth is but Truth, as it is Timed! Or, Our Ministry's Present Measures against the Muscovite Vindicated by Plain and Obvious Reasons: Tending to Prove that it is no less the Interests of Our British Trade, than that of Our State, that the Czar be not suffer'd to retain a Fleet, if needs must be that he should a Sea Port, in the Baltick.* Peter had assumed that having established a position of strength in northern Europe, he would be able to use it to his diplomatic advantage. Instead, he had merely frightened other states into ganging up on him. The 'suspicious' death of the Tsarevich Alexis had only confirmed the convictions of those who regarded Peter as a barbarian tyrant whose ambitions must be kept firmly in check.

The Baltic fringe nations now began to make their own arrangements without reference to Peter. In January, Hanover, Austria and Saxony formed an alliance to bargain over their mutual territorial boundaries and to drive Russia out of Mecklenburg. Britain expended considerable diplomatic energy in weakening Peter's position in the Baltic. George I sent out envoys with instructions to detach Prussia and Denmark from their compact with Russia, and also dispatched a naval squadron to patrol the Baltic. In Constantinople his ambassador endeavoured to stir up Turkish anti-Russian feeling. He even tried to induce British subjects working for the Tsar to return home. In July, Hanoverian troops marched into Mecklenburg, ostensibly to aid the aristocratic faction against the 'tyranny' of Duke Charles Leopold and to establish a protectorate in the name of the Emperor. Peter, unwilling to risk military conflict on behalf of his relative, withdrew his troops. The peace conference had resumed in June, and he was anxious not to do anything that would jeopardise it. But the participants were too far apart to allow for any meaningful dialogue, and talks were abandoned again in September. Britain and Sweden entered a formal alliance a few weeks later, and at the beginning of 1720, Prussia also sided with Sweden at the Treaty of Stockholm. Peter's achievements in the north had hitherto been helped by the preoccupation of the major powers with their own conflicts. Now, however, he could not rely on ancient animosities distracting France, Britain, Holland and the Empire. For a while, at least, a state of peace prevailed in much of Europe. Spain had come to terms with the Triple Alliance. France was involved in talks with Britain, and Denmark aimed at shoring up Sweden's power in the Baltic.

What all this meant was that something new had emerged in the political life of Europe: Russia, which a decade earlier had scarcely figured in the calculations of Western princes and ministers, was now a major force to be reckoned with – and feared. Nothing like this had happened since, almost exactly a century before, Gustavus II Adolphus had propelled Sweden into the military conflicts of Europe and laid the foundations of the modern Swedish state. This latest phenomenon was more worrying – or perhaps 'perplexing' would be a better word. Swedish expansionism had been a cause for concern, but at least Sweden was a Protestant state. It possessed a culture and a system of values that were understood by the other Western powers. Russia was still an almost entirely unknown quantity. It was vast. It possessed enormous resources, as yet almost untapped. It had an inexhaustible supply of potential soldiers and sailors. The Russian bear was a formidable beast, which, unchained, might come lumbering out of its lair, ready to maul nations that stood in its way. Even foreign residents who wrote books describing their experiences in Peter's employ could do little to dispel the widespread Western ignorance about the real Russia. Most of them had seen little of the life beyond Moscow and St Petersburg. They were inadequately aware of the internal divisions and powerful tensions that prevented Russia being the threat it was generally perceived to be. This explains the apparent discrepancy between popular attitudes towards Peter and towards his country. The Tsar was respected, even lauded, as an enlightened despot who had, against formidable odds, introduced civilisation to his people. But those people had as yet not emerged fully from barbarism and needed not only to be watched carefully but to be prevented from spreading beyond well-defined frontiers.

In 1719–20, it was borne in upon European leaders that there was, in fact, little they could do to contain Russian ambitions. The system of alliances designed to curb Peter's Baltic expansionism had little effect. It might be said to have actually exacerbated the problem. When the Tsar discovered that he could achieve nothing by diplomacy, he had no alternative but to continue the military offensive against Sweden. Confident now in his own naval supremacy in northern waters, he was ready to defy his enemy and whatever allies might come to his aid. It was not only the size and quality of Russia's navy that had improved. Trained largely by British officers, Peter's captains were emerging as skilful battle tacticians. In May 1719, Russia's first full-scale naval engagement took place when a group of seven ships led by Captain Sunyavin sailed out of Tallinn in search of a small Swedish flotilla. They encountered the enemy off Osel Island (modern Saaremaa) and a fierce gun battle ensued. In a duel between the Russian *Portsmouth* and the Swedish frigate *Karlskrona Vapen*, the former had its sails shredded but doggedly continued until its adversary was forced to surrender. Commodore Wrangel, in the Swedish flagship *Wachtmeister*, headed out for the open sea but was hotly pursued by two Russian ships of the line that brought him to action. The fierce exchange of broadsides went on for more than an hour, at the end of which Wrangel was forced to strike his colours. In the summer of 1720, Mikhail Golitsyn demonstrated his mastery of the art of galley warfare when he led a force of sixty-one oared ships to victory in an engagement off Grengham Island in the Åland chain. Golitsyn was confronted by a squadron of heavily armed vessels that had been sent to dislodge the island's occupants. The Russian commander had no possibility of outgunning the enemy ships. Instead he lured them into a pursuit that brought them on to a lee shore. While the Swedes were desperately concentrating on avoiding the rocks, Golitsyn brought his superior numbers to bear. Two frigates were driven aground and two more were grappled and boarded. When Peter received the news, he might very well have reflected that it justified his earlier educational programme. Golitsyn had been one of the young men he had sent to England to train as naval cadets. In common with other scions of boyar houses, he had deeply resented his temporary exile. In his letters he had complained of homesickness and difficulties with the language. He had also insisted that he hated the sea.

The Russians were the undoubted masters of the Baltic and the Gulf of Bothnia. The heirs of the Vikings no longer dominated northern waters, and when it came to the crunch, their British allies did not wish to engage their navy in serious action. As a result, the 'war' in its final phase consisted of little more than a succession of Russian raids on Swedish island and coastal settlements. Landing parties destroyed villages and towns and thrust far inland, meeting little opposition. Fires could be seen from the walls of Stockholm and a depressing procession of refugees streamed in through the gates. By August 1720, the Swedish king and his people had had enough. They were ready to receive envoys from St Petersburg.

Peter sent one of his most trusted minions. Alexander Rumiantsev had come up through the ranks of the Preobrazhensky regiment, served in the major campaigns of the reign, accompanied the Tsar on his travels in 1716–17, and had been trusted (along with Tolstoy) with the difficult mission of coaxing Alexis back to Russia. Now he travelled to Stockholm with Peter's peace proposals. His way was smoothed by Jean-Jacques Campredon, France's ambassador to St Petersburg. The latter had been charged by the Duc d'Orléans with brokering a peace, and he worked tirelessly at his brief. Peter was quite prepared to bargain away some of his conquests, but his trump card was his support for Duke Karl of Holstein's claim to the Swedish crown. Preliminary toings and froings continued through the autumn and winter, and formal talks were able to begin in the Finnish coastal town of Nystad (modern Uusikaupunki) in April 1721. The Swedes fought hard to regain as much as possible of their lost territory, but with Russia's military back-up to its diplomacy, and the major powers urging a settlement, it was inevitable that they would have to recognise that Peter was the new master of the Baltic. By the terms of the treaty signed on 30 August, Russia now took permanent possession of all the territories lining the southern shore of the Gulf of Finland – Ingermanland, Estonia and Livonia (modern Estonia and Latvia), with the large islands of Osel and Dagö (Saaremaa and Hiiumaa). To the north, it annexed part of Karelia with the strategic fortress of Viborg. Peter cheerfully abandoned his obligation to Duke Karl, restored the rest of Finland to Swedish control and pulled his troops out of the lands to the west.

The Tsar was sailing off the Finnish coast when he received the news of the treaty. Immediately, he steered his yacht back to St Petersburg. As it entered the harbour, he was to be seen standing in the prow and shouting, over and over again, 'Peace! Peace!' As the glad tidings spread, the nation went wild with joy, as well it might after such a long and devastating war. In the capital, celebrations were noisy, frenzied and long. Nystad was Peter's great vindication. It gave the lie to his critics and demonstrated triumphantly that all those who had plotted or harboured thoughts of rebellion had been enemies of the state who would anchor Russia to its dead past and prevent it sailing into a new, bright future. Peter was determined to drive the lesson home. He ordained that there should be three periods of thanksgiving and rejoicing: one immediate, one on 22 October (already a public holiday commemorating victory over the Poles in 1612) and one on 28 January. In fact, organised and spontaneous revels took place throughout the autumn and winter. Typically, they consisted of a mixture of the devout and the bizarre.

As soon as he arrived home, Peter attended a Te Deum in Trinity Cathedral. Then he delivered a speech to the crowd that had gathered in the square outside and ordered free beer and brandy to be available. For those too far away to have heard the news immediately, he sent out heralds, crowned with laurel wreaths and blowing trumpets, to spread the good news. More solemn church ceremonies took place on the days designated for celebration, but they were interspersed with masquerades.

One such, somehow considered appropriate, was a repeat of the Zotov wedding of 1715. Presumably it had been a great success within elite circles, and a new ceremony was staged for Peter Buturlin, who had succeeded Zotov as Prince-Pope. Once again, St Petersburg's finest turned out in fancy dress and toured the streets, led by the Tsar in his favourite costume as a naval drummer. The 'happy couple' were toasted many times over and were themselves obliged to drink from large vessels shaped like genitalia, before being escorted to bed in a specially erected cabin provided with peepholes for the entertainment of the guests. The following day's hilarity climaxed in a crossing of the Neva by Buturlin and his attendant cardinals in barrels. The Prince-Pope himself was conveyed afloat in a bowl within a larger barrel containing beer, into which he was, of course, tipped at the culmination of his perilous transit. A banquet for a thousand people went on for several hours, and though the Tsar retired at one point to sleep off his excesses, everyone else was obliged to stay – enjoying themselves by royal command! Gun salutes featured prominently in the noisy celebrations, as, of course, did firework displays.

However, the most significant element in the mixture of pious rituals, overindulgence and knockabout humour occurred during the October festivities. At the culmination of a service in Trinity Cathedral, Archbishop Feofan Prokopovich preached an adulatory sermon. Prokopovich was Russia's leading intellectual and a not inconsiderable orator. He had also been appointed by the Tsar to keep the church in order. His catalogue of Peter's achievements might have been official propaganda, but none could deny its essential truth.

> ... those who abhorred us as rude assiduously seek our fraternity; those who dishonoured us glorify us; those who threatened us are afraid and tremble; those who despised us are not ashamed to serve us; many European crowned heads are not only willing to ally with Peter, our monarch, but do not consider it dishonourable to give him precedence; they have repealed their opinion ... they have begun to speak and write about us differently. Russia has raised her head, bright, beautiful, strong, loved by friends, feared by enemies.[9]

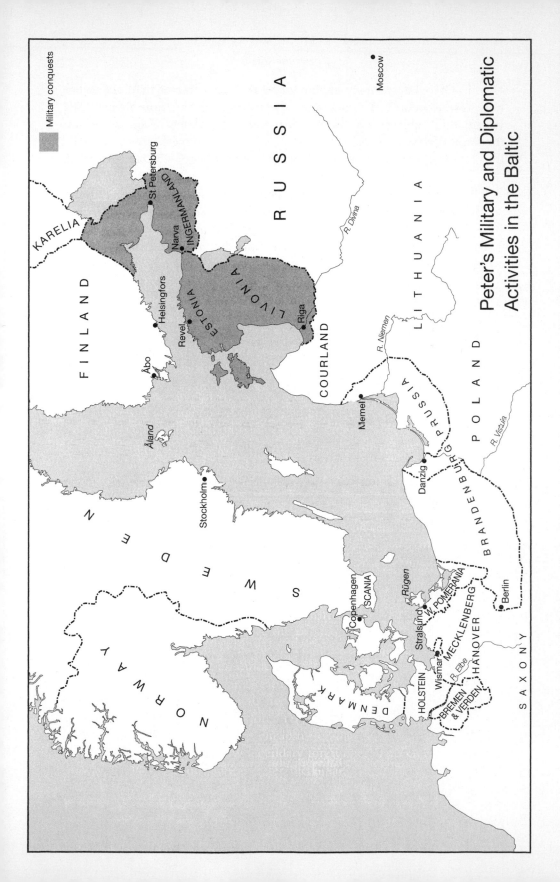

Peter's Military and Diplomatic
Activities in the Baltic

Military conquests

Gavrila Golovkin, recently appointed to the new post of state chancellor, now rose to address the congregation. He took up the same theme: 'We, your faithful subjects, have been thrust from the darkness of ignorance onto the stage of glory of the entire world, promoted, so to speak, from non-being into being and included in the society of political peoples.'[10] He continued:

> The Senate takes the liberty of begging Your Majesty to accept the titles Father of the Fatherland, Emperor of all Russia, Peter the Great ... We thought it right ... in the manner of the ancients, especially the Roman and Greek people ... also as was the custom of the Roman Senate in recognition of their emperors' famous deeds to pronounce such titles publicly as a gift and to inscribe them on statues for the memory of posterity.[11]

It had, of course, all been carefully prearranged, but if the thunderous cheers that greeted the announcement, accompanied by a salvo of trumpets and drums and gunfire from ships in the harbour, were well orchestrated, they were not entirely devoid of sincere enthusiasm. Peter was, indeed, a reincarnation of the rulers of ancient Rome. Had he not won for his people an empire? And had he not given them bread and circuses?

8

'Projects that I have not been able to carry out'

Peter was forty-nine when he celebrated the glorious Peace of Nystad. He might have been excused for resting on his laurels – for a while, at least – but that was not in the nature of the man. He was conscious of more essential work to be done, of long-maturing ideas to be turned into concrete reality. He was incapable of idleness. As we have seen, he took a portable lathe with him on many of his travels and frequently presented churches and guests with chandeliers, chairs and other items he had turned himself. Everything to do with navigation and astronomy fascinated him. He drew his own charts, plans and architectural designs. Whole rooms in the summer palace at St Petersburg were taken up with his tools and the mechanical devices he had collected in Europe or had had made for him. Peter's curiosity was boundless. He enjoyed anatomical study and sometimes had bodies brought to him for dissection. Nor did he confine his activities to the dead; he carried with him instruments that enabled him, at any time, to pull a tooth, let blood or carry out simple surgical operations. He needed little sleep, and 'relaxing' for him did not mean inaction. For example, music was for Peter something that demanded participation. He enjoyed beating a drum and energetic dancing but had no patience to sit listening to a performance or watching an opera or play. His hectic and irreverent revels, whatever they implied about Muscovite traditions and religion, were necessary outlets for his physical and mental energies. The essential restlessness that characterised the Emperor of All the Russias was exquisitely captured by the twentieth-century artist Valery Serov, who depicted him hurrying purposefully along a quayside while his attendants struggled to keep up. The historian has much the same problem – how to convey an accurate impression of this bustling, ever-active man, and specifically, how to understand his convictions and motivations.

The last years of the war had been frustrating for Peter because they were a distraction from his programme of internal reforms. We have already seen something of the changes he introduced into central and regional government. We know that he was concerned about the efficiency of the administration, particularly as it affected the provision of men, money and supplies to furnish the war effort. We have witnessed his ongoing struggle against corruption. We know that he instituted systems of checks and balances and constantly kept them under review. But what was it that he was trying to achieve? What was his vision for Russia? Did he simply stride from problem to problem, applying the solutions that occurred to him on the spur of the moment, or did he work towards the realisation of objectives that were clear in his own mind? Specifically, to what extent did he seek to Europeanise his empire? We will consider later the changing evaluations of history, but we need at this point to arm ourselves against the hindsight adulation of those writers of the Enlightenment who claimed Peter as one of their own; as, indeed, a model of the rationalist monarch: 'Within a few decades, Russia emerged from historical and intellectual "nonbeing", developed a rational and coherent code of laws and became in the eyes of western intellectuals a type of the model state ... The Muscovy of 1700 transformed itself into an enlightened empire, a nation of light, a [universal] example.'[1]

I believe we can take as our starting point Peter's natural ability in technical and mechanical pursuits. Though lacking any kind of intellectual training, he was a natural empiricist. Whether working at the lathe, assessing the efficiency of a government department or calculating how to provide water under pressure for the Peterhof fountains, he brought an open mind to the solution of problems. He regarded experience, not religious dogma or age-hallowed tradition, as the only source of knowledge. And having discovered what seemed to be the correct solution, he applied it doggedly, unemotionally and, when necessary, ruthlessly. This explains how a loving husband and father and a warm friend could display cold indifference to the human cost of building his paradisal capital city, carry out public executions and pursue his own son to death. Once he decided that something had to be done, it had to be done. Ends justified means.

So, what ends did Peter pursue in his creation of a new Russia? His earliest political impressions were entirely negative. Within the claustrophobic, small-roomed court in Moscow he experienced and was revolted by the Miloslavski–Naryshkin rivalry and its eruption into violence and bloodshed. Life at Preobrazhenskoe was an escape. As a child and teenager he could ignore the prevailing regime and largely be ignored by it. He received very little in the way of political education for his role as co-tsar and so his mind was not closed to the influences of the foreign quarter. What interested him most in what he learned from the Dutch, British and German residents was military matters, but he could not avoid discovery of the vastly different political world that lay to the west. National rivalries were played out in the microcosm of the foreign quarter, and the diplomats were under instructions to court the favour of the young Tsar. Thus, for example, Peter was persuaded by Patrick Gordon not to recognise the anti-Jacobite regime in Britain after the Glorious Revolution of 1688. The more Sophia's government, backed by the Orthodox clergy, opposed foreign influence, the stronger became Peter's attachment to his non-Russian friends. In 1689 he attended the wedding of Gordon's daughter, which was performed by a Lutheran minister because Jesuit priests had just been expelled. Every day he learned more about Western nations, their political, religious and commercial rivalries.

It was the commercial activities of his foreign friends that increasingly interested Peter. Not only did they have stories to tell of strange lands and exotic customs; not only could they show him the ingenious products of craftsmen from their own countries; but they were adventurous merchants competing hard for business in a land whose people had virtually no interest in commercial enterprise. Russia's economic potential was vast, and increasing as its frontiers were pushed eastward, but its people lacked the business skills to exploit its abundant natural resources. In a land where fewer than 5 per cent of the population were town dwellers, trade based on capital, as understood in the great commercial entrepôts, did not exist. It was, therefore, the travellers who arrived at Archangel during the summer months to buy furs, hemp, pitch and timber who set the pace – and took the lion's share of the profits. Peter was introduced at an early age to the writings of the influential Saxon philosopher-jurist Samuel Pufendorf, who spent many years at the University of Lund in Sweden. Pufendorf's *Introduction to the History of the Principal Kingdoms and States of Europe* (Frankfurt, 1682) described how small nations such as England and Holland had grown rich and powerful by developing long-distance trade. From this and other writings, as well as from discussions with his foreign friends, Peter came to understand the theory of mercantilism that governed seventeenth-century international trade. Its basic principle was that governments should regulate trade in such a way that exports exceeded imports. Such control, he realised, would never be possible in Russia, as long as it remained a landlocked nation, dependent on the activities of foreign merchants. It was Peter's desire to join the international community of trading states coupled with his fascination with the sea and ships that provided the initial impetus to challenge Swedish domination of the Baltic.

From this everything else followed – Peter's wars, his foreign travels, his industrialisation programme, his development of centralised bureaucracy, his importation of Western technologies, the sacrifices he made for the fatherland and the sacrifices he had no hesitation in demanding from every one of his subjects. Peter was no political philosopher. For him government was an essentially practical affair, rather than the application of any of the theories that were being discussed all over seventeenth- and eighteenth-century Europe. However, he was an eager student of the lexis and praxis of government (it took him, we may recall, on to the roof of the English parliament), and he was not oblivious to the contemporary debate on the rights and responsibilities of rulers and ruled. Peter could not avoid being impressed by the most eminent philosopher of the day, Gottfried Leibniz (1646–1716), and he received a visit from the great polymath in 1711. Leibniz's theory concerning social and political order had immediate appeal to someone with a technical bent; Leibniz likened the world to a divine machine that when properly operated produced a morally ordered society. It was the responsibility of absolutist monarchs to organise their states in harmony with the schema of God, the supreme rationalist. Peter fully accepted this concept. That explains why he struggled to reform and reform again, to refine and refine again the unwieldy administrative system (if such it can be called) he had inherited. He brought to civil government the same devotion to discipline that he applied to his military reforms. In 1718, when he expected the imminent end of his long struggle with Charles XII, he claimed, referring to himself in the third person, as he often did, that 'His Majesty, despite his own unbearable toil in this burdensome war ... has not neglected civil administration but, is labouring to bring it into the same good order as military affairs. Wherefore colleges have been instituted, that is assemblies of many persons instead of the bureaus in which the presidents or chairmen do not have the same authority as the old [administrators], who did what they wished.'[2]

'To bring it into the same good order' – the phrase well expresses the authoritarianism of the Petrine regime and brings us to the point where we need to consider Russian absolutism and how it differed from the absolutism practised in other European states. 'His Majesty is a sovereign monarch who is not obliged to answer for his acts to anyone in the world; but he holds the might and power to administer his states and lands as a Christian monarch, in accordance with his wishes and best opinions.'[3] The words are from the Russian Military Service Regulations of 1716. Interestingly, they are a straight translation from a statement drawn up by the Swedish *riksdag* in 1693 to describe the powers of the King. It was sometimes observed of classical culture that 'conquered Greece conquered Rome'. Much the same could be said of the relationship between Sweden and Russia. Peter openly acknowledged his indebtedness to his stubborn enemy in matters military. In 1716 he told a Swedish diplomat, 'for what he had learned about waging war and had taught his own people about war he was indebted to none other than [Charles XII]'. The Swedish king also won Peter's grudging admiration for his ability to continue fighting, year after year, receiving the necessary reinforcements and supplies without having to travel back to Stockholm in order to overawe the government in person. Charles had inherited a system that had emerged over the seventeenth century and seen the crown triumph over the nobility, the church and the *riksdag*. The executive was made up of five colleges, whose members were appointed by the King. This gave him direct control of the major organs of government, including – crucially in wartime – finance and military recruitment. It will readily be seen how closely Peter followed this pattern in his administrative reforms of 1718.

In practical terms, the two combatant nations were run on similar lines. The devil is in the detail. Sweden's administrative system evolved through various stages of negotiation between the estates of the realm. It was Pufendorf who gave it its philosophical backbone. His *On the Duty of Man and Citizen According to Natural Law* was a Hobbesian tract. It defined the good citizen as 'one who promptly obeys the orders of those in power' but argued that this master–servant relationship was arrived at by contract, the people bartering their independence for sound leadership and good government. The ruler, while answerable to no human agency, yet had the responsibility to govern wisely in the public interest. Peter could, and frequently did, claim to be such a ruler. He pointed out, with justification, the great pains he had taken for and the tireless energy he had devoted to the well-being of his people. Explaining his treatment of Alexis, he declared, 'by so doing I hope to have ensured the endurance of my great work, which is to make the Russian nation forever powerful and formidable and all my states flourishing'. He considered himself to be both the servant of the state and the father of the fatherland, the ultimate paternalist, who knew what was best for his people and pursued his objectives without being beset by doubts. But his absolutism was not one that had evolved and there was no suggestion that it had been arrived at by any sort of contract with the people. He had inherited absolute power, and he embellished it by his harsh, uncompromising treatment of dissent and his administrative reforms. If he adopted ideas and institutions from other countries, it was only to bolt them on to his own absolutist system to make it work better.

It is scarcely surprising that the majority of the people lacked any enthusiasm for Peter's brave new Russia. A report from the Polish border posts in 1724 spoke of 'fugitives assembled in large numbers who do battle with firearms and cudgels against dragoons as if they were enemies'. The problem was not new. Year on year, large numbers of Peter's subjects sought out weak points on the frontier in order to escape. The government's attempts to contain the population became increasingly heavy-handed. The Iron Curtain was not an invention of the twentieth century. In fact, long before Peter's time, thousands of families and even whole villages had tried to decamp. But the plethora of new, oppressive regulations, most of which were brought in after 1721, resulted in a dramatic growth of attempted exodus.

When, in October 1721, Peter responded to the Senate's offer of his impressive new titles, he thanked God for the coming of peace and welcomed the opportunity to bring to completion the 'reorderings begun in the state', which would bring inestimable benefits to the people, largely as a result of increased foreign trade. What he had in mind was an era of prosperity resulting from a growth of exports, increased manufacture, and some lightening of taxation now that the war was over. Paradoxically, however, the continued expansion of the nation's commercial life involved yet another armed conflict, which would cost Russia a further 30,000 lives and drain yet more money from the economy. The Persian War of 1722–3 was a further example of the application of logic to the accomplishment of the Petrine vision. The Tsar took little account of the problems that might be encountered. For him, the shortest distance between two points was always a straight line. In political affairs, bends and circuitous routes inevitably interpose themselves between the framing and the achievement of policy objectives, but Peter, who understood that simple mathematical rules applied in ship design, astro-navigation and architectural drawing, invariably took the straightforward approach. Having achieved his goal of a gateway to the West, he now turned his attention to the East. Russia lay between the hungry markets of Europe and the wealth of the Orient. Therefore, it must be possible for it to act as a commercial bridge. By establishing fortified trading posts on the farther shores of the Caspian, connected to St Petersburg by a network of rivers and canals, Russia could capture the lion's share of the trade in silks, gems, spices and other luxury goods so much prized in Europe. No one at that time possessed accurate maps of central Asia, and Peter had no precise information about the distances and the terrain involved in achieving his dream. But ignorance, far from being an obstacle, was simply a spur to endeavour. Like Henry the Navigator, who sent his ships out to circumnavigate Africa, or Columbus, who headed into the empty Atlantic in search of Cathay, or the English pioneers who sought north-west and north-east passages through icy Arctic waters, Peter was fascinated by the quest for that route that would transform intercontinental commerce. Ever since the sixteenth century, Europeans had come to Moscow seeking permission to explore potential trade routes to the East. Increasingly, Peter had taken the initiative away from foreigners by dispatching his own explorers and envoys to establish commercial contacts and to spy out the land.

The only political barrier between Peter's territory and the Indian Ocean sea lanes was the Persian Empire. Fortunately for the Tsar, the Safavid dynasty chose this moment to fall on evil times. An Afghan rebellion threatened to unseat the weak ruler, Shah Sultan Hussein, and he was, in fact, murdered in 1722. The resulting chaos provided the opportunity for an Ottoman invasion, and Peter was determined not to be left out in any carving-up of the empire. An attack on a Russian trading post at Semacha (west of Baku) in October 1721 provided a useful *casus belli*, and the following summer, Peter marched south with his invading army. In contrast with his earlier wars, this one was brief and completely successful. Derbent and Baku were taken with little resistance. The Persians were unable to fight wars against Turkey and Russia simultaneously, and envoys were soon on their way to St Petersburg to discuss peace terms. These involved the cession of the entire south Caspian lands from Baku to Mazandaran. In a subsequent treaty with Turkey, Russia's conquests were confirmed.

Though there had been comparatively few casualties in battle, the inevitable losses from disease and the hardships of campaigning very far from home were severe. This did not worry Peter greatly. His head was already bristling with ideas for the settlement of his new lands, the treatment of the local people and the exploitation of commercial possibilities. His attention was now as focused on south-eastward expansion, as it had been on gaining control of the Baltic. As usual, a stream of instructions issued from the Tsar's office. The inhabitants of Trans-Caucasia were to be treated with every consideration, so as not to necessitate further military action. However, where land was needed for settlement, existing residents were to be unceremoniously removed. Just as peremptorily, Russian communities were uprooted for transplanting to the far south. As soon as fortified bases could be firmly established, Peter intended to use them to launch commercial and military expeditions towards India. Meanwhile, he wrote to his Dutch trading partners assuring them that abundant supplies of silk would soon be reaching them by the overland route.

The extent of his imagination and ambition is demonstrated by the remarkable 'Madagascar Project'. The Indian Ocean island was at the time in the grip of pirates, of whom the chief was Caspar Morgan, self-styled King of Madagascar. In order to give his regime some legitimacy and a flag to hide behind, he offered sovereignty of the island to Charles XII of Sweden and claimed to rule as his viceroy. When the Tsar heard this, he decided to outbid Charles as patron of the sea brigands. He pursued this plan with all seriousness and extreme secrecy. In 1723, he fitted out two ships to make the voyage from Europe via the North Sea and the Atlantic. They were to travel the long way round Britain in order to avoid raising curiosity in the English Channel. If challenged, they were to pose as trading vessels bound for India but were really to 'persuade' Morgan to place himself under Russian protection. The bizarre enterprise came to nothing. One of Peter's ships foundered near Revel, and anyway, the criminal commune on Madagascar disintegrated. The only interesting point about the scheme is that it shows that Peter was in earnest about developing Oriental trade by all and any means possible. It was perfectly logical to him that once he had established access to the Persian Gulf, he would need a naval base in the southern seas. Artemy Volynsky, one of the Tsar's principal agents in dealings with Persia, was convinced that there was no limit to his plans: 'His concern was not for Persia alone ... if matters had succeeded for us in Persia and his exalted life had continued, of course he would have attempted to reach India and he nurtured intentions even to the Chinese state.'[4]

When peace came to Russia in September 1723, it was for the first and last time in the entire reign. Peter was now able to devote all his attention to internal affairs. Primarily that meant intensifying his legislative efforts aimed at creating the perfect state machine. Introducing the corpus of laws and the bureaucracy necessary to enforce them was something he had been working at since about 1715, when defeat of Sweden had seemed imminent. The process once embarked upon created its own momentum. Reform begat reform. Definition engendered yet more precise definition. The workings of new institutions had to be constantly refined. Thus, for example, fresh instructions were issued concerning the day-to-day workings of the colleges. The duties of every official were set down in detail, as were the conduct of meetings and the routines for drawing up agendas, for reaching decisions and for keeping an accurate record of those decisions. Even the furniture for the college rooms and the regular cleaning of the rooms was prescribed. Peter devised rules for everything. Nothing, down, as it were, to the last paper clip, was left to chance – or more to the point, left to maladministration, inefficiency or corruption.

To gain a flavour of the breadth of Peter's interests and the narrowness of his concentration on detail, consider this letter to Ivan Musin-Pushkin, head of the monastery departments, concerning the programme of book publishing:

I am sending you by this post the book on Swedish military law, which you should order to be printed in octavo. But first it should be revised, for in some places the translation is obscure and in other places the language is most crude. For this purpose you should employ the same translator who translated it in the first place – Schilling [Benedict Schilling, a Swedish prisoner of war working as a translator in the Foreign Office]; after amending the text, have it printed. We are also sending you a history of Troy, which should likewise be printed (there is no need to amend the text) in the same size, but in medium-sized type, such as was used for the books on sluices and on epistolary etiquette. The book that Golovkin was translating should be printed with the same medium-sized type. Take good care of the bindings, so that they bind them as well as your book of geometry.

P.S. When the book on geometry is ready, have about two hundred copies of it printed; don't let it be sold until you are ordered to do so, but have ten or fifteen copies of it sent here. It is also necessary to print three or four hundred copies of the book on architecture, like the one that has been sent to Mr Gagarin for correction; they are also not to be sold until the receipt of orders, and let ten or fifteen copies of them be sent here.[5]

To make doubly sure that every administrative department worked honestly and efficiently, Peter appointed a new overseer to be the Tsar's eyes and ears at meetings of the Senate and the colleges. This was the procurator general, and his installation is symptomatic of Peter's understanding of the state machine in two ways. The new officer was there to instil discipline and to provide surveillance. An edict of 1724 enjoined him to ensure 'that the regulations be followed in everything just as firmly as the military regulations and to enjoin them strictly on all members and subordinates'. Appropriate extracts were to be read as necessary, just as the articles of war were proclaimed to soldiers and sailors. Like a military campaign, every item of administration was to be planned and executed by the book. Individual initiative was discouraged, and since the procurator was there to check all procedures, and written records were carefully kept, few officials were tempted to depart from the rules. What Peter created was a bureaucracy that became progressively swamped by paper and red tape. But it is easy to see why he tried to strap the central administration into such a straitjacket. Overcontrol was preferable to the internal bickering, incompetence and corruption that had existed before.

However, when Peter extended the system of surveillance, he created a state-wide operation that was far more sinister. The procuracy was an open control agency. What the Tsar now placed alongside it was a secret bureau, the fiscality. It had been first instituted in 1711 as a response to corruption in the law courts and the tax-gathering system. The fiscals, whose number had risen to 500 by the end of the reign, were empowered to sniff out and report cases of bribery, extortion and other corrupt practices. There is no doubt that some means of stamping out malfeasance was urgently needed to prevent subjects being exploited and government defrauded. Since victims were naturally reluctant to fall foul of powerful local officials, the system made provision for secret denunciation. People prepared to inform on alleged wrongdoers were promised confidentiality. In the event of successful prosecution, which usually resulted in confiscation of land and property, informants were often rewarded with a percentage of the takings. Such procedures were open to abuse, and it was not long before the power of the fiscals was increased and their remit widened. They became agents of state control and social engineering. In a vast country, where the reforming activities of central government were widely resented and where outbreaks of revolt were ever-present possibilities, surveillance of some kind was prudent. But the dual system of procurators and fiscals created an atmosphere of suspicion and unease. A man could never know when he might be denounced for unguarded words spoken after too much vodka, or whether it was safe to enter into friendly conversation with a newly arrived stranger.

What made state control more oppressive still was the fact that the enforcement agency was the military. After the northern war, Peter had no intention of reducing the size of the army. That meant that he had to find work for it to do. One of its allotted tasks was to provide a police force. Much of the soldiers' time was taken up with routine enforcement of law and order – rooting out nests of brigands, apprehending criminals, defending property, etc. – but their responsibilities, as defined by the government, went much further:

> The police ... facilitates rights and justice, begets good order and morality, gives everyone security from brigands, thieves, ravishers, deceivers and the like, drives out disorderly and useless modes of life, compels each to labour and to honest industry ... guards against all illnesses that occur, brings about cleanliness on the streets and in houses, prohibits excess in domestic expenditure and all public vices, cares for beggars, the poor, the sick, the crippled and the needy, trains the young in sensible cleanliness and honest knowledge; in short, over all these the police is the soul of the citizenry in all good order and the fundamental support of human security and comfort.[6]

The soldiery represented the long arm of the state, reaching into every home, not just to combat antisocial or illegal behaviour, but to regulate the way ordinary people lived their lives. Peter intended by infiltrating the military into every locality to instil discipline, loyalty and all the 'virtues' of camp life.

His ideal was the creation of a militarised state in which the soldier/police-man did, indeed, represent the 'soul of the citizenry'.

This might, perhaps, have been bearable had it not been for corollaries attached to the policing system – taxation and billeting. To pay for the maintenance of a peacetime army, Peter swept away all existing imposts and replaced them with one simple poll tax, earmarked for the military and levied on the male heads of peasant households. To house the army, Peter located units in almost every area and gave the inhabitants the choice of having soldiers billeted in their homes or building separate quarters for them. Of all the intrusions of central government into the lives of the people, none was more resented than the billeting programme – and with reason. Rough soldiers did not make the best kind of lodgers. Complaints of rape, theft and damage were frequent – and commonly ignored by the men's officers. Furthermore, since the soldiers' pay came directly from the poll tax, they made sure that no one fell behind in making his contribution. For efficient tax collection it was necessary for the government to have accurate information about the populace. Peter therefore instituted the first Russian census. Information was collected between 1721 and 1724. By whom? By the military. Small wonder that the people were restless under these burdens.

Individuals, families and sometimes whole villages decamped from the homes in which their ancestors had lived for generations in order to get away from the census takers or tax collectors or bullying militiamen. Some became vagabonds or retreated into the forests and formed themselves into outlaw bands. Others tried to quit Russia altogether and reach Polish or German territory. The majority, however, made for distant, sparsely occupied reaches of the empire, such as the upper Don valley, where they hoped to settle and begin a new life. Peter's response was, typically, to issue fresh edicts and set his officials on an energetic witch hunt to track down those who chose to vote with their feet against his new Russia. The hue and cry was usually set up by the census takers. When they discovered empty homesteads, they interrogated the neighbours, often under torture. In the last years of the reign, tens of thousands of fugitives were forcibly returned to their original places of residence. No one could be allowed to create anomalies in the well-regulated, closely ordered, effectively policed state that Peter was creating.

Nor was it just the rural peasantry who found themselves reorganised in ways convenient to the central government. One fact that had become obvious to the Tsar on his foreign travels was the vitality of urban life in the West. The flourishing merchant communities of Amsterdam, London and Paris were based on guild and municipal organisations that had grown up over the centuries. If Russia was to enter fully into the international trading community, its craftsmen and entrepreneurs had to forsake their traditional ways of doing business and adopt Western patterns of communal organisation. In January 1721, the Main Municipal Administration assigned merchants and artisans to newly formed guilds and corporations. Government then had a simple means of communicating with the townsmen, imposing fresh regulations and making proper tax assessments. It was all very tidy. Or it would have been if it had worked. It was one thing to make sure that a butcher, baker or candlestick maker wore the right kind of coat. It was quite another to ensure that he and his colleagues made work a system of trade organisation that they were completely unused to.

When condensed into a few paragraphs, the account of Peter's social engineering seems inhumanly draconian and brutally insensitive. Judged by any modern criteria, it certainly was. But we have to compare what he was doing with what contemporary Western rulers were doing in their lands. Serfdom, standing armies, secret police, state control of morals and religious beliefs – none of these things was unique to Russia. From the Atlantic to the Urals, most societies were carried on the weighed-down shoulders of peasants, who had few rights and no privileges. The greatest fear of monarchical governments was rebellion among this class, which had no constitutional means of seeking redress of grievances. It was the Spanish satirist Francisco de Quevedo who warned his patron, 'A people that lies in hopeless poverty is an explosive charge, a danger, a menace, because the starving multitude knows no fear.' European history until well into the nineteenth century was punctuated with peasant revolts. The response of rulers, apart from ruthless suppression, was to tie the aristocracy securely into the workings of government on the understanding that they had as much to lose as their sovereigns from any disruption of the social order. By the mid-seventeenth century, standing armies had become the norm in most states. Gone were the days when troops were raised only in times of war and consisted solely of feudal levies, citizen militias and foreign mercenaries. Kings maintained (or, rather, the taxes levied by kings maintained) professional militias, trained and equipped to the highest standard and ready for any emergency – external or internal. Prussia was the prime example of a state grown independent and powerful by transforming itself into a military dictatorship. Frederick William, the 'Great Elector' (1620–88), had formed a standing army financed by direct taxation and had revoked the rights of the estates (Prussia's parliament) to grant revenue. The availability of an armed force, tied by oath of allegiance to the crown, was in itself an incentive to rulers to pressurise subjects into supporting their policies. The billeting of troops and their use as a police force was one of the many ideas Peter copied from Charles XII, and before the development of the Swedish system, Louis XIV had demonstrated how royal troops could be used to support state ideology. In the 1680s, the

French king, determined to stamp out Protestantism and enforce religious unity, had unleashed the notorious *dragonnades*, bands of dragoons billeted on Huguenot families with the intention of brutally enforcing conversions. The policing of morals had passed from the church to the state. The principle of freedom of conscience was, with painful slowness, gaining ground during the seventeenth and eighteenth centuries. The old assumption, *cuius regio eius religio*, that kings had the right to determine the religious (and therefore the moral) beliefs of their subjects, only reluctantly ceded ground. In England, Charles I lost his head defending his determination to impose a very Catholic form of Anglicanism on his people, and the victorious Cromwell used a system of military regional governors to enforce a Puritan regime. Wherever we look in Europe at the turn of the eighteenth century (with the possible exception of the more liberal Dutch and Swiss republics), we observe constitutions that were essentially based on the need of governments to maintain control, especially over the illiterate hordes who formed the lowest stratum of society. And the tools of repression – the secret tribunal, the paid informer and the torture chamber – had not passed into history with the disappearance of the Inquisition. So, was Peter's regime any different from that prevailing throughout Europe?

Before offering an answer to that question, we must consider two other major reforms: the establishment of the Holy Synod and the Table of Ranks. Peter had always resented the power and influence exercised by church leaders. His disdain had been shown in the irreverent, if not downright blasphemous, antics of himself and his hard-drinking cronies and in the restrictions he imposed on clergy, monks and nuns. In 1701, the Monastery Department had been set up under secular leadership, ostensibly to enable the religious more effectively to fulfil their vocations, but in reality to extract revenue for the Great Northern War. It was an act of semi-nationalisation. The patriarchate had recently fallen vacant with the death of Patriarch Adrian, and Peter, despite periodic protests, simply declined to fill it. Further decrees followed over the years designed to restrict the activities of churchmen and curb their criticism of the government (for example, the refusal to allow monks to have pens, ink and paper in their cells). By 1721, the Tsar was ready to include the church in his programme of administrative reform. In future, members of the Russian Orthodox communion were to be governed by a Holy Synod, appointed by the Tsar. This was another college following the pattern set up to regulate the civil and military administrations, as was made clear by the Spiritual Regulation describing the change: 'Perceiving in [the church] much disorder and great deficiency in its affairs, we have experienced in our conscience no idle fear that we appear ungrateful to the All-High if, having received from him so much good success in reforming not only the military rank but likewise the civil rank, we should neglect to reform also the clerical rank.'[7] Inevitably, there were howls of protest at the church being turned into just another state department, but Peter had at his elbow a churchman extremely well equipped to defend his actions and put a theological gloss on them. Feofan Prokopovich, the extremely erudite Archbishop of Pskov, was the Tsar's man to his very fingertips. In justifying the new arrangement, he represented it as the reformation of a church long sunk in error:

> The fatherland need have no fear of revolts and disturbances from a conciliar administration such as proceeds from a single, independent ecclesiastical administrator. For the common people do not understand how the spiritual authority is distinguishable from the autocratic; but, marvelling at the dignity and glory of [the patriarch], they imagine that such an administrator is a second sovereign, a power equal to that of the autocrat, or even greater than he and that the pastoral office is another, and a better, sovereign authority. Thus have the people, on their own, become accustomed to think.[8]

At a stroke, Peter and his ecclesiastical accomplice achieved that subordination of the spiritual authority to the temporal that most Western monarchs had striven to accomplish since the Reformation (mostly without complete success).

The Table of Ranks has been called 'the keystone of Russian absolutism'. In the monumental reorganisation of society that occupied Peter's last years, the upper echelons did not escape. He had always believed that a man's worth consisted of his service to the state rather than his wealth, heredity or family connections. He had set a personal example by proceeding, himself, through the military and naval ranks. He had chosen a peasant woman as his wife because of the stalwart qualities she manifestly possessed. His treatment of the Tsarevich Alexis was based on the boy's lack of inclination to serve the new Russia and his unwillingness to learn what it meant to be a tsar in the Petrine mould. He had promoted low-born men to prominent positions in the armed forces and the administration, Menshikov being the outstanding example. In his dealings with the nobility, he had stressed in numerous ways the importance of service. He had scrapped the rank of boyar. It was bestowed for the last time in 1699, and by 1718, there were only six boyars left. Peter alienated many of the Russian elite by sending their sons abroad to learn Western skills and attitudes, but his cultural ploughshare bit deeper into the soil of traditional upper-class life when he refused to permit adolescent nobles to marry if they had not studied at military or naval academy or other schools where they would be prepared for careers in the civil administration.

They had to present themselves regularly for examination, and at sixteen, begin their appointed careers. For them there was to be no idling their time away on their country estates or in the Moscow fleshpots. Nor could they expect to walk into a top army job. No longer did birth provide the only qualification necessary for admission to the officer corps. At the same time, the old boyar council decayed through disuse and had no place in the new patterns of government the Tsar was developing. But, of course, the old aristocratic families still existed, a network of proud clans enjoying court connections and influence. Inevitably they tended to look down on Peter's 'new men' and this he found intolerable. At the same time, he could not afford to neglect these 'top people'. They still formed the backbone of the state. His tidy mind reacted against the unclear relationships between people who handled the apparatus of military, civil and court life. How could a system be devised that would make clear the gradations of value inherent in the holders of various offices?

Inevitably he looked westwards for answers to this question. Over several years he gathered information from Poland, Sweden, Denmark, Austria, England, France, Spain, Prussia and Venice, the extent of his research indicating the importance of the social reordering he had in view. He was not planning simply to take the existing social 'canvas', sorely in need of restoration, and do a bit of cleaning and patching. He intended to obliterate the image and overpaint it with his own work of sociopolitical art. The result was the Table of Ranks, which went through several drafts between 1722 and 1724 and was issued in the latter year. It was, as the title suggests, a table, set out with mathematical precision. There were six columns, one for each area of public service: State (civil administration), Court, Navy, Artillery, Guards Regiments, Infantry. Within each column, office holders were listed in fourteen classes or ranks. By reading across from one column to another, it was possible to determine immediately an individual's status. Thus, for example, the president of a college was on a par with the senior chamberlain at the royal court, a rear admiral in the navy, a colonel in the guards and a major general of infantry or artillery. Everyone, of whatever social standing, had to begin on the bottom rung and work his way up. Promotion incentives included the appropriate perquisites of rank. A man's dress, his carriage, his house and the number of horses in his stable immediately proclaimed his status to all observers.

The new order was not a meritocracy *tout court*. It certainly encouraged men of humble origin to enter public service. It also obliged nobles to regard themselves as important, not simply because of the number of serfs they owned, but because of their contribution to the state. However, the Table of Ranks did not abolish existing social distinctions. Some classes were reserved for men of breeding. Thus, it was considered inappropriate for non-nobles in the civil administration to be promoted to ranks that would permit them to adjudicate in cases involving their betters. In practice, several other exceptions and adjustments had to be made to the new system, and in any case, it was always open to the Tsar to make appointments on his own initiative. The Table of Ranks did not introduce democratic principles into Russian life or promote an open society of equal opportunity. Its aim was to strengthen the state by providing it with efficient, conscientious and well-trained officials at all levels.

For Peter, the state, the fatherland, the empire was all. His great vision may have been to establish Russia among the leading Western nations, but his more fundamental concern was to make his vast and disparate realm governable. It was a monumental task and it could never be 100 per cent successful. Scarcely a year passed without reports of serious unrest in one region or another. Discontent usually presented itself as outrage against the Tsar's radical policies, but such protests should not distract us from observing the serious fault lines – racial, tribal, cultural, economic and religious – that lay below the surface of Peter's empire. When the Don Cossack Kondraty Bulavin revolted in 1707, his principal grievances concerned the forcible recapture of fugitives who had placed themselves under his protection and the encroachment of rival Cossacks on his territory. It was only when he sought to widen his power base that he deliberately appealed to a wide cross-section of Peter's disaffected subjects: 'we cannot be silent on account of the evil deeds of wicked men and princes and boyars and profitmakers and Germans and cannot let them off for leading everyone into the Hellenistic pagan faith and diverting them away from the true Christian faith'.[9] Peter's way of ruling his multi-ethnic empire – and it is difficult to see any practical alternative – was to establish strong central government and to ensure that its decrees were obeyed in all regions. He travelled widely in his territories, but this was not in order to understand the problems faced by Siberian fur trappers, Cossack fishermen or Ukrainian farm labourers; it was to ensure that his agents on the ground were carrying out to the letter the directives from St Petersburg. One of the failings of his reform programme was that it tried to establish blanket regulations to be applied in every part of the country. In fact, even if he had had the will to create a more flexible system, the sophisticated and complex administrative mechanism that would have made regional variations possible simply did not exist.

Peter the Great set himself the labours of Hercules. He reformed every aspect of a society that was incapable of gradual self-improvement under its own impetus. He bent every class of that society to his own will. He adopted and adapted Western models that he thought he could use to achieve his objectives. He collected political ideas as he collected mechanical devices, ship designs and architectural drawings. They were 'things' to be taken and applied in the Russian context. He had no interest in how Western practices and institutions had emerged over the centuries, any more than he cared about how a clock or an astrolabe had come to be developed. Either they had transplanting potential or they did not. So, for example, having seen the English parliament at work, he was able to dismiss it as being inapplicable in his own empire. He neither knew nor cared that monarchical power in France, Austria or Sweden existed in relation to municipal, guild, baronial and parliamentary institutions that had deep roots. The existence of revered bodies of law administered by independent or semi-independent judiciaries was of no interest to him. In the early eighteenth century, Peter was one absolute monarch among several, and in practical, day-to-day experience many of his oppressed subjects must have felt much the same about the prospects for themselves and their families as did their counterparts in Bourbon France or Vasa Sweden. If your daughter was being regularly raped by a guardsman for whom you were obliged to provide food and shelter, it would not matter whether you lived in Novgorod or Nantes or Norrköping. To that extent, the question whether Russian autocracy was or was not of a piece with that practised in other European states is academic.

It is only when considered in the long term that the question has relevance. For Peter to stride from a polity that, for want of a better word, we may call 'medieval' to one possessing some of the outward characteristics of modernity was to ignore forces of change that were active in those very countries he wanted to emulate. In those countries, even where absolute monarchs reigned supreme, individual enterprise and political ambition were not totally stifled. People, even people of humble origin, read books. Municipal communities developed their own forms of government. People aspired to higher living standards and travelled in increasing numbers to America to achieve them. Enterprise created new manufactories and the towns that grew with them. In Russia, things were different. There the individual was not free to contribute his talent and inspiration for the well-being of his fellows. He was the servant of the state and able to act only with the permission of higher authority. For the political system that bound him, the twentieth century invented the word 'totalitarianism'. Evgenii Anisimov adroitly describes the Petrine system:

> Peter's revolution possessed, however paradoxical it may sound, a distinctively conservative character. Modernization of the institutions and structures of authority for the conservation of the fundamental principles of the traditional regime appeared to be the ultimate aim. We are discussing the emergence of the autocratic form of rule that

lived on until the late twentieth century and that affected the structure of the new authority after 1917.[10]

Peter would have firmly rejected any suggestion that he suppressed personal initiative. He encouraged new industries by enabling them to acquire serf labour, offering financial incentives and bringing in foreign expertise to help Russian businessmen with their 'R and D'. But this very paternalism created an anti-enterprise culture. As long as entrepreneurs worked within a framework of rigid state control, they would not develop that skill essential to successful business – risk-taking. Again, the Tsar would have insisted that he was committed to the upholding of law. The massive, ubiquitous system of government agencies he built was like a series of aqueducts carrying 'law' to every region of the empire, and he worked tirelessly to prevent 'law' being subverted by corrupt officials. But, of course, what Peter meant by 'law' was not a sacred repository of sovereign legislation that existed to preserve the rights of all. It was the body of state directives. Such distinctions made the new Russia different from the old Europe.

In the long run, what would matter to Europe would not be what Peter took from it, but what he brought to it. This reality evaded the vast majority of contemporary and near-contemporary foreign observers. What they saw was a whirlwind of a tsar who had torn his country up from its barbarous and backward past and deposited it in the modern, enlightened world – which was, of course, the world trail-blazed by 'civilised' western Europe. For his eye-widening achievements they were prepared to forgive him his acts of brutality. To them, living as they did in an age well accustomed to absolutism, Peter's particular brand of it did not seem all that out of the ordinary. Voltaire set the mood:

> Who could have pretended to say, in the year 1700, that a magnificent and polite court would be formed at the extremity of the Gulf of Finland? that the inhabitants of Solikamsk, Kazan, and the banks of the Volga and Sok would be ranked among our best disciplined troops and gain victories in Germany, after defeating the Swedes and the Turks; that an empire two thousand leagues in length, almost unknown to us before, should in the space of fifty years become a well-governed state and extend its influence to all the European courts ... Peter the Great, therefore, who singly planned and executed this amazing and altogether unforeseen revolution, is, perhaps, of all princes, the one whose deeds are most worthy of being transmitted to posterity.[11]

In the last three years of Peter's reign, there was a detectable change of mood at the centre. He no longer had wars to organise (1724 was the only year of peace in his twenty-nine years of sole rule), and this seems to have deprived him of something that had become necessary to him. Sailing his beloved ships, visiting military encampments and planning campaigns had provided the excitement he craved, and while he welcomed the end of the northern war with exuberant celebration, it had left a gap in his life. As we have seen, he partially filled it with a prodigious programme of civil administration reform, but this induced a certain amount of frustration, forcing him to realise afresh how immense was the task he had undertaken. Reports from the regions frequently drew his attention to the difficulty of implementing government decrees. Wilhelm Henning, who was a long-serving and highly trusted agent, was sufficiently close to the Tsar to be able to write frankly. Sent on an inspection tour of mines and factories, he reported from Siberia, 'Terrible deeds are in evidence, the poor peasants suffer ruin at the hands of officials, and in the towns much oppression is caused by the local officials sent from the local finance office and the merchantry has been so badly damaged, that an artisan with any capital is scarcely to be found, which has led to a decline in revenues.'[12]

It was depressing for Peter to realise that whatever time he had left to him would be insufficient to change the soul of Russia. The age-old system of unpaid or underpaid officials making their money from peculation and exploitation was so ingrained that no amount of injunctions and threats from distant St Petersburg could make much impression on it. Many of the new officials the Tsar put in place to clean up and regulate the operation of government were no better than the men they replaced. In 1721, the Governor of Siberia was executed for massive corruption. Two years later it was the turn of Vice Chancellor Peter Shafirov to fall under scrutiny. Shafirov, like Menshikov, was a man who had risen from humble origins to a position of considerable power. In all probability his wealth was second only to that of Menshikov. In 1723 he was tried and found guilty of embezzlement. Peter decreed the death penalty, and on the appointed day Shafirov was brought to the scaffold. The headsman raised his axe and brought it down with a thud on the block close to the ear of the trembling ex-minister. Then a royal pardon was read out. Peter had commuted the punishment to exile and confiscation of all property. Such warnings failed to make the intended impact. Only months later the chief fiscal, Afanasy Nesterov, was put on trial for taking bribes. On one occasion, when Peter expressed his determination to deal ruthlessly with all corrupt officials, one of his friends commented, 'Then, do you wish to govern all by yourself?' As Professor Hughes has observed, 'it seems unlikely that by 1723 he had complete faith in anyone'.

Yet there was no let-up in the stream of directives that issued from the

Tsar's office. Day after day he bent himself to the task of cleaning up his realm and making the state mechanism more efficient. Whenever anything occurred to him that required attention, he issued a ukase, often without considering the implications. Thus, he ordered a change in the width of cloth being made by peasant artisans despite the fact that their looms could not produce material of the required dimensions. He paid much attention to transport, fully understanding how vital the infrastructure was in developing the economy of a country where distances between population centres were immense. He attempted to link Moscow and St Petersburg by a coach road, the existing road being, in places, little more than a track through forest and marsh and over perilously inadequate bridges. This undertaking proved too much for even Peter's drive and the labour of thousands of workers. He did, however, authorise the setting up of distance markers along the route and the provision of rest houses at regular intervals. He had a canal built beside Lake Ladoga, which was a notoriously storm-inflicted stretch of water. He sent out teams of cartographers to set about the first scientific mapping of Russia. Other regulations included the instruction to nobles to draw up clear wills, orders to printers to produce translations of Western books, the forbidding of men under fifty to enter monasteries and even the re-laying of untidy tombstones.

It goes almost without saying that one of Peter's major concerns was the codification of the law. Several times he set in train the process of tidying up the ever-growing volume of piecemeal directives, several of which simply could not be reconciled with each other. In 1700 he established a commission to bring the existing (1649) code up to date. It drowned in a sea of paper. A second attempt in 1714 met the same fate. In 1719, he tried a new tack: Russia's laws were to be codified along Swedish lines. A commission of native and foreign experts struggled manfully with this task. They were still struggling when Peter died, but they did eventually hand in their work of monumental revision. It was never published. The Tsar's passion for legislation and his unremitting publication of new regulations was eventually self-defeating. Amidst the confusion, it was easy for offenders to break the law either through ignorance or because they thought they would get away with it.

By way of a brief digression, it is interesting to note that Peter's vision of a body of law applying to all and impartially enforced was one shared by at least one other man at the opposite end of the social scale. Ivan Pososhkov was an ill-educated artisan who by his own industry had become a moderately wealthy businessman and the owner of seventy-two serfs (proof that the class system did not totally suppress men of talent). He also became literate and wrote down his observations on Russian society. In *A Book on Poverty and Wealth* (1724), he asserted that '... above all we must seek [to establish] justice in the law courts; for if justice is established among us, all people will shy away from wrong-doing. All that is honourable is based upon fair and impartial administration of justice; [if we achieve it,] even the tsar's revenue will be doubled. For this purpose a [new] code of laws must be drawn up with provisions for all kinds of cases ...'[13] In the unlikely event of this manuscript coming to his attention, Peter would have been pleased to have this confirmation of his own conviction from one of his subjects not involved in the administration. Pososhkov's fate is, perhaps, instructive. Months after the Tsar's death, he was thrown into prison for an offence now unknown. He died there in 1726.

Aware though he was of the inadequate response to his efforts on behalf of the fatherland, Peter's massive ego would not allow him to believe that he should change direction. When his impact on his people, even in St Petersburg, began to wane, his response displayed no suggestion of self-criticism. Citizens were growing tired of the constant round of celebrations, national and religious events, royal birthdays and bizarre public rituals. In May 1723, Peter ordered that his first ever boat, the dinghy in which he had learned to sail, be brought to the capital. He planned that it should be welcomed with great acclamation as the 'grandfather' of the Russian fleet, the sire that had generated the nation's naval supremacy. The populace were enjoined to turn out in their own boats and accompany the Tsar as he piloted his little craft around the great warships in the harbour, which fired their guns in salute. Peter was disappointed at the turnout, but instead of accepting that many people disliked aquatic events, he doled out fines to those who had not bothered to attend the party. Weeks later, another regatta was even more sparsely attended. Peter issued a ukase ordering the immediate payment of fifty roubles by anyone who refused to enjoy themselves when their Tsar told them to. One of the first offenders to be punished was Admiral Apraksin!

How was such an extraordinary reign destined to end? The answer is in anticlimax with an element of mystery. By 1724, everyone at court and most citizens of the capital knew that Peter's health was failing. Although he kept up his punishing daily routine and put on an energetic front, the telltale signs were visible. The monarch who lived his life in full view of his people was seen by them to be ageing and ailing. He was observed less often striding along the waterfront at a challenging pace. Now he sometimes relied on carriage or sledge to get him about. As for Peter himself, his schedule reflected an awareness of his declining health but also a reluctance to face up to his own mortality and its implications for the country. In January, he witnessed the execution of Chief Fiscal Nesterov. The wretched embezzler was broken on the wheel and several of his underlings received sentences ranging from flogging and consignment to the galleys to beheading. The Tsar turned from this latest evidence of the failure of his reform programme to his newest project.

It was obvious to him that education was absolutely fundamental to the building of a new Russia. The nations he so much admired had for centuries possessed universities and other centres of learning. From them had come the geniuses whose understanding of the physical world had led to technical innovations in every field of human endeavour. Russia could not possibly catch up until it had institutions where native talent and intellectual enterprise could be fostered. On the other hand, he had been encouraged by the optimism of Leibniz, who had told him that he enjoyed a unique opportunity: '... since in most parts of your empire all the studies are as yet in a large measure new and resemble, so to speak, a tabula rasa, it is possible for you to avoid countless errors which have crept in gradually and imperceptibly in Europe. It is generally known that a palace built altogether anew comes out better than one that is rebuilt, improved upon, and much altered through many centuries.'[14] Peter had corresponded with the philosopher, met him at least twice (1711 and 1716) and provided him with a pension. By picking the brains of Leibniz and other prominent intellectuals, and by closely studying the working of the Académie des Sciences in Paris, Peter had evolved a plan for the cultural improvement of his country The first fruit of this was the Russian Academy of Sciences, a centre of higher education offering courses in law, medicine and philosophy. Significantly, this was a secular institution. Western universities had mostly begun as places where men destined for ecclesiastical careers had submitted to those disciplines that led to the study of theology, the queen of the sciences. Peter had no intention of wasting state funds on the training of priests. The church could look after its own. His academy was intended to serve the state in very practical ways. He had begun recruiting staff from Europe (mainly Germany) in 1721, and now he was ready to announce the arrangements for the opening of the Academy (which took place in August 1725). Peter also worked on plans for regional libraries and museums.

In February, he and his court set off for Martsial'nye spa. At the conclusion of his stay, Peter presented one of his home-made candelabra to the local church as a thank-you offering for his cure. It is unlikely that any respite from his distressing symptoms could have been more than temporary, for later that same year he had to submit to a surgical operation. By late March, the Tsar was back in Moscow to make the detailed arrangements for an extraordinarily important event: the coronation of his wife. In 1721, Catherine had become empress, but that was only because Peter had exchanged the title of tsar for that of emperor. The ceremony that took place in May 1724 had an altogether different significance. In the Cathedral of the Dormition in Moscow, where the coronation of tsars and patriarchs always took place, amidst scenes of great pomp and before a congregation that overflowed on to Cathedral Square, Catherine, the Latvian peasant girl, was crowned as Empress of All the Russias. No expense was spared to render this unusual event wholly memorable. Peter ordered a gilded carriage (which survives in the Hermitage collection) to convey Catherine to the church. The jewel-encrusted crown, crafted for the occasion, was set with a ruby larger than a pigeon's egg. The Empress's crimson and silver gown was the last word in exuberant display. The coronation banquet was suitably sumptuous, and for those not invited, oxen were roasted and fountains gushing wine were set up in the streets. Only once before in the entire history of Russia had a woman been thus honoured, and Peter was obviously aware that what he was doing was of singular importance. But what *was* he doing? There is no direct evidence that he intended anything other than a public acknowledgement of Catherine's importance to himself and to the state. Yet it is difficult to believe that this elaborate show did not have some deeper significance. It seems more than likely that he was preparing Russia for the accession of a woman ruler. He had no male heir that he was prepared to trust. If his dynasty and his policies were to continue, it would have to be through the female line. It was obvious that there would be fierce opposition to the succession of a low-born foreign woman to the ultimate position. Was this investing of Catherine with the dignity of empress in her own right Peter's way of disarming the critics? The French diplomat Jean-Jacques Campredon certainly believed so. 'Contrary to custom,' he reported, 'the rite of anointing was executed over the tsaritsa so that she has thereby been recognised as ruler and mistress after the death of the tsar her husband.'[15] There must have been many other witnesses to the ceremony who thought the same, and whatever Peter intended, it was public perception that mattered.

The court remained in the ancient capital much longer than usual, possibly because Peter was too unwell to face the arduous journey back to St Petersburg. It was late June before he returned to his 'paradise'. Catherine followed at her leisure and did not reach St Petersburg until 8 July. But what a reception she received! To the sound of church bells and cannon fire, her yacht sailed down the Neva and was met by her husband at the head of a naval flotilla. Church services were ordered to celebrate Catherine's return, now as Russia's anointed empress. The elite attended a special banquet that continued into the small hours. And, of course, there were fireworks. It is difficult to see this as anything less than a carefully prepared propaganda exercise designed to accustom citizens to accord Catherine the full honours due to a head of state.

Given Peter's attitude to his own crusading reign and to the inadequacy of the heirs he had spawned, the options for the succession had dwindled to one. Early in 1722, he had issued a decree that reserved to the reigning monarch the right to nominate his heir, so that the torch he had lit could be entrusted to worthy hands and not pass automatically to the next available male. Yet he gave no intimation of whom he wished to succeed him. The next in line was little Peter Alexeevich, but the Tsar showed no interest whatsoever in his grandson. Though he bestowed the title of tsarevni on his daughters by Catherine, Alexis' son was not nominated as tsarevich. He was simply 'Grand Duke Peter'. If he assumed that the boy would be tainted by association with his 'martyred' father or manipulated by his grandmother's relatives, the remedy was in his own hands. He could have had young Peter 'properly' reared and tutored. As it was, he made no such arrangements. All his affection was centred on Catherine and their daughters. He was well aware of the chaos that usually followed the failure of a dynasty. The death of the childless Fedor I (1598) had been followed by fifteen years of family and aristocratic rivalries and challenges for the throne by impostors. Only a drastic change to the customary laws of inheritance could ensure the continuance of the Tsar's family, and the safeguarding of his legacy.

Within days of Catherine's elaborate welcome, Peter was again laid low with illness. It could have been any one of a number of ailments that prostrated him. For most of his adult life he had waged constant war on his liver and his digestive system. His numerous affairs had left him with venereal disease (possibly gonorrhoea). This and the inaccuracy of eighteenth-century medical diagnostics make it difficult for the historian to be precise about what afflicted Peter at any given time. However, it seems to have been the return of an infection of the bladder and urinary tract that now troubled him. His condition was serious enough to call for surgery, and he underwent an operation that left him weak for several weeks. But no illness was allowed to put him out of action for long. At the end of August, he set off to inspect progress on the Ladoga canal, his only concession to disability being the decision to travel by water rather than land.

He was back in the capital by the end of October and it was then, according to legend, that there occurred an incident that began the final undermining of his constitution. At the nearby fishing village of Lakhta, he saw some soldiers in difficulties in a boat that was foundering close to the shore. Without hesitation, he joined the rescue party and waded into the icy waters of the gulf. This brought on a chill, but he brushed aside his physician's order to rest.

In any case, he soon had something to think about that caused him much greater distress than a throbbing head and a high temperature. Someone, impelled by either duty or a desire to prevent the crown passing to Catherine, relayed some information designed to cause a rift between husband and wife. William Mons (brother of Peter's first mistress) was Catherine's chamberlain. This handsome and accomplished twenty-eight-year-old man was the perfect courtier, and the forty-year-old Empress was very fond of him. But how fond? Tongues wagged in the imperial household. What came out beyond any doubt in the ensuing investigation was that Mons had used his influence with Catherine to offer favours for sale. That in itself was enough to throw Peter into one of his terrible rages. He was reported as having smashed furniture in his fury. Mons and his associates were arrested on 8 November, tortured, convicted of receiving bribes and sentenced. Within a week, Mons had been executed and several other court officials – male and female – had been flogged, exiled or condemned to hard labour. Peter published the names of all those involved in the dead man's peculation. They included Menshikov and even the Duke of Holstein, currently paying court to Tsaritsa Anna. In a cruel, bizarre corollary to this sombre event, the self-pitying Tsar sent Mons' head to Catherine in a jar.

That gesture, and the speed with which Mons was dispatched, seem at first sight to be the work of an enraged, cuckolded husband. His love for his wife was genuine and deep. He had frequent liaisons with other women, but throughout all the years they had spent together, no one had ever challenged Catherine for his affections. He took her with him whenever possible on his travels and campaigns, and when they were separated by affairs of state, he wrote frequent letters telling her how much he missed her: 'for God's sake come soon and if, for some reason it is impossible to be here soon, do write, because without you it is sad for me'. Catherine replied in similarly affectionate vein. Describing a recent party, she told him, 'We were all very happy. If my "old man" had been here there would have been another little nipper born next year.' Peter was never happier than when living in simple domesticity with his wife and children at Monplaisir. Catherine was the perfect foil for him, able to match him in the consumption of alcohol, enjoyment of practical jokes and telling of risqué stories. She calmed his rages and often interceded for unfortunates who had incurred his wrath. All this Peter appreciated. When he honoured her publicly for her untiring support, it was not political window-dressing. So her betrayal hurt him deeply. He hit back by ordering his officials to ignore any instructions from the Empress. He blocked the supply of money to her, so that she was obliged to borrow from her ladies. Diplomats reported that the royal couple were completely estranged, no longer eating or sleeping together.

But was Peter angry at having been displaced by a younger man in his wife's affections? Would the canny ex-peasant girl, who knew better than anyone else how fatal it could be to cross her husband, have been foolish enough to be unfaithful to him? Might there not have been some other reason for Peter's extreme reaction? A different explanation is certainly possible. It relies on an understanding of faction politics in the court of the ailing Tsar. Rival groups were positioning themselves for what would happen when Peter died. The most powerful clique was that headed by Catherine and Menshikov, supported by Fedor Apraksin, Chancellor Gavrila Golovkin and Peter Tolstoy. It was a formidable team, and the traditionalists could not match it. But that is not to say they did not try. The Mons affair was a shrewd move. It created a scandal, news of which spread rapidly beyond the capital. Peter must have recognised it for what it was, and that probably explains why he dealt with it so rapidly. Normally, investigation of high-level corruption went on for months, its ripples spreading wider and wider as time went by. This time the Tsar clamped the lid firmly on the affair. But he was extremely angry. Whether or not he had decided to nominate Catherine as his successor, there can be no doubt where his favour lay. Only the Catherine–Menshikov alliance could ensure the continuance of his policies. Their success had now been compromised. A struggle for the crown was distinctly possible. His achievements might be under threat.

Yet there could have been deeper reasons for his angst. Nothing infuriated Peter more than corruption in high places. He regarded it as a criminal betrayal of trust. He never wavered in his determination to clean out Russia's Augean Stables. In recent months he had condemned several senior officials to public humiliation and death. Only Menshikov had been able to get away with bribery, embezzlement and fraud on a massive scale. Though relations between the two old friends were not as strong as they had once been, Peter could not bring himself to deal with Menshikov as his crimes deserved. But Menshikov did at least understand the sordid underworld of Russian politics. Poachers made the best gamekeepers, and it would be good for Empress Catherine to have their old friend at her elbow. Now, however, serious accusations had been levelled against her, of all people. Torture of Mons and his accomplices had revealed that she was hand-in-glove with them. Peter must have been racked with disappointment and doubt. The tendrils of duplicity and deception had snaked their way even into his own bedchamber. Was Catherine worthy of the succession, or had she, like Alexis, ruled herself out? If Mons had been able to involve her in his sharp practices, might not others follow in his wake? The succession issue now became a nightmare and he could not decide how to resolve it.

Whatever turbulent emotions Peter and Catherine were experiencing, they kept up appearances. On 22 November, the engagement, after a two-and-a-half-year on-off courtship, of their daughter Anna to the Duke of Holstein was celebrated with a ball. Christmas came, with its usual round of religious observations and carousings. Soon afterwards, Peter took to his bed. Physical inaction did not stop his brain buzzing, as he explained to one of his agents. 'My poor health has forced me to keep to my room. I have, therefore, had time to reflect and I have remembered several projects that I have not been able to carry out.' He was, he wrote, determined to initiate several reforms to adorn Russia with institutions dedicated to the arts and sciences. They were destined not to materialise. The Tsar's condition deteriorated rapidly. By 21 January he was in intense pain because of an inability to urinate. After three days of excruciating suffering, which caused him to shriek and groan, the doctors decided to perforate the bladder. They drew off a litre of foul-smelling urine carrying fragments of putrid flesh. Any relief was brief. Gangrene set in to the diseased organ, bringing on fever and delirium. Catherine sat by him during his ordeal. What she and everyone else wanted to know was Peter's intention for the succession, but they waited in vain. According to one legend, shortly before lapsing into unconsciousness, he called for pen and paper and managed to scrawl an unfinished sentence: 'Leave all to ...' At six o'clock on the morning of 28 January 1725, Peter the Great, Emperor of All the Russias, died.

Epilogue

An Unsilenceable Trumpet

alf a century after Peter's death, the Russian poet Alexander
Sumarokov wrote a eulogy containing the following lines:

> It is not appropriate in Christianity
> To revere creatures as gods;
> But if still during paganism
> Such a tsar had occurred,
> As soon as his fame had spread
> The entire universe would have been shaken
> By his most marvellous deeds:
> Fame, like an unsilenceable trumpet,
> Would have proclaimed God, not tsar,
> That warrior who ascended the throne.[1]

Since 1725, Peter's reputation has been at the mercy of that gallery of distorting mirrors we call history: now ballooned to dominating proportions; now reduced to a wavering insignificance; now, his barbarities exaggerated to monstrous proportions, appearing as the worst kind of tyrant; now assuming the kindly shape of the most benevolent of dictators; now the rescuer of his country from the dead hand of the past; now an oppressor of the people, indistinguishable from the despots of earlier centuries; now the ruler who brought his country into the community of leading nations; now a traitor to everything truly Russian. What is beyond question, and what every argument about him confirms, is that his fame (or notoriety) has sounded in every age like an unsilenceable trumpet. Viewed from a Western standpoint, the enigma that is Peter Mikhailov is part of that larger enigma that is Russia – an enigma we still live with. By focusing on the fifty-two years and eight months of Peter's life, we gain an insight into the institutions, beliefs, social and political structures and culture of the largest land empire on the face of the planet. That is one of the reasons for the existence of this book. But only time can offer clues to the *significance* of historical figures, so we must now enter that gallery of distorting mirrors to see what posterity, inside and outside Russia, has made of this prodigy of nature.

Peter's reputation towered over succeeding generations just as he had physically dwarfed those among whom he moved while alive. The men and women who succeeded him in the eighteenth century (and they were mostly women) could not match his stature. They allowed some of his reforms to fall into abeyance and deliberately reversed others. To outside observers, the 'new' Russia looked like a very fragile construct. 'After all the pains which have been taken to bring this country into its present shape, by which it is so nearly connected with the rest of Europe, and has so great a weight in the affairs of it, I must confess that I can yet see it in no other light, than as a rough model of something meant to be perfected hereafter, in which the several parts do neither fit nor join, nor are well glued together.'[2] So wrote a British observer in 1741. For thirty-seven years Russia was ruled by nonentities more interested in enjoying the pleasures and privileges of power than planning and providing for the prosperity and progress of the people. And yet, each of them in turn purposefully donned the mantle of their great predecessor. While lacking Peter's vision, they claimed to be moved by his spirit and appealed to his memory when seeking popular support.

Like all great reformers, Peter died in the knowledge that his work was unfinished. At the same time – and perhaps this is also typical of great reformers – he made no provision for the continuation of his programme. He was so caught up in his own activities, plans and dreams that the future – over which he would have no control – did not loom large in his thinking. What he had done, by repeated acts of terror, was to weaken the forces of reaction, and, by putting in place new government institutions (albeit inadequate and prone to endemic corruption), to free the crown from ecclesiastical and aristocratic restraints. The result was that the reform programme stalled but the dynasty survived – for almost two centuries. That left successive governments with no overall vision as they struggled with external relations and the changes – cultural, social and political – that inevitably followed in their wake. Russia had become part of Europe. There could be no going back – for either Russia or Europe. Henceforth they would shape each other.

Yet for more than three decades, Peter's achievements seemed repeatedly to be at risk. Short reigns, lack of male Romanovs and palace intrigues dominated Russian politics, as they had before 1689. The navy, which had been Peter's pride and joy and the battering ram that had demolished Sweden's Baltic empire, was allowed to decay. The great ships, the frigates and the galleys lay rotting in harbour. Despite its successes, the navy had never won the hearts of the people. Its decline was symbolic. There existed a stone wall of incomprehension that resisted the thrust of radical ideas. If a prolonged period of internal stability was needed to consolidate the gains of recent years, that was the very thing the country was denied. Peter's death without a proclaimed heir threatened to throw back into the melting pot all that he had worked for. But Catherine and Menshikov had everything well in hand. To what extent the late Tsar was a party to the arrangements for the succession we shall never know. What is clear is that those arrangements were so carefully made that the Empress' coup worked with well-oiled precision. Proclaimed by the Preobrazhensky and Semenovsky guards and supported by the favourite and his clique, Catherine became sole ruler of all Russia. From peasant girl to empress of a vast territorial empire – surely this is the greatest ever rags-to-riches story. But it was Menshikov who emerged the real winner. He ruled in Catherine's name. His power and cupidity now knew no limits and his ambition very few. When the Empress died after only two years on the throne, fourteen years of intrigue and confusion ensued, threatening to revive the Time of Troubles. Menshikov championed the claim of the twelve-year-old Peter Alexseevich, with the intention of continuing his own reign and marrying his daughter to the Tsar. But at long last, the great favourite had overreached himself. A court coup in September 1727 toppled him from power, stripped him of all wealth and titles and dispatched him to Siberia. Now it was the turn of the Dolgorukis to become 'top family' as guardians of the young Tsar. But their reign too was brief. Peter II died of smallpox in 1730, and once again the crown was back on the green baize of the St Petersburg casino. The royal tree was suffering from a complete lack of male twigs, and the aristocratic establishment struck a deal with Peter the Great's niece, Anne, Duchess of Courland.

This seemed to be the opportunity for the leading families to claw back power. A council of nobles attempted to impose conditions on the sovereign, assuming responsibility for all major affairs and even forbidding the Empress to marry. This would have destroyed the platform on which Peter had built his autocracy, and Anne was wise to the implications of the deal. Once in power, she lost no time in tearing up the agreement and assuming full authority. For ten years she ruled through favourites brought from Germany, and before she died, she nominated an infant great-nephew as her successor. The time was ripe for another military coup. Moscow's elite had had quite enough of the Germans, and the guards backed a bloodless takeover by

Peter's Successors

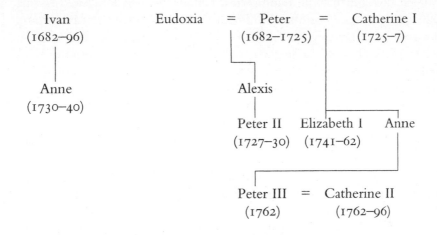

Elizabeth, the only surviving daughter of Peter the Great and Catherine. It says much for the strong imprint Peter had left on the Russian memory that Elizabeth was welcomed as the harbinger of a returned golden age. She did manage to occupy the throne for twenty years, but then she too died childless. Now, the German Romanovs took over. The heir apparent, who came to the throne as Peter III, was the son of Peter the Great's eldest daughter, who had been married off to the Duke of Holstein. He was also mad, a condition that revealed itself in violent, cruel behaviour. He hated Russia, and the Russian elite hated him. Within months of his accession he fell to another palace coup, was forced to abdicate, then assassinated. But what marked his removal as different from that of several of his predecessors was that it was engineered by his wife, who was born Princess Sophie of Anhalt-Zerbst. She managed to have herself crowned as the Empress Catherine II, and her name was destined to be coupled with that of Peter I by her acquisition of the title 'Great'.

All visitors to St Petersburg have the Bronze Horseman on their sightseeing itinerary. The equestrian statue of Peter gazing out across the Neva is imposing. It has had and continues to have a profound influence on the Russian people. Catherine the Great brought Etienne Falconet from France to create this symbolic tribute to her predecessor, but what is particularly interesting about it is the inscription: 'To Peter I, Catherine II'. The Empress erected the statue in 1782, and it encapsulated her determination to be seen in the same light as her by now legendary forerunner. This German woman, who was not even born when Peter died, had a profound – though not uncritical – admiration for the reforming Tsar and deliberately associated her reign with his. She was buying into a well-established cult. It might have been thought that the traditionalist families who had resented having foreign customs foisted on them and being forced to move to St Petersburg would have gleefully thrown off the galling Petrine yoke, but this was not the case. The Dolgoruki faction who had held sway during the brief reign of Peter II moved the capital back to Moscow and rescinded some of the late Tsar's edicts, but Anne had promptly put a stop to that when she came to power. She and Elizabeth both set in hand lavish building programmes in St Petersburg and permanently re-established the court there.

In her attitude to Peter, Catherine the Great was by no means solely motivated by sheer reverential awe. She used the reforming Tsar's reputation as a mounting block for her own. She needed to be accepted, respected, perhaps even loved by the political nation if she was to carry through her own reforming programme. She was an Enlightenment monarch influenced by the new liberal philosophies of Rousseau and Montesquieu. It suited her to emphasise Peter's progressive policies, while privately deploring his legislative programme, based as it had been on autocratic diktat supported by fear of punishment. She wanted to be loved by her people, and had brave schemes for constitutional reforms and, most radical of all, the abolition of serfdom. Catherine discovered through hard experience that her idealistic plans were impracticable, and in the second half of her reign she became much more like Peter, imposing change *de haut en bas*, instituting major building and cultural projects, completing the state takeover of the church, giving new meaning to the expression 'conspicuous consumption' and dispatching successful armies to fight against Turkey.

However, other changes were taking place in Russia as a result of Peter's initiatives that were, in the long run, more important than impressive victories, palaces and parties. A Westernised intelligentsia was emerging. In 1755, Moscow University was founded. It was the logical development of the Academy of Sciences and Peter's desire for Russia's brightest sons to match their European counterparts. Tsarina Elizabeth was careful to point out the connection:

> Our ... beloved father and sovereign, Peter the Great, emperor and reformer of his fatherland, did his utmost to bring the enfeebled Russia, sunk in depths of ignorance, to an understanding of the true welfare of mankind ... His most useful enterprises were not brought to perfection ... in his lifetime; however, by the benevolence of the Almighty, we have constantly applied ourselves ... to bring to completion all his glorious enterprises, as well as to promote [new ones] for the benefit and welfare of our whole country ... All that is good proceeds from an

enlightened mind, which also serves to eradicate evil; for this reason it is a matter of urgent necessity to strive to increase every kind of useful knowledge in our extensive empire through fostering appropriate sciences ...[3]

Two years later, the Academy of Arts was founded to 'enhance the glory of this empire' and encourage native exponents whose work could be commissioned by the state and private individuals. Heretofore, as the decree setting up the institution stated, such activity had been dominated by 'foreign artists of mediocre talent', who had pocketed 'enormous fees' and returned home without passing on the secrets of their craft.[4] Around the same time, Elizabeth had state theatres built in St Petersburg and Moscow. Italian operas and French plays were performed in these prestigious venues, but royal and aristocratic patronage made possible the formation of Russian troupes performing Russian dramas. Ballet, which later Russian musicians and choreographers were to bring to such heights of perfection, had its origins in France and had made its first tentative appearances during the reigns of Alexis, Sophia and Peter, but it was taken up with greater enthusiasm by the eighteenth-century tsarinas. The Imperial Ballet was founded in 1738. By the end of the century, St Petersburg could boast four theatres dedicated to the performance of opera and ballet, and while the popularity of the latter was declining in the West, in Russia it was being developed as a primary art form. It is doubtful whether Peter, who was seldom able to sit through a whole stage performance, would have appreciated all this. But the development of the performing arts was a direct consequence of the increased contact of the Russian elite with the sophisticated courts of Europe that he fostered.

If literature was to develop its full potential, the first requirement was the codification of the language. For this, Russia was indebted to Mikhail Lomonosov (1711–65), who would undoubtedly have been a man after Peter's heart. Indeed, he was precisely the kind of new Russian the Tsar's reforms were meant to produce. He came from a fishing family near Archangel. Having heard of the educational opportunities being provided by the Tsar, he made his way on foot to the capital and, despite opposition from aristocratic snobs and bullies, managed to enrol himself in the Academy of Sciences. Voraciously lapping up everything he could learn from books and teachers, Lomonosov developed into a remarkable polymath. He wrote and translated works on various aspects of physics and chemistry, geography and maritime affairs, metallurgy and astronomy, history and economics. In addition he was a poet and an educationalist and closely involved in organising the new university. He travelled widely to meet foreign scholars, becoming particularly friendly with Voltaire (it goes almost without saying that he mastered the leading European languages). Yet amidst all the accomplishments of this remarkable scholar, perhaps his most important was his publication of the first Russian grammar. This single work was the decoagulant that set the blood of a vigorous language coursing through the veins and arteries of vernacular literature. Lomonosov never wavered in his admiration for the first emperor:

> He was a god, he was your god, Russia,
> He assumed in you corporeal forms,
> Having descended to you from on high;
> Among heroes, above the stars
> He is now shining in eternity,
> Looking joyfully at his grandson.[5]

It is unfortunate that the dedicatee of this ode was the vile and short-lived Peter III.

Undoubtedly there was a great deal of political correctness displayed in such works. Men writing during the reigns of Elizabeth and Catherine II knew what they were expected to say about Peter the Great. But the liberal ideas and freedom of expression that Russia was importing from the Enlightenment were intrinsically opposed to the blind hero-worship that was the approved 'party line', and by the end of the century, the strain was beginning to tell. Historians were discovering that not everything pre-Petrine was darkness and barbarism and that Peter's reforms were not above criticism. Ivan Boltin (1735–92) was one who took a longer view of Russian history and of Peter's place in it:

> When we began to send our youth abroad and to entrust their education to foreigners, our morals entirely changed; together with the supposed enlightenment, there came into our hearts new prejudices, new passions, weaknesses and desires that had remained unknown to our ancestors. These extinguished in us our love for the fatherland, destroyed our attachment to the faith of our fathers and to their ways. Thus, we forgot the old before mastering the new and, while losing our identity, did not become what we wished to be.[6]

Boltin was addressing a serious question, one that went to the heart of Peter's personality and his clash with the forces of tradition: what has the Tsar done to the soul of Russia? A more critical historian, Mikhail Shcherbatov (1733–90), probed deeper. Answering the claim that Peter had stripped the church of superstition, he acknowledged that this was, in principle, good.

But when did he do that? When the people was still unenlightened; and thus, taking superstition away from an unenlightened people, he was taking away their belief in the divine law itself ... Thus cutting down superstitions injured the most fundamental parts of faith; superstitions declined but faith declined also; the slavish fear of hell disappeared, but the love of God and of his holy law disappeared too; and morals, corrected by faith in the absence of another enlightenment and having lost that support began to turn into debauchery.[7]

Undoubtedly Shcherbatov was overstating the case, but he was giving a more eloquent voice to the traditionalists, who had by now convinced themselves that a golden age had existed in Russia before Peter corrupted the land by introducing an alien culture.

Meanwhile, on the other side of the fence, the 'aliens' had also been reflecting on Peter's legacy. In general terms, Western responses were remarkably similar to those within Russia – decades of adulation, slowly giving way to more critical assessment. Two factors shaped these reactions: Russia's emergence as a major European power, and the continuing ignorance of Western observers about what was happening in the vast empire outside St Petersburg and Moscow. Thus, while there was increasing contact at all levels – political, diplomatic, commercial, intellectual and cultural – it tended to be superficial in nature. The tsarist government established permanent representation in all the major capitals, and this helped considerably to oil the wheels of international trade. For example, the long-sought-for Anglo-Russian commercial agreement was signed in 1734.

All the European chancelleries recognised that Russia was now a force to be reckoned with. It was closely involved in most of the important political events of the century and maintained a system of alliances that was remarkably consistent. When conflicts broke out, Russia was usually to be found on the side of Austria and Britain against France. Relations with Prussia were more complex, largely because both countries were emerging military powers with unfinished business to attend to in Sweden and Poland. In 1741, Sweden made a last attempt to regain Baltic supremacy. Within two years Russia saw off that challenge, with the support of Austria. The political landscape of northern Europe became fixed. Or almost. It was the expansionist ambitions of Frederick the Great that now threatened the peace of the area. Brandenburg-Prussia sought to consolidate its position in northern Germany, and this involved conflict with Austria and Poland. Russia could not stand aloof from these quarrels. The death of the Emperor Charles VI in 1740 provoked another round of territory-grabbing confrontations, known collectively as the War of the Austrian Succession. Russian troops played a fairly inconsequential part as an ally of Austria, and could not prevent Frederick the Great grabbing mineral-rich Silesia and holding on to it at the Congress of Aix-la-Chapelle (1748).

The Seven Years War (1756–63) was more significant in the emergence of Russia on to the world scene. This conflict has been called 'the first world war' because the colonial expansion of France and Britain carried their arguments across the eastern and western oceans. It brought about, if not the birth, certainly the post-natal sustenance of those empires whose development would convulse international relations until the mid-twentieth century. Within Europe, conflicting ambitions in 1756 resulted in the radical redrawing of alliances known as the 'Diplomatic Revolution'. Russia found itself in concert with Austria, France, Saxony and Sweden against Prussia and Britain. Austria's primary objective was the regaining of Silesia, but Russia aimed at a larger goal. Elizabeth's advisers pointed out that it was vital to nip Prussian pretensions in the bud. Frederick was emerging as a new Charles XII, militarising his state and using the mineral wealth of Silesia to equip his armies. Any extension of his Baltic territories would be a direct threat to the supremacy Peter had so painstakingly won. But did Russia still have enough of Peter's spirit to withstand this new menace? A French traveller through Russia during the war, the Abbé Chappe d'Auteroche, was scathing about the nation's progress. Russia, he averred, had sunk back into unimaginative sloth since the departure of Peter. The great days of Poltava were a distant dream that the sad state of the army and navy would make it impossible to revive. But even while the Abbé was compiling his notes, Russia's generals were giving the lie to his gloomy analysis. They brought the Prussian king to his knees with victories at Zorndorf and Kunersdorf. They occupied Berlin. 'All is lost' – so read Frederick's scribbled note from the bloody field of Kunersdorf. Had it not been for events in distant St Petersburg, that prophecy would have been fulfilled and Europe's history would have been dramatically different. But in the Russian capital, Tsarina Elizabeth died and her place was taken by mad Peter III. He hero-worshipped Frederick, and ordered not only the end of hostilities, but also the placing of Russian troops at Frederick's disposal. This allowed Frederick that recovery from which he never looked back. The overthrow of Peter III came too late to reverse the situation. History must regard this as one of the great missed opportunities in the evolution of modern Europe.

Studies of eighteenth-century colonial expansion often confine themselves to the seaborne activities of France and Britain in the Americas and Asia, but by 1800, it was Russia whose territory had expanded the most dramatically. It had conquered the Crimea and the Danube estuary, thus gaining access to the Mediterranean, crossed the Bering Strait into North America and gobbled up the greater part of Poland. Historian Norman Davies described the latter proceeding in justifiably emotive language: 'The partitioning of Poland, effected in three stages in 1773, 1793, and 1795, was without precedent in modern European history ... Poland was the victim of political vivisection – by mutilation, amputation, and in the end total dismemberment; and the only excuse given was that the patient had not been feeling well.'[8] Poland was indeed sick, rent as it had been for centuries by internal divisions. But weak states inevitably become power vacuums, sucking in the ambitions and designs of their neighbours. Peter the Great had made of Poland a client state. It was his territorial buffer against the West, a land he could dominate without having to pay to rule. Catherine II was happy to maintain this situation. It was Frederick the Great's ambition that precipitated the carving-up of Poland. He was anxious to unite the two halves of his kingdom, East and West Prussia, separated from each other by Polish territory. While Russia and Austria were preoccupied with Turkey, he proposed his land grab and suggested that the other two powers reinforce their own borders with similar takeovers. It was something Peter the Great would never have agreed to. Twenty years of internal instability and constitutional experiment followed. Eventually, Russia wrested all of eastern Poland from its quasi-independent government, establishing a new frontier on the Niemen and the Bug, which made Russia a central European power, and compensating Austria and Prussia with similar acquisitions. Poland had ceased to exist, and no other state raised its voice in protest. Europe had other things to worry about as the forces of revolution gathered in France and threatened the old autocratic world order.

Voltaire set the tone for most of the numerous biographical treatments of Peter in the eighteenth century. For the French philosopher, it was the Tsar's civilising crusade that placed him among the greats. 'Naught ... remains in history worthy of fixing the attention of mankind,' he insisted, 'but those striking revolutions which have wrought a change in the manners and laws of great states; and upon this principle the history of Peter the Great is worthy of being known.'[9] Having established that *raison d'être* for his work, Voltaire was ready not only to explain the conduct of his hero, but also to excuse it: '... though he had faults, they never obscured his princely qualities ... though, as a man, he was liable to errors, as a monarch he was always great. He everywhere forced Nature, in his subjects, in himself, by sea and land; but he forced her only to render her more pleasing and noble.'[10] It was all a question of emphasis. Dr Johnson's take on Peter's 'errors' was somewhat different: the Tsar, he claimed, 'amused himself in digging canals and building cities; murdering his subjects with insufferable fatigues and transplanting nations from one corner of his dominions to another, without regretting the thousands that perished on the way; but he attained his end, he made his people formidable ...'[11]

For the most part, however, writers – and there were a great many of them – eulogised the great Tsar. Peter was a favourite subject for authors of biography and history, and had so grabbed the imagination of Western readers that every book on the subject could be assured of healthy sales. Foreign writers with no access to original documents or understanding of the Russian language relied largely on anecdotal material and the accounts of travellers. What emerged was, unsurprisingly, a one-sided view. Material that did not fit the image was all too easily ignored. Jonas Hanway, merchant, traveller, explorer, author and self-publicist, made an epic journey through Russia and Persia in the 1740s and described his experiences in *An Historical Account of the British Trade over the Caspian Sea*. In it he countenanced no breath of criticism of 'the immortal Peter'. 'He might commit some acts of severity,' Hanway conceded, 'but that he put men to death with his own hand, I am persuaded is not true.'[12] The Reverend Dr Thomas Birch, Fellow of the Royal Society, contributed a biography to the compendious *General Dictionary, Historical and Critical* in which he airily dismissed an account of the All-Drunken Assembly:

> ... it would be perhaps an injustice to the merit of that illustrious person to regard it in any other light than that of calumny and detraction. It is the voice of envy and revenge and proceeds, it may be, from those only who could not endure his glory or who hated to be civilised; who were sottish enough to imagine that the disgrace and ruin of a people must be the consequence of deviating from the customs or even the barbarity of their forefathers.[13]

These were men writing during the last decades of the *ancien régime*. What they believed or accepted without critical enquiry was that hereditary monarchy was the best form of government. Kings might be assisted by representative bodies from among the better sort of their people and must govern according to just laws, but it was in their hands that the welfare of their subjects ultimately lay. If, in some places at some times, this resulted in autocracy and benevolent dictatorship, well, that was far better than weak leadership or anarchy. Given this premise, it was obvious, as another writer insisted, that 'Peter was a pattern of imitation to every prince who aims ... to be truly great.'

But the times they were a-changing. In 1762, Rousseau published his *Social Contract*. Between 1752 and 1780, the new intelligentsia of the Enlightenment produced the Bible of rationalism, the *Encyclopédie* or *Rational Dictionary of the Arts and Sciences*. In 1775, Britain's American colonists rebelled, refusing to obey laws passed without their consent. And in 1789, the French revolutionaries took their bloody axe to the tree of absolutism.

Rousseau asserted that sovereignty is vested in the people: 'It is not a convention made by a superior with an inferior; it is a convention made by the whole Body with each of its members – a convention which is just, because it rests on the social contract; equitable because it is common to all; useful because it has no other object than the general good; and permanent because it is guaranteed by the public force and the supreme power ...'[14] Absolutism was, for Rousseau and the *philosophes* of the Enlightenment, the ultimate heresy. However, Peter the Great presented something of a problem for them for two reasons: he had, undoubtedly, brought his people to a higher level of civilisation, and he had defended his exercise of supreme power, not by reference to his sacral function (which he habitually downplayed, even to the point of irreverent parody), but by his own endeavours for the good of the state. He had certainly achieved a degree of enlightenment in Russia that would otherwise have taken centuries to bring about – but he had done it by force. It was the discrepancy between the will of the people and the will of the Tsar that Rousseau condemned.

> Some of [Peter's] measures, indeed, were proper enough, but most of them were ill-timed or ill-placed. He saw that his subjects were mere barbarians, but he did not see that they were not ripe for being made polite. He wanted to civilise them, when he should only have checked their brutality. He wanted to make them at once Germans and Englishmen, whereas he ought to have begun by making them first Russians.[15]

It was not one of Rousseau's more convincing arguments.

Catherine II for long years enjoyed the reputation of being a kind of Peter I in drag. By victories against the Turks and by engineering the demise of Poland, she added 520,000 square kilometres to Russian territory. She secured her country's access to the Black Sea. She reformed central and regional administration. She instituted new educational initiatives. She presided over a glittering court that attracted inquisitive and awestruck celebrity-seekers from all over Europe. For all that, the question of whether Catherine II can be called an enlightened despot has long been debated among historians. She patronised Voltaire, Diderot and other advanced thinkers of the age. She corresponded with Europe's intellectual leaders and brought many of them to St Petersburg. For the first time the Russian elite were in a position to exchange ideas as well as works of literature and music with their Western counterparts. The interaction was particularly strong during the years of the French Revolution, which brought an influx of émigrés to Moscow and St Petersburg, but cultural activity was no longer a one-way street; writers like Nikolai Karamzin travelled extensively in Europe, absorbing Enlightenment ideas but also contributing concepts that were essentially Russian. Catherine came to power with her head full of enlightened ideas. She would emancipate the serfs and introduce constitutional reform. However, when she realised the opposition such policies would provoke among the landowning class, she abandoned her principles without much apparent difficulty. That indicated a marked difference between her and Peter. He had never permitted mere pragmatism to interfere with his plans. Towards the end of her reign, reeling from the shock of the French Revolution, the Empress performed a complete policy U-turn. She actually extended serfdom, notably in the Ukraine, and tightened control of the peasant population.

The movement for liberty, equality and brotherhood drew a sharp philo-sophical line in the sand. It forced men to decide for the old order or the new. And it made historians review their opinions about Peter the Great. There is something of a paradox here. Writers praised the Tsar for encourag-ing that engagement with wider cultural movements that enabled them to develop their own political thinking, but that thinking actually led them to downgrade Peter's significance. Nikolai Karamzin (1766–1826), who wrote a twelve-volume history of Russia, was one of the leading lights of a new nationalist school that now tended to see Peter as just one figure in an on-going outworking of native genius. In some respects indeed, Karamzin reck-oned, he had actually inhibited that development. His attacks on traditional customs had undermined national self-confidence. Russia was the equal of other states and had no need to apologise for long beards, native costume or activities others might consider barbaric. For Russia to take its place among the brotherhood of nations, it was not necessary for it to submerge its own identity.

> Two states may stand on the same level of civil enlightenment although their customs differ. One state may borrow from another useful knowl-edge without borrowing its manners. These manners may change natu-rally, but to prescribe statutes for them is an act of violence, which is illegal for an autocratic monarch ... We became citizens of the world but ceased, in some respects, to be citizens of Russia. The fault is Peter's.[16]

Radicalism inevitably seeped into Russian intellectual life, and with it the redefinition of such concepts as 'state' and 'fatherland'. The disciples of the

Revolution spoke and wrote about the 'people' and the necessity of government representing the will of the majority. The challenge to a government that regarded itself as paternalistic, that governed the lives of a huge serf population that had no means of expressing its will, was obvious. Alexander Radishchev (1749–1802), a pioneer social and political reformer, returned from Leipzig with his head buzzing with liberal notions, and his publication of *A Journey from St Petersburg to Moscow* in 1790 was a ringing denunciation of serfdom. Yet even he was held captive by the Petrine legend. Profoundly moved by the unveiling of the Bronze Horseman, he described in glowing terms the statue and the demigod it represented – a hero who 'having overcome the strong vices which opposed his reforms extended his protection to all who were called his children'. This adulation did not protect Radishchev; Catherine had him packed off to Siberia.

Politically, the Revolutionary and Napoleonic Wars created problems for the Russian government and further defined the nation's relationship with Europe. In 1793, Catherine became the first crowned head to join the First Coalition formed by William Pitt to contain the spread of revolutionary France. But the Empress avoided direct involvement, preferring to use her neighbours' preoccupation with France to extend her own control of Poland. It was not until the Second Coalition, to which Catherine's son Paul became a signatory in 1798, that Russia was committed to military action. An autocrat of autocrats who despised his mother's flirtation with liberal ideas, Paul threw himself enthusiastically into the conflict and, in concert with Austria, won significant victories in Italy over the next few months. But then he switched sides and negotiated a peace with Napoleon. In 1801, Paul, like his father, was assassinated in a palace coup.

Alexander I, who succeeded his father, was just about the last man one might have considered likely to dramatically change the face of Europe. Influenced by liberal ideals and Christian mysticism, strongly laced with traditional absolutism, his mind was a whirl of conflicting impulses, which resulted in 'policies' (if such they can be called) that defy close analysis. Yet he was destined to deliver Europe from the military and political domination of one of the greatest leaders in its history. Alexander abandoned Paul's French alliance and was drawn into the War of the Third Coalition in 1805. The immediate consequences were disastrous. Napoleon smashed his enemies at Austerlitz (1805) and forced Austria and Prussia out of the war. Alexander, despite heavy losses, refused to quit until he too was humiliated by the French at Friedland (1807). The ensuing Treaty of Tilsit did at least enable Alexander to turn his attention south-eastwards and bring to a successful conclusion a long-running war with Persia, which resulted in the addition of Georgia to the Russian empire. Expansion in the far east, beyond the Bering Strait, saw bases planted in Alaska and California. The two emperors, Napoleon and Alexander, now dominated the whole of Europe and there was talk of a marriage alliance between Bonaparte and the Tsar's sister. Alexander might have settled down to maintaining his own sphere of influence, but relations between the emperors were strained and broke down altogether when Napoleon married Marie Louise of Austria. In the summer of 1812, he made the fateful decision to invade Russia.

The defeat of the Grande Armée is the stuff of legend. Napoleon crossed the Niemen with 420,000 men (later augmented to almost 600,000). In late November, he struggled back into French territory with fewer than 30,000. He had been defeated by the early onset of the winter and by the difficulty of protecting his extended supply lines from Russian attack. But he had also failed to take account of the tenacity of the people and their mystical relationship with their land. Like Charles XII, Napoleon discovered the hard way that the combination of a harsh terrain and a large population able and willing to sustain heavy losses was formidable. The one-eyed veteran General Mikhail Kutuzov retreated before the invaders, drawing them into a land that had been despoiled of crops and livestock and refusing to offer a pitched battle. Only at Borodino, 120 kilometres from Moscow, did he face the French, and though he lost a pitched and bloody battle, he inflicted severe losses on the invaders. Alexander's refusal to discuss terms, even after the city was taken, left Napoleon with no option but to return through the snow with troops of Russian horsemen and civilian guerrillas mercilessly harassing his line of march. It was now the turn of Russia and its allies to go on the offensive. The recent sacrifices gave Alexander immense moral authority, and he became the acknowledged leader of the allied cause. His call to the other nations to rid Europe of the scourge of Bonaparte could not be ignored. The advance of Alexander's army right across Europe was, for Russians, an even more important event than the frustrating of Napoleon's invasion – almost another Poltava. The seventy-seven-year-old Kutuzov died still campaigning as his army marched westwards (the Soviet government created the Order of Kutuzov in his honour at a time when Russia was facing yet another tyrant in 1942), but its impetus was irresistible. In the following October, Napoleon suffered his worst defeat to date at the Battle of Leipzig (or Battle of the Nations). Peace might have been negotiated at that point had not Alexander insisted on the complete humiliation of his enemy. Napoleon had occupied Moscow. Alexander would occupy Paris. On 31 March 1814, he led his troops into the French capital. It was, he said, the happiest day of his life.

Alexander was now the arbiter of Europe. At the Congress of Vienna (1814–15), his was the most insistent voice, not only in the process of redrawing the map, but also in laying down the Congress System, designed to create a new order that would maintain autocratic governments while providing for the development of constitutional initiatives. The Tsar claimed, 'We are Europe,' by which he meant that sovereignty and power rightfully resided in the crowned heads acting in concert. He further attempted to enshrine his continental vision with the creation of a 'Holy Alliance', by the terms of which the rulers of Russia, Prussia and Austria agreed to consider themselves as divinely appointed to govern three branches of one family, in the belief that 'the Christian world, of which they and their people form a part, has in reality no other Sovereign but Him to whom power really belongs'. Most of the sophisticated delegates at Vienna were prepared to endorse this attempt to revivify the medieval concept of Christendom simply in order to please Alexander, while privately dismissing it, in the words of the British foreign minister, as 'a piece of sublime mysticism and nonsense'. Yet it would be a mistake to brush aside the Tsar and his pious declaration as wholly irrelevant. A new entity had come into existence. After two centuries of intermittent and violent interstate rivalries, 'Europe' was now a political reality within which the component nations were pledged to regulate their relationships by peaceful means. Russia was a part of that reality and committed to its cultural, commercial and political development.

But political truth did not by any means reflect intellectual unity. Over the next century the continent would be repeatedly convulsed not by wars between rival states, but by the clashing interests and aspirations of rulers and ruled. There was no country in Europe in which liberalism and nationalism did not come into conflict with the forces of reaction. Russia was no longer insulated from the high-voltage ideas surging through the intellectual cables of the continent. More young men were receiving education. Many were travelling abroad and being stimulated by the exciting concept of 'freedom', which their foreign friends were discussing in pavement cafés and *bierkellers*. When talk turned to action and the barricades went up (for example, in 1830 and 1848), governments were forced to 'negotiate', some with paper constitutions, some with drawn sabres. Tsar Nicholas I (1825–55) stood at the extreme right of the political spectrum. He suffered from none of the abstruse mystical speculations and otherworldly concerns of his brother. He was a soldier and every inch the military martinet, who believed that the heterogeneous Russian empire could only be held together by the iron bands of unyielding centralised control. He had no truck with progressive ideas or anything that might undermine absolute monarchy. He exercised a rigid press censorship, demanded unthinking personal loyalty and set his face against reform.

Oppression inevitably influenced the way thinkers defined the nation's problems. The absence of an approved forum where the pressing issues of the day could be debated drove opponents of the regime into more extreme expressions of opinion, and sometimes into more extreme methods of demonstrating their opinions. One way that writers who were burning to make political comment could do so without risking arrest was to confine themselves to history. In the process of reassessing the past, writers were involved in tortuous – sometimes even tortured – reformulations of the Petrine legends. The most famous product of this process is Alexander Pushkin's remarkable poem, *The Bronze Horseman* (1833), which is still learned by heart in all Russian schools. It is a complex, multilayered work, in part celebration of St Petersburg and encomium of the city's founder, but also containing more than a hint of menace. Yevgeny, the tragic hero of the piece, loses his beloved Parasha when the Neva overflows its banks. He wanders the streets, a dishevelled tramp, deranged with grief – or perhaps with an overmastering sense of futility:

> … Was life also
> An idle dream which in derision
> Fate sends to mock us here below?

He finds himself in the shadow of Falconet's statue and rails upon it. Now the poem surges to its melodramatic climax:

> For now he seemed to see
> The awful Emperor quietly,
> With momentary anger burning,
> His visage to Yevgeny turning!
> And rushing through the empty square,
> He hears behind him as it were
> Thunders that rattle in a chorus,
> A gallop ponderous, sonorous,
> That shakes the pavement. At full height,
> Illumined by the pale moonlight,
> With arm outflung, behind him riding
> See the bronze horseman comes, bestriding
> The charger, clanging in his flight.
> All night the madman flees; no matter
> Where he may wander at his will,
> Hard on his track with heavy clatter
> There the bronze horseman gallops still.[17]

Whatever other messages Pushkin's poem may contain, it certainly conveys powerfully the sense that, for Russians, there is not and never can be any escape from Tsar Peter I and his legacy. Like an Everest in the intellectual landscape, Peter is 'there' – impressive, challenging, daunting. Pushkin had been commissioned by Nicholas I to write a biography of the first emperor, and the convolutions of *The Bronze Horseman* represent the poet's conflicting impressions of his subject. What his calm reflection might have produced we shall never know, for Pushkin was killed in a duel in 1837, his biography no more than a bundle of notes.

Pushkin's friend and close contemporary Peter Chaadaev (1794–1856) also struggled with his interpretation of the great Tsar who dominated the past and had directed Russia towards that ambiguous present in which it now found itself. Depressed by the thought that 'we are not related to any of the great human families; we belong neither to the West nor the East',[18] Chaadaev wrote a pessimistic *Philosophical Letter*, which drew upon him the opprobrium of the establishment. Nicholas pronounced the author to be 'mad' and had him placed under surveillance. That experience prompted further reflection and a more positive assessment. Chaadaev's final position seems to have been that Russia was not lost in a barren no-man's-land, but was free to seize its own destiny without slavishly following Western patterns. This involved a drastic reappraisal of Peter's role and, it must be said, a selective use of sources. So far from imposing alien ideas on an unwilling nation, the Tsar had simply led the people in a direction they wanted to go. Russia 'had long recognised the superiority of the countries of Europe, especially as regards military matters; tired of its old routines, bored with its isolation, its one aspiration was to enter the great family of Christian peoples ...'[19]

This somewhat ambiguous conclusion made it possible for Chaadaev to be claimed as a supporter of both rival schools of nineteenth-century thought – the Westernisers and the Slavophiles. Just as in Britain the surge of technological progress, with its clangorous city streets and smoke-belching factories, provoked Gothic revivalism, so in Russia Slavophiles conjured up a vision of golden-age innocence in which serf and master had lived harmoniously under the benign supervision of the Orthodox church. Westernisers dismissed this as not only naïve but also obscurantist. It ignored the brave mission to which Russia was being called. This was nothing less than to be the saviour of Europe; the standard-bearer of humanity. The West was suffering from political confusion, moral decline and cultural barrenness. In 1812–13, Russia had saved the European body. Now it was called upon to save the European soul. If that strikes us as pretentious, we need to remind ourselves that contemporary British and French overseas expansion was being fired by the same high-sounding oratory. Missionaries and merchants were moving through Africa and Asia under the banner of 'Christianity, Commerce and Civilisation'.

Culturally, it would be difficult to deny the outstanding contribution of Russia's sons to European life in the nineteenth century. The flood of talent was prodigious. St Petersburg and Moscow became artistic centres on a par with Paris, London, Berlin and Rome. In 1859, the Maryiinsky Theatre, named in honour of the wife of Alexander II (reigned 1855–81), was opened, its audience capacity of 1,800 indicating the importance opera and ballet had assumed in the life of the St Petersburg *haut monde*. In the following decade, music conservatoires were founded in Moscow and St Petersburg by the brothers Anton and Arthur Rubinstein. Through their portals passed a brilliant cavalcade of teachers and students – Glinka, Balakirev, Borodin, Mussorgsky, Rimsky-Korsakov, Tchaikovsky. The field of literature was not lacking geniuses of equal distinction – Turgenev, Tolstoy, Gogol, Dostoyevsky, Chekhov. These were but the more brilliant luminaries of an artistic galaxy that, whether or not it saved the soul of Europe, certainly made Europe aware of much that was in the soul of Russia. They were doing what Peter had done in his own way; as the leading literary critic Vissarion Belinskii (1811–48) said, 'Peter was the full expression of the Russian spirit.'

That spirit was now receiving very mixed receptions in Europe. Culturally the atmosphere could scarcely have been warmer. For example, when Tchaikovsky made a conducting tour of Leipzig, Hamburg, Prague, Paris and London in 1888, he played to packed houses and was feted by fellow composers such as Brahms and Grieg. In 1832 appeared *Memoir of the Life of Peter the Great* by Sir John Barrow, one of the most engaging Englishmen of the age, who served over thirty years as secretary to the British navy, travelled widely and yet found time to research and publish books and articles on a wide range of subjects. His biography ran to several editions and was the most popular in Britain throughout the nineteenth century. It was Barrow who, for the first time, wrote a coherent account of the Great Embassy, based on careful study of contemporary newspaper reports and letters. Beyond this there was little new in his account. For Barrow, Peter was 'one of the most extraordinary characters that ever appeared on the great theatre of the world, in any age or country'. It was Peter's patriotism that most impressed this English gentleman:

> Russia was to him all in all; her welfare and her glory engaged his daily thoughts; and those excesses and little eccentricities which appear childish and frivolous, as well as those more ... serious acts of severity, which all must condemn, had each of them a motive pointing to some end, and that generally a benevolent one. In the execution of

his great designs for the improvement of his country, no difficulties or dangers stood in his way; his indefatigable activity – the perseverance and intrepidity which enabled him to overcome all obstacles, and brave the most imminent perils – and for the love of country – are the proud qualifications that entitle him to the name of GREAT.[20]

Yet there were others who saw Peter's devotion to the well-being of his country in a more sinister light. The emergence of Russia as an equal partner in the affairs of Europe left no room for patronising attitudes. No longer was it appropriate to regard Russia indulgently as a backward country trying to catch up with her more sophisticated neighbours. It was a huge empire, which in recent years had encroached westwards over thousands of square kilometres, extending its own brand of slavery to its subject peoples, and systematically suppressing liberal movements. Moreover, its ambitions were manifestly not yet satiated. The current regime clearly had designs on the crumbling Ottoman Empire and planned to dominate the Mediterranean, as it dominated the Baltic. Fears of the 'Russian threat' were fostered by an extraordinary canard that appeared in various forms throughout the first half of the century.

After the decline of French and Austrian dominance, it was Russia that emerged as the bogeyman of Europe. It was, perhaps, inevitable that the counterattack should begin in France, which had suffered the humiliation of invasion by Alexander I's army. In 1839, the Marquis de Custine grabbed the market with his sensationalist exposé, *La Russie en 1839*. He dismissed the people as 'nothing better than well-dressed barbarians' and referred to Peter as 'that too-highly lauded man' whose beneficial achievements had proved transient and whose evil legacy was permanent and irreparable.[21] Custine's diatribe was translated into English and reprinted in 1854 when the two Western nations went to war with Russia in the Crimea. But what was even more damaging was the circulation of a fraudulent document purporting to be the political testament of Peter I. Designed to stir up Russophobia, it was quoted in various books published around the middle of the century, and claimed to reveal the step-by-step process outlined by the first Emperor whereby his successors could achieve complete world domination. Like all effective propaganda, it mingled historical fact with highly coloured fiction. Thus, the dismemberment of Poland and the cultivation of 'useful' commercial relations with Britain were posited as plans laid down in advance by Peter, who had regarded them as elements of a Machiavellian military and diplomatic offensive that would lead by stages to the annexation of the Ottoman Empire and Persia. Subtle diplomacy would then set the major Western powers at each other's throats, and when they were weakened by their own conflicts, 'Two immense fleets, laden with Asiatic hordes, and convoyed by the armed squadrons of the Euxine and the Baltic [would] set sail simultaneously from the Sea of Asof and the harbour of Archangel. Sweeping along the Mediterranean and the Atlantic they will overrun France on the one side while Germany is overpowered on the other. When these countries are fully conquered, the rest of Europe must fall easily under our yoke.'[22]

Like all conspiracy theories, the 'Testament' and the books that uncritically propagated its absurdities ignored the changes and chances of history and wove the events of the century following Peter's death into an elaborate, sinister tapestry whose design had been carefully pre-planned. However, if the forgery was widely believed, it was because the world of the late nineteenth century was a battleground of competing national and colonial rivalries. While Britain, France and the new German empire 'scrambled' for territory in Africa and Asia, and the USA was reaching out across the Pacific, Russia extended its southern borders towards the frontiers of Afghanistan and India, while in the Far East its engagement with the rivalries of China and Japan won it northern Manchuria and the port of Vladivostock (construction of the monumental Trans-Siberian Railway, linking European Russia with its distant Pacific base, began in 1891). By the beginning of the twentieth century, the major powers were regarding each other with suspicious eyes and forming 'protective' alliances that, with a sickening inevitability, would lead to world war.

Ironically, when the rulers of Russia really did begin to indulge dreams of world domination, it was only after they had firmly turned their back on Peter the Great and his legacy. Following the 1917 revolution, which swept away the last Romanovs and the political order they represented, history had to be rewritten. Everything to do with the tsarist regime was expunged from the public record. Marxist-Leninism saw the past in terms of the deterministic outworking of forces leading to the inevitable rule of the proletariat. There was no room for the contribution of individuals. When party-line scholars did turn their attention to the first Emperor, it was only to bury him beneath mounds of hatred and contempt. Peter was portrayed as

An abnormal man, always drunk, a syphilitic, a hypochondriac, who suffered from psychopathic seizures of depression and violence, who with his own hands choked his son to death. A monarch who could never restrain himself in anything, who did not understand that one must control oneself, a despot. A man who had absolutely no sense of responsibility, who despised everything, who failed to understand to the end of his life either historical logic or the physiology of the life of the people. A maniac. A coward. Frightened by his childhood, he came to hate the old world; blindly he accepted the new; he lived with foreigners who arrived for easy gain, he obtained a barracks upbringing; he looked up to the ways of a Dutch sailor as his ideal. A man who remained a child to the end of his days, who loved play above all – and who played all his life: at war, at ships, at parades, at councils, at illumination, at Europe. A cynic who despised the human being in himself and others. An actor, an actor of genius. An emperor who loved debauchery above all, who married a prostitute, Menshikov's concubine – a man with the ideals of the barracks. The body was enormous, unclean, very sweaty, awkward, in-toed, thin-legged, eaten through and through by alcohol, tobacco and syphilis. With years the cheeks began to hang down on the round, red, old-woman's face, the red lips became flaccid, the red – syphilitic – eyelids would not shut tight, and behind them gazed mad, drunken, wild, child's eyes ... He fought for thirty years – he played at a mad war – only because his mock-soldiers had grown up and his fleet found itself cramped on Moscow River and on the Preobrazhenskii pond. He never walked – always ran, swinging his arms, his thin legs intoed, imitating Dutch sailors in his gait. He dressed dirtily, tastelessly; he did not like to change underwear. He liked to eat much, and he ate with his hands – the enormous hands were greasy and calloused.[23]

Such angry products of the Communist cultural revolution were, of course, propaganda and not historiography. What is interesting is the lengths the educators of the new order had to go to to expunge from Russian minds the heroic image of the first Emperor. It was not enough to decry his policies, to expose his cruelties; scorn also had to be poured on his personal morals and even his disregard of etiquette. The name of Peter's city had to be changed, and in 1924, St Petersburg (Petrograd since 1914) became Leningrad. Any objective, scholarly reappraisal of the Russian past and Peter's place in it was subject to a censorship every bit as strict as that operated by the secret police of Nicholas I. I wonder whether any scholar sufficiently close to the Politburo to understand its personalities and inner workings ever pondered ruefully on the similarities between Stalin and the Tsar for whom he never conceded any more than a grudging admiration. Both men had the same manic energy, the same huge appetites, the same calculated ruthlessness, the same bonhomie that could turn on the instant into frightening rage. Both forced through massive reforms, many of which were destined to fail. Both ruled autocratically through reformed bureaucracies that ultimately could not deliver the results demanded of them. Many commentators have seen Peter the Great as Joseph Stalin's most obvious ancestor.

There were many in Europe who looked to the Soviet regime as the world's champion against the evils of fascism as the continent drifted towards war in the 1930s, but, like Peter, Stalin's only interests were those of the state. The pact he made with the German dictator in 1939 enabled him to reconquer Poland and Lithuania, regions lost to Russia in the aftermath of the First World War, and to grab territory in Latvia, Estonia, Romania and Finland. He was apparently genuinely surprised by the German invasion of 1941 and had no alternative to throwing in his lot with Britain and the USA. Yet in the next four years, the Soviet Union really did become the saviour of Europe. It maintained the largest army in the field, suffered immeasurably more military and civilian casualties (some 27,000,000) than any other combatant state and, by absorbing the shock of German invasion, fatally weakened Hitler's war effort (75 to 80 per cent of Nazi losses in men and materiel were incurred on the Eastern Front). The fate of Leningrad symbolises that determination of the government and that capacity of the Russian people for self-sacrifice that had defeated Charles XII and Napoleon. In September 1941, the Germans began a siege that was destined to last for 900 days, reduce the historic city to rubble and see between 700,000 and 1,000,000 citizens killed by famine, cold, disease and enemy action. This confrontation of biblical proportions, in which the rival war leaders outbidded each other in their frenzied quest for victory and inflicted unimaginable hardships on their own people as well as the enemy, was, by a very long way, the major military element in the Second World War. Yet its true significance has seldom been understood in the West. Britain and America celebrated their own campaign achievements and grew their own legends, but the Cold War effectively stifled appreciation of the contribution made by the Soviet Union in the overthrow of the Nazi regime.

The superpower conflict and the nuclear arms race that dominated world affairs for three decades diverted attention from Russia's relations with its Western neighbours. Like the Orthodox leaders of old, the Communist rulers in Moscow sought to isolate themselves and their satellites behind the Iron Curtain from the corrupting influences of bourgeois capitalism. NATO was America's front line of defence against the 'red menace' – although 'grey' might be a better colour to designate Soviet society in the sixties, seventies and eighties. Peter the Great might well have envied the effective centralised power of the state, the authoritative bureaucracy, the insidious influence of the KGB, the effective power that backed the law, and the gulags where dissident citizens were disciplined and had their thoughts 'corrected'. But Europe was changing, uniting, recovering economically. More and more Soviet citizens envied the material prosperity they could only gaze at, like deprived children with their faces pressed to the shop window. They were waiting – whether or not they realised it – for a radical leader who would have the prescience and the courage to open frontiers, both geographical and psychological.

Mikhail Gorbachev is an unlikely figure to compare with Peter the Great, but if we are right in detecting similarities between Stalin and the first Emperor, it is also permissible to find points of reference between Peter and that other leader who led the nation in a new direction. Gorbachev saw, and more importantly, was prepared to admit, that the Soviet system was inadequate to the needs of Russia and its satellites in the late twentieth century. In his vision (and that is not an inappropriate word to describe it), Europe, far from being regarded as an alien and potentially hostile land, could become a bridge between Moscow and Washington and, more immediately important, could provide his country with valuable economic markets. Yet not even the premier could foresee the speed with which the Soviet edifice would collapse once pressure was applied to it. In 1988, Gorbachev made a world-changing speech at the UN, in which he announced drastic Soviet demilitarisation and renounced the threat of force as an ingredient of diplomatic relations with Russia's Western neighbours. Within three years the revolution that swept him from office also removed Communist regimes from power throughout the Eastern Bloc and actually declared Communism illegal in Russia. By a vote of its citizens, Leningrad became, once more, St Petersburg.

What is post-Soviet Russia like? More to the point for this book, what is post-Soviet Peter like? When Boris Yeltsin was asked on TV to designate his favourite Russian hero, he unhesitatingly answered 'Peter the Great'. A portrait of the Tsar in the Pavlosk Palace torn up by the Nazi occupiers was reassembled. The wind-blown fragments were collected up and preserved and the painting has now been lovingly restored. The version of the Tsar being offered to today's citizens is accessible, friendly and without much of the awe that characterised attitudes in earlier times. His face gazes out from cigarette packets and beer labels. The palaces and parks he created have been restored at vast expense. His modest cabin never lacks for visitors. He is regarded with mingled pride and familiarity. In today's open Russia, Peter has become an important tourist attraction and earner of currency. But he is much more than a valuable economic asset. Scholars have once again ventured into the realm of 'Peter studies' and are continuing the process of re-evaluation. But the image that strikes me most forcibly comes not from a book but is fashioned in bronze. In 1991, they put up a new statue to Peter in the grounds of the Peter and Paul fortress. Created by Mikhail Shemiakin, it could not be more different to the Bronze Horseman. It shows a seated figure, described by one critic as 'an ill-formed freak, unnaturally small-headed, bald, bug-eyed and spindly limbed'. It has become a custom for young Russian ladies to be photographed sitting in the statue's lap. The great autocrat, it seems, has been fully democratised.

And in Europe? In reality, most people are as unaware of this extraordinary human being as they are of the 'real' modern Russia (whatever that might mean). Television and newspaper headlines draw attention to our relations with that country when diplomatic waters have been ruffled by some crisis. Then memories of the Cold War and fear of mushroom clouds come flooding back. We are aware that capitalist, democratic Russia is still different from its Western neighbours. It is distinctly in Europe but not of Europe. Yet perhaps that should not be difficult for British people to understand. Are we not also part of a cultural entity we call 'Europe' – but only when it suits us? At other times do we not easily fall into the habit of referring to EU member states as 'them'? This matters because our destiny is a common destiny. Historically and culturally we have much more in common with a greater Europe than we do with our transatlantic friends. In attempting a greater understanding, we may be helped by reflecting on the phenomenon that is Peter the Great. Men and women of stature all have their place in the historical record. But there are very few who need to be reinterpreted for every age, who are so significant that their significance has to be periodically reassessed. They are the ones who are truly 'great'.

Bibliography

The following is a list of the best books and articles in English currently available on Peter the Great and Petrine Russia. The place of publication is London unless otherwise indicated.

Anderson, M.S., *Britain's Discovery of Russia 1553–1815*, 1985

Anderson, M.S., 'Peter the Great, Imperial Revolutionary', in A.G. Dickens, ed., *The Courts of Europe: Patronage and Royalty 1400–1800*, 1977

Anisimov, E.V., *The Reforms of Peter the Great*, Armonk, 1993

Banks, J., *A New History of the Life and Reign of Czar Peter the Great, Emperor of All Russia ...*, 1740

Barany, G., *The Anglo-Russian Entente Cordiale of 1697–1698*, New York, 1986

Barrow, J., *A Memoir of the Life of Peter the Great*, 1832

Bell, J., *Travels from St Petersburg in Russia to divers parts of Asia*, Glasgow, 1765

Benson, S., *The Role of Western Political Thought in Petrine Russia*, CASS 8 (1974)

Black, C.E., 'The Reforms of Peter the Great', in C.E. Black, ed., *Rewriting Russian History*, New York, 1962

Bruce, P.H., *Memoirs of Peter Henry Bruce, Esq., a military officer in the service of Prussia, Russia and Gt. Britain ...*, 1782

Bruyn, C. de, *Travels into Muscovy ...*, 1737

Burnet, G., *Bishop Burnet's History of His Own Time*, Oxford, 1823

Bushkovitch, P., *Peter the Great: The Struggle for Power 1671–1725*, Cambridge, 2001

Cook, J., *Voyages and Travels through the Russian Empire, Tatary and Part of the Kingdom of Persia*, Edinburgh, 1770

Cross, A., *Peter the Great through British Eyes*, Cambridge, 2000

Cross, A.G., *By the Banks of the Neva: Chapters from the Lives and Careers of the British in 18th Century Russia*, Cambridge, 1996

Crummey, R.O., *Aristocrats and Servitors: The Boyar Elite in Russia, 1613–1689*, Princeton, 1983

Davies, N., *God's Playground: A History of Poland*, Oxford, 1981

Deane, J., *History of the Russian Fleet During the Reign of Peter the Great*, 1899

Dmytryshyn, B., *The Modernization of Russia under Peter I and Catherine II*, New York, 1974

Gordon, P., *Passages from the Diary of General Patrick Gordon of Auchleuchries, AD 1635–AD 1699*, (ed J. Robertson), 1859

Grey, I., *Peter the Great Emperor of All Russia*, 1960

Grey, I., 'Peter the Great in England', *History Today*, 1956

Hartley, J., *England Enjoys the Spectacle of a Northern Barbarian: A Window on Russia*, Rome, 1996

Hartley, J., ed., *The Study of Russian History from British Archival Sources*, 1986

Henshall, N., *The Myth of Absolutism: Change and Continuity in Early Modern European Monarchy*, 1992

Herd, G., 'General Patrick Gordon of Auchleuchries – A Scot in 17th Century Russian Service', Aberdeen PhD thesis, 1994

Hughes, L., *Peter the Great: A Biography*, New Haven, 2002

Hughes, L., *Russia in the Age of Peter the Great*, New Haven, 1998

Hughes, L., *Sophia, Regent of Russia 1657–1704*, Yale, 1990

Kirby, D., *Northern Europe in the Early Modern Period: The Baltic World, 1492–1772*, 1990

Le Donne, J.P., *Absolutism and Ruling Class: The Formation of the Russian Political Order, 1700–1825*, New York, 1991

Lednicki, W.A., *Pushkin's Bronze Horseman: The Story of a Masterpiece*, Berkeley, 1955

Lentin, A., 'Voltaire and Peter the Great', *History Today*, 1968

Lewitter, L.R., 'Russia, Poland and the Baltic, 1697–1721', *Historical Journal*, 2, 1968

Longworth, P., *Russia's Empires*, 2005

Luttrell, Narcissus, *A Brief Historical Relation of State Affairs from September 1678 to April 1714*, Oxford, 1857

Monod, P.K., *The Power of Kings: Monarchy and Religion in Europe, 1589–1715*, New Haven, 1999

Motley, J., *History of the Life of Peter I, Emperor of Russia*, Dublin, 1740

Neuville, F. de la, *An Account of Muscovy as it was in the Year 1689 ...*, 1699

Perry, J., *The State of Russia under the Present Czar*, 1916

Putname, P., ed., *Seven Britons in Imperial Russia, 1698–1812*, Princeton, 1952

Rasmussen, K., *Catherine II and Peter I: The Idea of a Just Monarch*, Berkeley PhD thesis, 1973

Riasanovsky, N.V., *A History of Russia*, 2000

Riasonovsky, N.V., *The Image of Peter the Great in Russian History and Thought*, Oxford, 1985

Rothstein, A., *Peter the Great and Marlborough: Politics and Diplomacy in Converging Wars*, Basingstoke, 1986

Sumner, B.H., *Peter the Great and the Emergence of Russia*, 1950

Vernadsky, G., *A Source Book for Russian History from Early Times to 1917*, 1972

Voltaire, *History of Charles XII, King of Sweden*, 1976

Voltaire, *History of the Russian Empire under Peter the Great*, Edinburgh, 1906

Weber, F.C., *The Present State of Russia*, trs. W. Taylor, 1968

Whitworth, C., *An Account of Russia as it was in the year 1710*, 1758

Wortman, R.S., *Scenarios of Power: Myth and Ceremony in Russian Monarchy*, Princeton, 1995–2000

References

Introduction

1 See L.E. Berry and R.O. Crummey, eds., *Rude and Barbarous Kingdom: Russia in the Accounts of Sixteenth Century English Voyagers*, Milwaukee, 1968, 84.

1: Survival

1 Burnet, IV, 397.
2 See Bushkovitch, 137.
3 Vernadsky, II, 362.
4 Hughes, *Peter the Great*, 19.

2: The Third Rome

1 R. Hakluyt, *The Principal Navigations Voyages Traffiques and Discoveries of the English Nation*, Glasgow, 1908, III, 384.
2 Cited in Riasanovsky, *A History of Russia*, 196.
3 See ibid., 202.
4 See C. Hinrichs, *Preussen als Historisches Problem, Gessamelte Abhandlungen*, Berlin, 1964, 53.

3: The Travels of Peter Mikhailov

1 See Hughes, *Peter the Great*, 34.
2 Herd, 92.
3 See Hughes, *Russia in the Age of Peter the Great*, 66–7.
4 Ibid., 294.
5 Hughes, *Peter the Great*, 40.
6 Vernadsky, II, 314.
7 See Cross, *Peter the Great through British Eyes*, 10–11.
8 Vernadsky, II, 313.
9 Luttrell, IV, 330.
10 Barrow, 97.
11 See Hughes, *Peter the Great*, 49.
12 Charles de Marguetel, seigneur de Saint-Èvremond, *Works*, 1714, II, 85.
13 John Evelyn, *Diary,* ed. S. de Beer, Oxford, 1959, 1023.
14 See Barrow, 81.

4: Avenging Angel

1 See Hughes, *Peter the Great*, 51.
2 Voltaire, *History of the Russian Empire under Peter the Great*, I, 121.
3 Burnet, IV, 398.
4 Ibid., IV, 396–8.
5 D. Defoe, *Review of the State of the English Nation*, Columbia, 1922, XIX, 23 August, 1711.
6 See Dmytryshyn, 10.
7 Vernadsky, II, 347.
8 Ibid., II, 350.
9 Luttrell, IV, 723.
10 Ibid., IV, 685.
11 Ibid., IV, 697.
12 Quoted in H. Troyat, *Peter the Great*, 1988, 133, without source reference.
13 See Bushkovitch, 228–9 note.
14 See Hughes, *Russia in the Age of Peter the Great*, 64.
15 Perry, 279.
16 Ibid., 204.
17 Ibid., 268–9.
18 Ibid., 269–70.

19 Ibid., 246–7.
20 Ibid., 197.
21 Ibid., 250.

5: 'An army of veterans beaten by a mob'

1 Alexander Pushkin, *The Bronze Horseman*, trs. W. Lednicki, Berkeley, 1955.
2 Vernadsky, II, 347.
3 Perry, 261–2.
4 See Bushkovitch, 243–4.
5 See Hughes, *Russia in the Age of Peter the Great*, 37.
6 Ibid, 40.
7 Defoe, *English Nation*, XV, 233.
8 *The Balance of Europe*, 1711, 25–6.
9 See Hughes, *Russia in the Age of Peter the Great*, 47.
10 See Anisimov, *The Reforms of Peter the Great*, 130.

6: Unhappy Families

1 See Hughes, *Russia in the Age of Peter the Great*, 403.
2 Weber, II, 101–2.
3 See Bushkovitch, 347.
4 See ibid., 261.
5 Ibid., 256.
6 See Hughes, *Russia in the Age of Peter the Great*, 56.
7 *Further Reasons for the Present Conduct of Sweden in Relation to the Trade in the Baltick...*, 1715, 18.
8 See Hughes, *Russia in the Age of Peter the Great*, 52.
9 J. Juel, *An Embassy in Russia Under Tsar Peter*, trs H. Troyat, Copenhagen, 1893, 47.
10 See P. Bushkovitch, 321–2.
11 Hughes, *Russia in the Reign of Peter the Great*, 253.
12 Hughes, *Peter the Great*, 112.

7: 'The horizon is clear'

1 *The Northern Crisis, or Reflections on the Policies of the Tsar,* 1716, 9–18.
2 A. Hill, *Northern Star,* 1718.
3 Weber, II, 109.
4 See Bushkovitch, 370.
5 Ibid., 376.
6 Ibid., 409.
7 Weber, II. 164.
8 See Bushkovitch, 415, transliterated.
9 See Riasanovsky, *The Image of Peter the Great,* 12.
10 Ibid.
11 See Hughes, *Peter the Great,* 159.

8: 'Projects that I have not been able to carry out'

1 F. de Labriolle, 'Le prosvescenie russe et les lumières en France (1760–1798)', in *Revue des études slaves,* 1966, 75.
2 See Anisimov, *The Reforms of Peter the Great,* 144.
3 Vernadsky, II, 365.
4 See Anisimov, 263.
5 Vernadsky, II, 364.
6 Ibid., II, 217–18.
7 See Anisimov, 204.
8 Ibid.
9 See Hughes, *Russia in the Age of Peter the Great,* 456.
10 Anisimov, 298.
11 Voltaire, *History of the Russian Empire,* I, 5.
12 See Hughes, *Russia in the Age of Peter the Great,* 121.
13 Vernadsky, II, 359.
14 Ibid., II, 366.
15 See Anisimov, 280.

Epilogue: An Unsilenceable Trumpet

1 See Riasanovsky, *The Image of Peter the Great,* 29.
2 Vernadsky, 381–2.
3 Ibid., 388.

4 Ibid., 390.

5 See Riasanovksy, *The Image of Peter the Great*, 34.

6 Ibid., 60.

7 Ibid., 62.

8 Davies, I, 386.

9 Voltaire, *History of the Russian Empire*, I, 11.

10 Ibid., II, 234.

11 Cross, *Peter the Great through British Eyes*, 77.

12 Ibid., 74.

13 Ibid., 66.

14 C.E. Vaughan, *The Political Writings of Jean Jacques Rousseau*, Cambridge, 1915, 34–5.

15 See Cross, *Peter the Great through British Eyes*, 82.

16 Riasanovksy, *The Image of Peter the Great*, 71–2.

17 Lednicki, 150.

18 R.T. McNally, *The Major Works of Peter Chaadaev*, 1969, 27.

19 R.T. McNally, 'Chaadaev's evaluation of Peter the Great', *Slavic Review*, xxiii, 1, 44.

20 See Cross, *Peter the Great through British Eyes*, 109.

21 Ibid., 112–13.

22 Ibid., 115–17.

23 B. Pilniak, *Ego Velichestvo Kneeb Piter Komondor*, 1919; see Riasanovsky, *The Image of Peter the Great*, 249–50.

Index